THE LORD **PROTECTOR** AND HIS WIVES

THE LORD PROTECTOR AND HIS WIVES

Catherine Filliol, Anne Stanhope and Edward Seymour

REBECCA BATLEY

PEN & SWORD HISTORY

AN IMPRINT OF PEN & SWORD BOOKS LTD.
YORKSHIRE – PHILADELPHIA

First published in Great Britain in 2025 by
PEN AND SWORD HISTORY
An imprint of
Pen & Sword Books Ltd
Yorkshire – Philadelphia

ISBN 978 1 39903 274 2

A CIP catalogue record for this book is available from the British Library.

Typeset in Times New Roman 11/14 by
SJmagic DESIGN SERVICES, India.
Printed and bound in the UK by CPI Group (UK) Ltd.

The Publisher's authorised representative in the EU for product safety is Authorised Rep Compliance Ltd., Ground Floor, 71 Lower Baggot Street, Dublin D02 P593, Ireland.
www.arccompliance.com

For a complete list of Pen & Sword titles please contact
PEN & SWORD BOOKS LIMITED
George House, Units 12 & 13, Beevor Street, Off Pontefract Road,
Barnsley, South Yorkshire, S71 1HN, England
E-mail: enquiries@pen-and-sword.co.uk
Website: www.pen-and-sword.co.uk

or

PEN AND SWORD BOOKS
1950 Lawrence Road, Havertown, PA 19083, USA
E-mail: uspen-and-sword@casematepublishers.com
Website: www.penandswordbooks.com

FSC www.fsc.org
MIX
Paper | Supporting responsible forestry
FSC® C013604

For Rory – My baby brother.

Contents

Acknowledgements

There are many people I need to thank for their help and support in writing this book. My first thanks must go to Laura, Sarah-Beth and all the team at Pen and Sword who have been so wonderfully supportive. I also wish to thank my editor, Sarah, who has been amazing, thorough and very patient with me.

I must also thank Sarah at Syon House who supplied me with images and was very kind, as well as Christine at Westminster Abbey who was very helpful. The historian community on Twitter has also been extremely supportive and I must thank a few individuals: Sylvia Barbara Soberton for agreeing to read this book and Helene Harrison and Beverley Adams for being so kind and inspirational. Most thanks must go to fellow author and all around amazing human being Amy McElroy, without whom this book would not exist. Her constant support, help and friendship has meant the world to me. I'm so glad I don't have to write without your help.

I must also thank everyone at BTR who have all listened to me worry and waffle on about this book for the past two years. Elaine – I'm so happy we got to keep you. Jo H you are my favourite; Jo E – you're alright and make us all smile on a daily basis. Craig, thanks for being an amazing support human; Dee, Paul, Lisa, Emily, Carole, Ben, Kirsten, Lisa – you are all awesome.

As always special thanks must go to Louise, for being there – always and for longer than either of us would like to admit. Jeg elsker dig darling. I must also thank Toyah, for always replying and for being amazing – thanks lovely. Thanks must also go to my friend, Adam, for his support; you can definitely show your friends that you got a mention in here. Donna and Cerys thanks for the support and Tudor food chat.

Finally I must thank my family – my Mum for her unfailing support and love and my sister-in-law, Sam – you are far less annoying than Rory.

Finally thanks must go to Jem, my long suffering, Napoleon obsessed secretary – who I promised to note typed a few sections of this from my dictation. He is a rather hesitant member of the Richard III Society, and the Mortimer Society. I like him quite a lot – and love him more than anything in the entire universe.

List of Illustrations

Key Characters

The four Tudor monarchs whose reigns form the backdrop to this book:

King Henry VIII: 1509–1547
King Edward VI: 1547–1553
Queen Mary I: 1553–1558
Queen Elizabeth I: 1558–1603

The Seymours

Sir John Seymour (born c.1474). He was knighted by Henry VII and served Henry VIII accompanying him to the Field of the Cloth of Gold. He married Margery Wentworth in 1494 and they had ten children. He was the father of Queen Jane, Edward and Thomas Seymour, and was Catherine and Anne's father-in-law. He was grandfather to Edward VI. Died 1536.

Margery Wentworth (born c.1478). She grew up in the household of the Countess of Surrey and was the muse of poet John Skelton. She married John Seymour in 1494, becoming the mother of Queen Jane, Edward and Thomas Seymour amongst others. She was Catherine and Anne's mother-in-law and lived largely at Wulfhall. She was grandmother to Edward VI. Died 1550.

Sir Edward Seymour (born 1500). One of our protagonists, he rose to become 1st Duke of Somerset, 1st Earl of Hertford, 1st Viscount Beauchamp and Lord Protector of the realm. He was the brother of Queen Jane Seymour, Thomas Seymour and the husband of both Catherine and Anne. Uncle to Edward VI, he was imprisoned twice in the Tower and ultimately was executed for felony in 1552.

Sir Henry Seymour (born c.1503). He was the son of John and Margery Wentworth and brother to Edward and Jane, therefore uncle to Edward VI. He served four Tudor monarchs but did not seek to rise at court and continued his career largely in obscurity. Made a Knight of the Bath in 1547, he married Barabara Wolde and had issue. Died 1578.

Sir Thomas Seymour (born c.1508). 1st Baron Sudeley and brother to Edward and Queen Jane, therefore uncle to Edward VI. He married Katherine Parr in 1547 but was jealous of his brother Edward's position as Lord Protector. Later involved in a sexual flirtation with the young Princess Elizabeth, he was executed in 1549.

Queen Jane Seymour (born c.1508). She was the daughter of John Seymour and Margery Wentworth. She was sister to Edward and sister-in-law to both Catherine and Anne and would have had a first-hand view of Catherine's fate. She married Henry VIII in 1536 and Anne served as her lady in waiting. Jane bore Henry VIII a son, Edward VI, but died soon afterwards in 1547.

Margery Seymour. Died young in 1528, age unknown.

Elizabeth Seymour (born c.1518). She was a daughter of John Seymour and Margery Wentworth and sister of the above. She served in the household of Anne Boleyn, Anne of Cleves and Catherine Howard. Though sister to Queen Jane, she is not listed in the members of her household. She married firstly Sir Anthony Ughtred, secondly Gregory Cromwell (the son of Thomas Cromwell) and lastly John Paulet and had issue. She was close to her brothers and Anne, her sister-in-law. Elizabeth died in 1568.

Dorothy Seymour (born c. early 1515s). She was the daughter of John Seymour and Margery Wentworth and sister to the above. She married firstly Clement Smyth and then secondly Thomas Leventhorpe and had issue. Died 1552.

The Fillols

Sir William Fillol (born c.1451). He was Anne and Catherine Fillol's father and owned estates at Woodlands Horton and Fillols Hall in Essex. He was keen to forge a connection with his powerful neighbours, the Seymours, and made a marriage alliance with them whereby Edward Seymour would marry Catherine. At some point following the marriage he had an argument with his daughter and son-in-law, serious enough for him to make a will disinheriting them. Sir William died in 1527.

Dorothy Ifield (born c.1475 in Standon). She was Catherine's mother. It is uncertain whether or not she was also Anne's mother. Little is known about her, except that she married John Rogers in 1532 after William's death and died in around 1539.

Anne Fillol (born c.1496). Catherine's older sister, it is uncertain whether she was the daughter of Dorothy or whether she was William's daughter from an earlier marriage. She married Edward Willoughby and had issue. Anne died in 1541.

Catherine Fillol (born c.1501). Catherine is one of our protagonists, the daughter of Dorothy Ifield and Sir William Fillol. Catherine was the first wife of Edward Seymour. Following a family argument which caused her to be disinherited, and after bearing her husband two sons, her marriage was repudiated. She almost certainly retired to a nunnery but her ultimate fate remains uncertain. She died before 1532.

The Stanhopes

Sir Edward Stanhope. (born sometime around 1474) A loyal servant of the Tudor monarchs, he fought at the Battle of Stoke and was knighted following the Battle of Blackheath. His first wife was Adelina Clifton and by her he had two sons, Richard Stanhope and Sir Michael Stanhope. His second wife was Elizabeth Bourchier by whom he had a daughter, Anne. He died in 1511.

Elizabeth Bourchier (born sometime before 1473). Elizabeth was the mother of Anne Stanhope by her third husband, Edward Stanhope. The daughter of Fulk Bourchier and Elizabeth Dynham, Elizabeth boasted illustrious ancestry. She married four times, firstly to Henry Beaumont, secondly to a man with the surname Verney, by whom she had a daughter,

Catherine Verney. Her third husband was Sir Edward Stanhope by whom she had a daughter, Anne. After Sir Edward Stanhope's death in 1511 she married Sir Richard Page, and had another daughter, Elizabeth. As Lady Page she was close to Lady Mary and she remained loyal to her daughter Anne, visiting her in the Tower of London. She died in 1557 and was buried at the Priory of Clerkenwell.

Anne Stanhope (born c.1510). The daughter of Sir Edward Stanhope and Elizabeth Bourchier. She is our final protagonist and the final wife of the Lord Protector, Edward Seymour. A close friend of Queen Mary I for over thirty years, Anne served each of Henry VIII's six wives. She married Seymour sometime before March 1535 and bore him ten children. During the reign of Edward VI she was the foremost lady of the land but when her husband fell from favour she was imprisoned for over two years in the Tower. Upon becoming queen, one of Mary's first actions was to release Anne from the Tower, before even Stephen Gardiner. Mary granted her Hanworth Manor and Scion House and she managed to recover the majority of her position and power. Anne married her second husband, Francis Newdigate, in 1558/59 and raised her two grandsons. She died in April 1587 and was buried in Westminster Abbey on the orders of Elizabeth I.

Sir Michael Stanhope (born before 1508). The second son of Sir Edward Stanhope and Adelina Clifton. Thus he was Anne Stanhope's elder half-brother. Following the death of his elder brother, Richard, in 1529, he succeeded to the majority of the family's estates and by 1535 he had entered Henry VIII's service. He helped put down the Pilgrimage of Grace. He was appointed Groom of the Stool to Edward VI and became a leading figure at court. When his brother-in-law, Edward Seymour, fell from favour Sir Michael went down with him. Imprisoned in the Tower, he was convicted of conspiring to kill the Duke of Northumberland and was beheaded in January 1552. He had married Anne Rawson and had issue. Later Mary I reversed his attainder so his children could inherit.

The Children of Edward Seymour and Catherine Fillol

John Seymour (born 1527). Eldest son of Edward Seymour and Catherine Fillol. In 1540 he was excluded from both his paternal and maternal inheritance in favour of his father's children by his second wife. However he remained loyal to his father and was sent to the Tower with him in 1551. He petitioned for the restoration of his maternal inheritance, which was finally given to him but he died in the Tower eleven months after his father. His lands passed to his younger brother.

Lord Edward Seymour (born 1529). He was the second son of Edward Seymour and Catherine Fillol. He too remained loyal to his father and was sent to the Tower in 1551. However he managed to escape execution and inherited his mother's lands following his elder brother's death. In 1555 this included the manor of Berry Pomeroy Castle. He married Margaret Walshe and it is from him that the current Dukes of Somerset are descended. Died 1593.

The Children of Edward Seymour and Anne Stanhope

The order and names of Anne and Edward's children is not always clear. This issue will be explored fully in the text. These dates and birth order are therefore only very approximate.

Edward Seymour (born 1537 and died two years later as an infant). He was Anne and Edward's first born son and was styled Viscount Beauchamp from birth.

Anne Seymour (born c.1538). Edward and Anne's eldest daughter and a great scholar, she married John Dudley, 2nd Earl of Warwick, in an attempt to shore up the alliance between the two families. Anne married secondly Edward Unton and had children. Towards the end of her life she suffered from poor mental health and died just after her mother in 1588.

Edward Seymour (born c.1539). Anne and Edward's eldest surviving son, he was described as wilful and spent much of his life in and out of the Tower. He married three times, the first time disastrously to Katherine Grey by whom he had two sons. Secondly he married Frances Howard, and thirdly Frances Pranell. Largely thanks to his mother's support he eventually regained his freedom and the title Earl of Hertford. Edward lived to prosper in the reign of James I, dying in 1621.

Henry Seymour (born c.1540). He married Lady Joan Percy and quarrelled with his mother over his management of the family land and estates. His date of death is unclear.

Margaret Seymour (born c.1540). Margaret, along with her sisters, was a noted scholar and published author.

Jane Seymour (born c.1541). Jane was a great scholar and published author along with her sisters. She became a maid of honour to Elizabeth I who greatly favoured her. Jane was the only witness to the marriage of her elder brother and Katherine Grey. Her premature death meant that there was no witness to testify to the nuptials. Jane died, much mourned, in 1561 and is buried in Westminster Abbey alongside her mother.

Catherine Seymour (born c.1548). Little is known about her but she lived to see the reign of King James, dying in 1625.

Edward Seymour (born c.1548). Edward never married and died young in 1574.

Mary Seymour (born c.1552). Like her eldest brother, Mary married three times – to Andrew Rogers, Sir Henry Peyton and Francis Cosbie. She died in 1620.

Elizabeth Seymour (born c.1552). Elizabeth married Sir Richard Knightley of Northamptonshire and had issue. She died in 1602, just before the dawn of Stuart England.

Introduction

On 22 January 1552, Edward Seymour, the Duke of Somerset and uncle of King Edward VI was beheaded on Tower Hill between the hours of eight and nine in the morning. Despite the fact that the citizens of London had been ordered to stay in their houses, a great number gathered to witness the end of a man who many still called the 'Good Duke'. The day before, inside the walls of the Tower of London, he had written his final religious devotions, the words 'Fear of the Lord is the beginning of wisdom. Put thy trust in the Lord with all thine heart', and signed off with the poignant words '(written) from the Tower the day before my death 1551' followed by his signature, all of which was written in a steady, slanting hand.[1] On the morning of 22 January he was led out of the Tower to Tower Hill accompanied by a guard of the king's men, Tower warders and two London sheriffs. As was custom he was permitted to address the crowd and in a clear voice spoke the words:

> Dearly beloved masters and friends, I am brought hither to suffer, albeit that I never offended against the king neither by word or deed and have been always as faithful and true unto this realm as any man hath been. But for so much as I am by a law condemned to die, I do acknowledge myself as well as others to be subject thereunto. Wherefore to express and testify my obedience which I owe unto the laws, I am come hither to suffer death, whereunto I willingly offer myself, giving most hearty thanks unto the divine goodness, as if I had received a most ample and great reward.[2]

Unusually he maintained that he was innocent of the charges against him, but stated that he was prepared to die, nonetheless. The condemned man went on to say that he was proud of everything he had done to return the Church of England to its earlier form and that if people embraced it they would please God. It was at this point that Chronicler and Windsor Herald, Charles Wriothesley, writes that although he 'tooke his death byer patiently, but there was (now) such feare and disturbance among the people suddenly, before he suffered, that some tumbled downe the ditch and ranne towards the houses and thereby fell, that i was marveile to see and hear; but howe the cause was, God knoweth'.[3] It appears that loud noise had caused some to think that the Tower guns had fired, which could have signalled that Seymour had been pardoned at the eleventh hour, or that more guards were coming. In the confusion people panicked and the cry rose from the crowd 'Jesus save us! Jesus save us!' When Sir Anthony Browne was glimpsed riding towards the scaffold, fear turned to joy as many thought he had indeed come to bring Somerset a pardon. The man himself, however, knew better; he knew that he had too many enemies, too many powerful men calling for his downfall for a pardon to be possible. Instead he waited and asked the crowd to quiet stating that 'if you fall into tumult, it will be the greater trouble unto me'.[4]

He then knelt and Dr Cox handed him a paper continuing a confession. He read it then shook hands with those on the scaffold and, as was tradition, paid the executioner in gold coins before removing his own gown and kneeling in the straw, which had been spread to absorb his blood when it was spilt. An eerie silence fell over Tower Hill and the executioner was heard to ask Somerset to stand again to remove his doublet, probably because it was covering the back of his neck. This done, he lay down again and spoke his final words: 'O Lord Jesus preserve me'. Moments later he was dead, his neck severed by a single heavy blow of the axe. People rushed forward to dip handkerchiefs and cloth into his blood. His body was placed into a coffin and quickly taken back inside the Tower to be buried in the north side of the quire in the Church of St Peter ad Vincula.[5]

As the coffin bearers clattered towards the church, perhaps staggering with their heavy burden, the flesh of which would still have been warm, a woman would have heard them. She would also have been formally brought the news that her husband, the Duke, was dead. Somerset's second wife, Anne Seymour nee Stanhope, the Duchess of Somerset, was herself being held somewhere inside the Tower having fallen from favour alongside her husband. She shared his imprisonment although where she was held and what level of contact they had been permitted is unclear. It was reported that this indomitable lady would soon share her husband's fate because she was 'said to bear the principal part in all this mischief'.[6]

Fate though had other plans for Anne Seymour.

Both the wives of Edward Seymour, whose life ended that day, were reviled by some at the time and have been widely ever since. Their names were Catherine Fillol and Anne Stanhope and between them they stand accused of having been adulterous, scandalous, ambitious, unfeminine, and proud. These two very different women were bound together by the life and actions of Edward Seymour, the man they both married. His life in turn was dominated by the actions and fate of yet another woman: his sister Jane Seymour, who became the third wife of King Henry VIII. Her marriage had accelerated his journey to power and prosperity but had also sown the seeds of his downfall and destruction. The two wives who accompanied him on this journey are usually dismissed as largely irrelevant to his life and career; if they are considered at all, it is usually negatively. Catherine lies at the heart of a Tudor mystery and Anne Stanhope has been accused of contributing to his downfall through her lack of feminine modesty. Katherine Parr called her 'that hell', but Mary I called her 'my good Nann'. History similarly has judged these women to be either saints or sinners, but as always the truth lies somewhere in between. Neither Catherine Fillol or Anne Stanhope deserve to be forgotten; their actions may be largely hidden and indeed Catherine still remains largely obscure yet their influence was great both on the husband they shared and on the children they bore him.

I propose here to tell the story of Edward Seymour and his two wives, to examine their origins, their influence and their fates.

Chapter 1

Three Families

The Seymours

Edward Seymour was born around 1500 and was the second son of John Seymour and Margery Wentworth, His parents had married in 1494 and soon after his elder brother, John, had been born. Edward was therefore initially the Seymour 'spare'.

The family of Seymour was an old one and their ancestors are traditionally said to have come from the village of St Maur sur Loire. The village is said to have been named after a black hermit who lived there and was famous for his piety, rather than for the more established Abbott Maur who was canonised and has numerous churches dedicated to him. The hermit was said to be descended from the race of Solomon and the Queen of Sheba and to have fled to what is now France after the massacre of his family in Abyssinia.[1]

By the year 679 we are on slightly firmer historical ground and the records suggest that by this time the St Maur family, having taken their name from the village, were on the rise. The head of the family was one Richard de St Maur who was mentioned in a grant from Queen Fredegunde to the Abbey of Villers. In 701 Guy de St Maur, perhaps Richard's son, performed his 'fealty and homage' at the same abbey. He was followed by Ludo St Maur who was mentioned in 919.[2] By 1000, Goscelin de St Maur, a descendant of Ludo, was declared to be hereditary possessor and Lord of the Castle of St Maur by the grace of God in a charter issued by Foulque Martel, the Count of Anjou.[3] Nine years later Goscelin de St Maur married a woman by the name of Aremburg and together they had four sons, Josbert, Guillaume, Hugues and Goscelin.[4] Josbert appears to have been the eldest and he became a priest; Guillaume and Hugues married but remained in Normandy. Guillaume, however, is of particular interest to us because he had a son named Wido St Maur who it is said accompanied William the Conqueror on his invasion of England. This cannot be proven beyond a shadow of a doubt simply because the lists of men accompanying the Conqueror which do still exist are incomplete. However he does appear in Holinshed, as Sent More, and in Stowe's later Chronicles, as Seint More, which claim to be based on earlier records.[5] That Wido St Maur did in fact accompany William the Conqueror is highly likely as following the conquest he received a large barony and lands in Somerset, Wiltshire and Gloucester. Such a reward suggests that he was on a par with the conquerors extended band of companions. Men such as Raoul II of Tosny who, as one of the proven companions of William the Conqueror, was given widespread lands in Hertfordshire, Gloucestershire and Leicestershire as a reward following the conquest.[6]

The vast lands were inherited by his son, William FitzWido, sometime before the Domesday survey was taken in 1086 although the exact nature of the barony is not clear, with the historian, I. J. Sanders stating that there was no such FitzWido barony in existence.[7] According to tradition the St Maur's in England were buried in the Church of St Lawrence in Rode, although it is only tradition that assigns a recessed wall tomb to them. William FitzWido had a son called Roger sometime before 1100 and in 1129 Roger witnessed a charter of Richard de Cormeil given to the Priory of Monmouth. He was going by the name of Roger St Maur rather than FitzWido. It has been suggested that he settled at Penhow and that he held a position of responsibility in the Welsh Marches and although this is supposition and cannot be proven we know that Roger built a fortified manor house on his Penhow estate.[8] In 1170 Roger's son, Bartholomew, witnessed a charter from William, Earl of Gloucester to Keynsham Abbey and his son William was appointed as one of the king's esquires five years later.[9] The St Maur familial descent continued with William's son, Milo, who rebelled with many other barons against King John and who together forced him to sign Magna Carta in 1215. He was clearly active at King John's court, appearing in the fine rolls of King John, but otherwise nothing is known about his political life. Milo had at least two sons, Geoffrey and William, who both had families.[10] It was from William's familial line that Edward Seymour descended.

Geoffrey married the daughter of William de Rughdon and together they had at least one son, Laurence de St Maur. In 1274, Laurence obtained permission from King Edward I to hold a market at his manor of Rode in Somerset every Thursday and a fayre on the 'eve, day and morrow of St Margaret the Virgin'.[11] Laurence St Maur, it is said, lived at a house called Seymours Court which lay to the east of the church.[12] He married a woman called Sibilla and he paid one-third of a knight's fee to gain her inheritance which was based in Northumberland. Geoffrey served the king and he fought for him against the Welsh and abroad, in 1297 being recorded as having done 'service across the seas'.[13] He and Sibilla had one son called Nicholas. Nicholas was summoned by the king, in July 1297, to perform military service, and a year later fought in the north against the Scots. Henry III seems to have favoured him, making him a present of money so he could buy a horse and wine.[14] He served in the retinue of Henry of Lancaster and of Edmund Crouchback, King Henry III's second surviving son, whose name famously does not derive from his crooked shoulders but rather due to the fact that he was a crusader. The original 'Cross back' being corrupted over time to crouchback. Nicholas appears to have been active in the Welsh Marches and in 1313 he was granted a pardon for having participated in a manner which is unspecified in the execution of Edward II's favourite, Piers Gaveston. Following his pardon he was summoned to Parliament as the representative of Gloucester and then saw further military service fighting against the Scots.[15] He appears to have married twice, the first time to Eve de Meysi who died young but through whom he inherited a good deal of land and property, including the Manor of North Molton in Devon and half the Manor of Gatesen in Hertfordshire which Eve herself had inherited upon the death of her father.[16] Nicholas' second wife was Helen, a daughter of Alan de la Zouche of Ashby, who brought to her marriage yet more property for her husband, including lands in Cambridgeshire, Gloucestershire and the Manor of Poulton, the Manor of Eton-Meysi in Wiltshire and of Northam in Devon.

Geoffrey's brother, and Roger's second son, William, settled at Penhow and David Loades speculates that the two men might have been born to separate mothers explaining why the inheritance was split so evenly, as it evidently was, and also why either side seemed to want to have nothing to do with the other, going as far as choosing completely separate coats of arms and denying that they even knew each other.[17]

Nicholas St Maur died in 1317 and he was succeeded by his son with Helen, Thomas, who was only 9 years old when his father died. Given his age he was made a ward of the king and his wardship was granted to Hugh le Despenser the elder. Thomas appears to have founded a priory at Dulton in Wiltshire, which was annexed as a cell to the Priory of Semplingham. Semplingham Priory was an important site of religious pilgrimage due to the fact that St Gilbert had established the Gilbertine order there in 1131, and because many miracles were said to have taken place at his tomb. The Gilbertine order was traditionally made up of women, suggesting that perhaps he founded it as a place where his female relations could reside or retreat to. Sometime before 1330 Thomas married and had a son, Nicholas, before himself dying young. This Nicholas freed the St Maur family from their legal obligations to the Despensers and attended Parliament from 1352 onwards before serving in the wars with France in the retinue of the one-eyed (by 1360 at least) Thomas Holland, the 1st Earl of Kent. Perhaps Nicholas was with Holland at Caen when famously he and his retinue showed one of the rare proven instances of medieval mercy when they protected both the surrendering nobleman and the women and children from other 'pitiless men'.[18] Nicholas married the heiress of Lord Lovel, Muriel, and they had two sons: Nicholas and Richard. Nicholas appears to have died young for it was Richard who was of age and inherited his father's lands when the latter died sometime in 1361. These estates were vast and included one in Dorset, five in Devon, four in Gloucestershire, eight (and a bit) in Somerset and the moiety of the hundred of Westbury in Wiltshire.[19] For twenty years he attended Parliament regularly and he followed his father by serving in France, this time in the retinue of the Earl of Arundel. He and his wife Ela had three sons and were buried side by side in the chapel of Stavordale Priory in Somerset. Richard was buried in 1400, at which time there were eight canons in residence.[20] Ela died in 1409 and left her son, Nicholas, twenty pounds, John, her second son, a coral necklace garnished with gold and her granddaughter, Alice, was made her female heir. Another son, Richard, who presumably was the eldest son, had been serving in Ireland under the Duke of Surrey since 1399, and then in France where he was recorded as being in 1402. Alice was Richard's daughter and when her father died in 1408 she inherited his property, which then, as was law, became the property of her husband, William de la Zouche of Totnes, when she married him in 1409. This branch of the St Maur family therefore came to a natural end so we must go back to the other brother, William St Maur, to trace the descent of Edward Seymour. It is important that we trace the family as a whole, however, to gain a full understanding of the family inheritance, pedigree and history that Edward himself would have been fully aware of. The seeds of conflict and fratricide which would dominate Edward Seymour's life can perhaps be seen in this familial history of fratricidal conflict.

William St Maur, the second son of Milo, was known as William of Penhow, and we have details of a fortified manor house which had been present there since 1129, and which was presumably where he lived. In 1235–6 he entered into an agreement to take the manor of Undy from the Welshman, Morgan ap Howell, with the support of Gilbert Marshal, a kinsman of Earl William Marshal.[21] As one of Gilbert Marshal's men, William St Maur was linked to the Earl's actions in the region, and amongst other things he would have had to deal with native Welsh discontent and, according to Matthew Paris, 'such deluges of rain … never seen before in the memory of anyone'.[22] It appears, though, that he preferred to remain at Penhow where he enlarged the castle, created a large deer park, and dedicated a church there to St Maur. The building at Penhow was essentially a keep, which was about 32 feet by 22 feet in size, with 3 metre thick walls and it stood 3 storeys high.[23] His close relationship with Gilbert Marshal continued; William witnessed four charters between 1234 and 1244. The first is a charter of Gilbert Marshal, Earl of Pembroke, which concerned wood for the tannery of Tintern Abbey; the second concerned Walter Marshal, Earl of Pembroke from 1241–45, who gave the monks at Tintern 10 acres of land. The third and fourth were charters of Richard de Clare and William Derneford respectively. William was later knighted, probably for service in the war against Llywelyn ap Iorweth, under Richard de Clare, Earl of Gloucester which indicates that their military presence and loyalty was important.[24] Following his knighthood, Sir William St Maur witnessed five more charters between 1245 and 1267, most of which were concerned with Tintern Abbey. According to tradition and three later sources William married Sybil Marshal, third daughter of William Marshal, 1st Earl of Pembroke, but this is incorrect as Sybil had married the Earl of Derby, William de Ferrers, by May 1219. The identity of William's actual wife is unknown but we know that he had two sons, Roger and William. Sir William St Maur was dead by 1271 and his son Roger St Maur inherited his lands and estates.

Roger St Maur must have been born sometime between 1216 and 1223, given that he witnessed a charter on his father's behalf, dated between 1236 and 1240. He was certainly of age in 1245 when he and his father gifted 24 acres of land to Tintern Abbey. This land had already been gifted to them by Nicholas de St Bride, whose daughter Roger almost certainly married.[25] He seems to have died by 1276. William de St Maur's second son, William, is a figure somewhat more difficult to pin down and the father-son inheritance is unclear. However we do know that in 1271 the lordship of Penhow was held by another Roger de St Maur, after the death of another William de St Maur. David Loades suggests that this Roger was the grandson of the Roger mentioned above, but this is by no means a certainty. Whoever his father was, on 4 August 1301 Roger witnessed a confirmation by Roger Bigod, Earl of Norfolk and Marshal of England.[26] Roger is said to have married Margaret Devereux of Devonshire, although this is also uncertain. A man of clear ability, he served overseas and in 1306 he was one of the jurors at Striguil who determined what lands Roger Bigod held at the time of his death. He had two sons, including his eldest John, who must have been born around 1302, and another Roger. John de St Maur was definitely an adult by 1325 and in 1337 he was described as Lord of Penhow.[27] John died in April 1358 of the plague, leaving a son, Roger. John's younger brother, yet another Roger, became lord of the manor at Undy and married Cecilia, daughter of John Beachamp of Somerset, a descendant of William Marshal. Cecilia was the young widow of Sir Gilbert de Turberville, and was a great heiress, bringing a large amount of property to the match. Again, the chronology of inheritance becomes unclear here as there are a large number of St Maurs in the area, no doubt all siblings and cousins; individuals whose familial connections remain unclear. Roger died relatively young and Cecilia outlived him, dying in 1393. Their eldest son, William, served alongside Edward, Prince of Wales (later Edward II) in Gascony. He lived at Undy and married a woman called Margaret who was the daughter of Simon de Blackburn of Hereford.[28] Together they had a son, Roger, who ended up inheriting both his parents' lands and those of his grandmother which meant that he became a man of considerable wealth and it is at around this time that the name St Maur begins to appear as Seymour in the records. Likely because of this considerable inheritance he was able to marry Maud, who was the daughter, and heiress, of Sir William Esturmy, who was a knight of Wulfhall. The spelling of Wulfhall varies greatly in the sources and changes over time; for clarity I have chosen to use the earliest spelling – Wulfhall – here, Wulf being the Old English word for Wolf. The Esturmys were famous for having patronised the hospital of the Holy Trinity at Easton and for having been, in the words of Camden, 'the bailiffs and guardian of the forest of Savernake … from the time of Henry III'.[29] Savernake forest lies to the south of Marlborough and had been owned in 934 CE by King Athelstan. In the twelfth century it was established as a royal forest and appears to have been favoured by monarchs ever since.[30] When Maud's father died, Roger inherited this considerable position and property in right of his wife and according to historian, David Loades, moved to Wulfhall from Undy at about this time, bringing into the Seymour family the hall that would play such an important part in Edward Seymour's life. Roger and Maud's son, John Seymour, was born in around 1402 and in due course he inherited everything upon his father's death.[31] He became sheriff of Southampton and Wiltshire in 1431 and twenty years later can be found in Parliament representing Wiltshire when it met in Reading. He was knighted and served again as sheriff of Wiltshire in 1457 but the exact nature of his career remains unclear, although it appears that he was an able administrator. His later life was dominated by the outbreak of the civil war known today as the Wars of the Roses, during which he was charged with maintaining the beacon system in his district and from 1437–9 with raising troops for the Lancastrians, although his only direct involvement seems to have been suppressing local men who supported Richard, Duke of York. When Edward IV took the throne he seems not to have penalised Seymour for any of these actions from which we can likely infer that he was not deeply involved.[32] John Seymour had married Isabel Williams, the daughter of a Bristol merchant, and they had a son, unhelpfully also called John. He predeceased his father but left behind two sons, John and Humphrey, who remained in the care of their mother, Elizabeth, who was a daughter of Sir Robert Coker. The elder son, John, inherited Wulfhall. It was at about this time that the dynasty that was to make and break the family fortunes was rising to power but John was initially no supporter of the invading Henry Tudor. In June 1485 he was tasked by King Richard III to root out any traitorous activity in Wiltshire but he did not join his king to fight at Bosworth, something which it seems earned him the favour of Henry Tudor who allowed him to keep his lands, titles and position. It appears that John Seymour, like many others, had simply hedged his bets. John married Elizabeth Darrell in around 1473 and over fifteen years she bore him eight children. The eldest of whom was yet another John Seymour, who was born in 1474, and who would go on to become Edward Seymour's father. John had four other brothers, Edward's uncles, who all featured in his later story. His three younger brothers were George, William and Robert. George would follow in the family footsteps and become sheriff of Wiltshire, William would be knighted at the marriage of Prince Arthur to Katherine of Aragon, and Robert would become a gentleman usher.

Edward's father was not of age when his own father died in 1492 and so his wardship was granted to Sir Henry Wentworth on 20 December 1493.[33] Sir Henry's lands were centred at Nettlestead in Suffolk and it is likely that it was in the gentle rolling fields of Suffolk that John Seymour spent his minority. The Wentworths were an eminently respectable family who claimed royal descent, albeit well diluted, from Edward III via a daughter of Henry 'Hotspur' Percy.

Why the issue of his wardship took a year to settle is unclear; perhaps his mother opposed it or more likely the matter was simply not important enough for the court to give it priority. From an early age he seems to have been destined for a military career and served, largely in a voluntary capacity, in the king's forces when they met with Cornish rebels under the command of James Tuchet, Lord Audley, at Blackheath in 1497.[34] He served with such bravery that he was knighted on the battlefield.[35] John Seymour's star was in the ascendancy and he forged powerful connections, such as one with Edward Stafford, the Duke of Buckingham, whose steward he was in 1503. By 1507 he was sheriff of Wiltshire; two years later he attended the funeral of Henry VII and under Henry VIII he became a Knight of the Body. A certain personal closeness with the new king can perhaps be implied by the fact that John Seymour was one of the pallbearers at the burial of Henry VIII's infant son Henry, Duke of Cornwall, in 1511 and later he is listed as an official mourner.[36] Despite earlier intentions he was apparently not a military man and did not choose to joust, however he still accompanied the king on campaign in France when the young and warlike king finally browbeat his reluctant council into granting him the necessary funds for war, helped in no small part by the equal belligerence of the Pope who wanted revenge on the French King Louis.

John Seymour had married Margery Wentworth, daughter of Sir Henry Wentworth, on 22 October 1494.[37] Their first son, John, was probably born in around 1494/5 but he died in July 1510, just before the king's own son and perhaps that was the root of their camaraderie. Older than the king by some years, perhaps Henry looked to John Seymour for guidance in his grief. John's son was likely around 5 or 6 when he died and he was buried in Great Bedwyn church in Wiltshire where his brass monument can still be seen bearing the inscription:

> Here lyeth the body of John Seymour son and heir of Sir John Seymour, Knight and of Margery one of the daughters of

> Sir Henry Wentworth, Knight, which deceased the 15th day of July in the year of our Lord 1510 on whose soul Jesus have mercy and of your charity say a Pater Noster and a Ave Maria.

Unlike the king, however, John Seymour had other sons, and his second son, Edward Seymour, had been born in around 1500, followed by Henry in 1503, Thomas in 1508, John, who died as an infant, and Anthony. John and Margery also had four daughters, Jane, Elizabeth, Margery, named after her mother, and Dorothy.

John's wife and Edward's mother was by all accounts a remarkable woman. Margery Wentworth, as we have seen, was the daughter of Sir Henry Wentworth. Her great grandfather, Sir Philip Wentworth, had married a daughter of John, Lord Clifford and his mother had been Elizabeth Percy, the daughter of Henry 'Hotspur' Percy who boasted royal blood, being the great granddaughter of Edward III through her mother's side. Edward Seymour could therefore legitimately claim that he possessed, in a minor way, the blood royal. Margery Wentworth had other illustrious connections too – she was the first cousin of Thomas Howard, 3rd Duke of Norfolk, and his sister, Elizabeth Howard, who would go on to marry Thomas Boleyn. Such a pedigree had given Margery the opportunity to take up a place in the household of the Countess of Surrey, who was her aunt, at Sheriff Hutton castle. Whilst she was there she caught the attention of the poet, John Skelton, who appears to have admired her greatly. Margery is one of the ten gentlewomen that Skelton describes in his most famous poem *The Garland of Laurel*, the others being Elizabeth Howard, Muriel Howard, Anne Dacre, Margaret Tylney, Jane Blener-Hasiet, Isabel Pennell, Margaret Hussey, Gerturde Statham and Isabel Knyght. Their surname speaks to the illustrious circles in which Margery was moving. Skelton was very taken with Margery and likened her to a primrose and columbine. He admired her gentleness, shy demeanour and favoured her with a poem of her own which is much more tender than that which he bestows on the other ladies, reading:

> Wiþh margerain gentle,
> The flower of goodlihead,
> Embroidered the mantle
> Is of your maidenhead.
> Plainly I cannot glose;

Ye be, as I divine,
The pretty primrose,
The goodly columbine.
Benign, courteous, and meek,
With wordes well devised;
In you, who list to seek,
Be virtues well comprised.
With margerain gentle,
The flower of goodlihead,
Embroidered the mantle
Is of your maidenhead.

Where and when John Seymour met Margery Wentworth is unclear but it seems likely that they had grown to know each other when he was in her father's household and she was an excellent match for the up and coming courtier. The frequency with which Margery fell pregnant suggests that they were close and often together.

Margery remained at Wulfhall during their marriage, raising their ever-growing brood of children whilst John Seymour's star under Henry VIII continued to rise. By January 1512, Henry VIII was intent on war and John Seymour raised 100 men from Wiltshire to serve on Sir William Sydney's ship *The Dragon*, a 100-tonne ship, which was heavily armed.[38] He accompanied them to France where Henry VIII aimed to recover Guienne and master the seas. Howard was ordered to escort the Marquis of Dorset and his 10,000 men for that purpose and they were in Brest by 6 June where they 'made war not peace' with the French.[39] Seymour was paid off in October and although the English fleet sailed again the following year, he did not. This was because Henry VIII wanted him to instead serve in the royal army, where he can be found again in charge of 100 men in the king's force for his planned invasion of Picardy. He served under Lord Lisle, Henry VIII's closest friend and marshall of the army, Charles Brandon, who had been granted the title on 15 May 1513 when he had become betrothed to Elizabeth Grey. A marriage which would famously never take place when Brandon married the king's sister, Mary, instead. Brandon was exceptionally close to the king with Margaret of Savoy referring to him as a 'second king'. Seymour's proximity to him therefore implies a degree of closeness to the innermost royal circle. Seymour was present at the siege of Therouanne and the Battle of the Spurs, at which it is said the French ran away so fast that only their spurs were visible to the advancing Englishmen. During the battle, in the words of the St Maur chronicle, 'he succeeded in providing such signal services that the king who was present conferred upon him the honour of Knight Banneret'.[40] By October he had returned to England with the king and was once again paid off.[41]

In the patriarchal world of Tudor England it is reasonable to assume that John Seymour was held up to the infant Edward Seymour as the ideal to which to aspire. From the earliest moments of his consciousness he would no doubt have been told that his largely absent father was a great man, a brave warrior, a friend of the king and that he must do everything possible to equip himself to follow in his father's footsteps and honour the family name.

Whilst his father was away Edward Seymour grew up at the family's relatively recently acquired seat of Wulfhall. As mentioned earlier, the house was located near Savernake forest, of which the Seymours were ancestral wardens. We know that the house that Edward Seymour grew up in was built of stone and was medieval in date; it is likely it had been built over a much earlier dwelling. Edward was raised under the supervision of his mother, which was usual at the time. As a young child he would have learnt to read and write and possibly owned books such as a primer, which was 'the equivalent of an elementary textbook' from which he could learn 'his ABC's and prayers [it was] likely illuminated or illustrated with woodcut pictures'.[42] There are many records of such books being given to children of the nobility. He could also have learnt less academic pursuits from an early age such as riding and hunting. We know that Henry VIII himself was riding at 3 years of age and that he valued such accomplishments amongst his courtiers.[43] It would make sense then that an ambitious man such as John Seymour would school his son in a way that was likely to impress his sovereign.

The Fillol's

While Edward Seymour was growing up, so too was another child, this time a girl. Catherine Fillol's date of birth, like much about her life, remains unclear. It is most likely that she was born sometime in around 1500–1503, making her roughly the same age as her future husband Edward Seymour. The *History of Parliament* states that Catherine was 20 in 1527, when her father was making provision for the settlement of his estates, but that would place her date of birth sometime in 1507, which would have made her only 7 years old when she married. The fact that the marriage agreements contains a specific term which both fathers had to agree to: the idea that if Edward Seymour 'disagrees with the marriage' within three years then John Seymour would pay 200 marks towards her next dowry, suggests that Seymour was hedging his bets to see what sort of woman Catherine would grow into.[1] Whilst this is not impossible, child betrothals and marriages after all were nothing new, it would mean that she was just 11 years old when she bore her first child as his date of birth is established. This would have been extremely unusual, as the age at which a married couple were permitted to sleep together was 12 and this certainly did not mean that they did so with most 'believing that twelve was far too young for a girl to be participating in sex'.[2] Most young girls were expected to wait until at least age 14, something which became even more well-established following the example of Margaret Beaufort who was only just 13 years old when she gave birth to her only child, Henry Tudor. The labour did so much damage to her immature tissues and slight body that she never fell pregnant again, despite marrying twice more. She went on to 'enumerate a set of proper procedures concerning the delivery of potential heirs' and to specify the age at which their mother should be, something she must have felt strongly about.[3]

Based upon all this, historian Audrey Locke has suggested a birthdate for Catherine of 1504, meaning that she would have been 15 when she bore her first child, something much more acceptable to Tudor sensibilities and biological reality.[4] Given all this a date of somewhere between 1500–1504 for Catherine Fillol's birth seems most likely.

Catherine was the daughter of Sir William Fillol of Woodlands, Horton in Dorset and Fillols Hall, Kelvedon in Essex and Dorothy Ifield, who would marry John Rogers in 1532 after her first husband's death.[5] The Fillol family was an old and noble one who had shared a remarkably similar path to prosperity with the Seymours, although they were not quite on a par with them. The two families would certainly have known each other though as Woodlands is barely fifty miles from Wulfhall.

The Fillol or Filliol family (the spelling varies) are first mentioned in England at the time of the Norman conquest, their name appearing on the Roll of Battle Abbey. According to legend this Fillol was a bastard son of the Conqueror but this seems unlikely; far more likely they hailed from

Argentan in France. Just over a century later one Baldwin Fillol held three knights' fees in Kelvedon Essex according to the Pipe Rolls in 1206 and 1216.[6] The Fillols split into many branches and those based in the south east made a series of advantageous marriages and acquired a good deal of land in East Anglia, including estates at Coggeshall, Feering, Braxted, Inworth, Messing, Bradwell, Easthorpe, Copford, Tolleshunt Knights, Terling, Baddow, Bergholt, Little Oakley and Boreham.[7] They seem to have spent little time at Fillol's hall though when they were engaged in fighting for the king in France, Scotland and Wales during the thirteenth and fourteenth centuries.

Down in Dorset the Fillol family held the manor at Woodlands near Horton, since at least the twelfth century. By the late 1300s we are on historic ground and we know that Catherine's great grandfather, William Fillol, was born in around 1380 and owned the manor. He made several grants to the local priory, which was a Benedictine cell of Sherborne Abbey. It had existed in the district of Woodlands, Horton since 961 CE during the Anglo Saxon period when it gained prestige following the placement of St Wolfryth or Wolfrida as abbess, a woman who was related to King Alfred's royal line. The priory was involved in the working of two mills and a six acre meadow.[8]

William Fillol married Joan Frome, a daughter of John Frome, a Lord of Bickingham who served as a Knight of the Shire in three parliaments and then as sheriff of Dorsetshire. William died young, in his mid-thirties, and his lands passed to his son, John Fillol, who was born in around 1409. He married Margaret Carent of Silton in Dorsetshire. They had at least one son, Catherine's father, William ,who was born in around 1453 and who married Dorothy Ifield. Quite how he came to inherit Fillol's Hall in Essex, and how it came into the family's possession is something of a mystery, but it seems most likely that the East Anglian and Dorset branches of the family shared common ancestry and that at some point the rules of inheritance based upon primogeniture meant that the East Anglian inheritance came into the possession of their distant relations.

Catherine had a sister, Anne, but it is not known where the two girls grew up.[9] As the daughters of a nobleman, however, they would have received an education as befitted their status and prepared them for their future role as wives and mothers. Girls in the early 1500s would have mostly been taught informally at home. This would change in the 1530s when highly educating one's daughters became fashionable amongst the nobility following the examples set by Thomas More and Erasmus, with the aim of girls being later able to assist their husbands in creating virtuous, learned homes. When Catherine was growing up, however, the main focus of a woman's education was on equipping her for her future role as a wife and mother. To this end she would have been taught how to read, write and manage a household. She would also have been taught feminine accomplishments such as how to play music, dance and sing. It might well have been that the Seymour and Fillol families planned an alliance between the Seymour boy, Edward, and Fillol girl, Catherine, early on, suggested again by the fact that there was a 'get out clause' in the marriage agreement. Catherine may well have grown up, in the manner of Katherine of Aragon, knowing exactly who her future husband would be.

Religion would have also played an important role in Catherine's upbringing. Everyone was taught to be pious and to honour God. Going to church was compulsory and only illness would excuse you from attendance at Mass. Catherine, of course, was growing up thirty years before Henry VIII began the Reformation, so her faith would have been that of the 'old religion' – Roman Catholicism. The church that Catherine attended would therefore have been colourfully adorned with wall paintings and coloured wall hangings. Inside, the church would have been filled with candles and smelt of incense. There were between 40 and 50 important Church festivals in the Roman Catholic calendar and these were almost compulsory, with exceptions being made only for those such as fishermen, those tending the land or servants who had not obtained permission. There were two services a year dedicated especially to children: Saint Nicholas' day on 6 December and the Feast of the Holy Innocents on 28 September. The services which Catherine listened to would have been given mostly in Latin with a verse in English to remind them of baptism.[10] The key feature of the service which everyone in this book grew up with was the moment of transubstantiation when the priest would raise the host, and the bread and wine would be transformed into the literal body and blood of Christ.

The Stanhopes

Whilst Catherine was growing up so too was another girl, who had been born in around 1505–1510. Her name was Anne, and she was the daughter of Sir Edward Stanhope and his second wife, Elizabeth Bourchier.[1] Sir Edward

Stanhope was from an old and well-established family, in the manner of the Seymours and Fillols. The Stanhope name is said to derive from the town of Stanhope in Durham. In the reign of King Henry III, Sir Richard de Stanhope held lands in the north and his son, another Richard, was Lord of Estwyche and Mayor of Newcastle. He served against the Scots and received lands at Paxton from Edward III as reward for his service. His son, John, married the daughter and heiress of Stephen Mauvel, inheriting the manor of Rampton in Nottinghamshire. Sir Edward Seymour's great great grandfather was Sir Richard Stanhope of Rampton who was created a Knight of the Bath at the coronation of Henry IV and had served Nottingham in parliament. The identity of his first wife is unclear, but she was called Elizabeth, and was possibly the heiress of John Longvilliers. Richard secondly married Joan Staveley, the spelling being given as Johanna on her gravestone in Rampton church where she was buried in 1440, four years after her husband. Together they had five children, the eldest of which, Robert, died without issue. His son, Richard, meanwhile married twice and it was his son, John, by his first wife, Elizabeth Markham, who inherited the family lands and property in 1436 upon Richard's death. We know that these lands included those of Rampton, Ansty, Skegby, Southcotam, Egmanton and Tuxford. John had married Elizabeth Talbot in 1425, a daughter of Sir Thomas Talbot of Yorkshire, who it appears after her husband's death took a vow of chastity before the Archbishop of York at Scrooby where she swore that:

> In the name of God Amen, I Elizabeth Stanhope promise and vow to God, and our Lady, and all the Saints to be chaste from this time forward. In the presence of you, most revered father in God. Whom be the grace of God Archbishop of York, primate of England, and legate of the court of Rome and I promise to live stability in the vow during my life. And in witness thereof with my own hand make here this inscription – In nomine Patris, et Filii, et Spiritus Sancti, Amen.[2]

John and Elizabeth had at least two sons, Thomas and Henry, but there was some controversy regarding the estate inheritance and his lands seem to have passed in part to his cousin Edward Stanhope.[3] The rest went to his sons, of whom Thomas was the eldest, having been born in around 1445 in Rampton. He married Mary Jeringham of Somerleyton and they also had two sons – Anne's father, Edward Stanhope, and her uncle John. Sir Edward Stanhope was born in 1474 and as a teenager fought at the Battle of Stoke Field which saw the rebellion against Henry VII in the name of Lambert Simnel, and orchestrated by amongst other the Earl of Lincoln, crushed. He was noted as 'one of the principal (soldiers) who vanquished John Earl of Lincoln'.[4] Sir Edward was a career soldier and is known to have fought at the Battle of Blackheath in 1497, after which he was knighted for his valour and loyalty to the king for whom he was made a Knight of the Body and who created him Constable of Sandal Castle.[5] Anne's father was married twice, firstly in about 1500 in Nottingham to Adelina Clifton, a daughter of Sir Gervase Clifton.[6] Together Edward and Adelina had six children: Anne's older half siblings, Richard, Michael, Marmaduke, Thomas, John and Elizabeth. The eldest of which, Richard and Michael, would go on to play an important role in their half-sister's life. Adelina died young, possibly falling victim to death in childbirth which saw one in three women die even amongst the nobility, and Edward Stanhope then married Anne's mother, Elizabeth Bourchier, a family with far more illustrious connections than the Stanhopes.[7] Anne's mother was a daughter of Fulk Bourchier, 10th Baron FitzWarin (1445–1479) and descended from Edward III through his youngest son, Thomas of Woodstock, and his daughter Anne of Gloucester. This degree of royal descent was not particularly uncommon, Edward III had numerous children and dozens of descendants but it was something of which Anne would later be extremely proud and it is likely that the status it bequeathed would have been impressed upon her throughout her childhood. Fulk's wife and Anne's grandmother was Elizabeth Dynham, who after being married and widowed three times took a vow of celibacy in 1510 before Bishop Fisher and devoted herself to the religious life.[8] Elizabeth Bourchier had been married before; her first husband had been Henry Beaumont, her second a gentleman named Verney by whom she had a daughter, Anne's half-sister Katherine Verney. Anne's father was Elizabeth's third husband, but Edward Stanhope died in 1511, likely before Anne was even a year old. This did not leave Anne, as is sometimes suggested, as a great heiress. Her father's heirs were her half-brothers Richard and Michael from his first marriage and her own share of the Stanhope inheritance appears to have been insufficient for her to be appointed a royal ward. Instead she was left in the care of her mother, who in 1512 married again, this time to Sir Richard Page by whom she soon had another daughter, Elizabeth. The marriage was an advantageous one; Richard Page was a presence at the court of Henry VIII being, at the time, a member of Cardinal Wolsey's household, and later his chamberlain. In 1516 he was knighted and made a gentleman of Henry VIII's privy chamber, although as we shall see his career at court was far from smooth sailing. This connection was one that Anne's ambitious mother recognised the importance of and from an early age it seems that it was intended that Anne should serve at the royal court. As well as this connection and her drop of royal blood, Anne had the advantage of being born almost a decade after Catherine Fillol and as such she is much more likely to have been formally educated. By the 1520s many noble families were beginning to educate their daughters along humanist lines. Prominent scholars such as Erasmus, Juan Luis Vives and Thomas More were now recommending that girls be educated in more than just the ways of the Church or household. Anne, and her half-sisters, would therefore have likely been taught not just to read and write but also schooled in the basics of subjects such as philosophy, poetry and languages such as Latin and French. Thomas More's daughter, Margaret Roper, was held up as the best example of the benefits of educating women and the embodiment of this new approach to female education.[9] Richard Hyde, who translated Vives work into English, argued that women should be educated 'to the increase of her virtue/she hath taken and taketh no little occasion of her learning'.[10] Anne's education would have been supervised by her mother, around whom everything in her world would have revolved. As we shall see, there is evidence that Anne and her mother were close in later life suggesting that as a child Anne was strongly attached to her and that they spent a good deal of time together.

Chapter 2

Edward and Catherine

The royal court of Henry VIII was at the centre of all three of these children's worlds. Catherine and Anne were being raised to be the sort of wives and mothers who were capable of making an illustrious marriage. Catherine's future husband was likely already known to her; Anne, however, would have to catch a husband herself.

Edward Seymour meanwhile was seeking preference and advancement, and the best way to achieve this was to secure the support of an influential patron and through him serve the king. John Seymour, whilst a regular figure at court, had no particular influence there to wield on behalf of his son but at some point Edward Seymour came to the king's attention and at just 14 years old he was, in October 1514, appointed as page of honour to accompany the king's sister, Mary, when she married Louis XII, King of France.[1] This was a hugely prestigious appointment and there seems no obvious reason why he was chosen, so perhaps it should be attributed to his personal merit. He was appointed alongside two other pages, the sons of Lord Roos and Lord Cobham. Together they accompanied Mary when she sailed from Dover to Calais to marry the ageing French king. Edward Seymour would have witnessed their elaborate wedding at Abbeville church. Louis and Mary had already been married at a proxy wedding held in the Great Hall at Greenwich which saw the Duke of Longueville stand in for the French king, and at which the princess had worn 'a gown of purple satin and cloth of gold in chequers; she wore a cap of cloth of gold and chains and jewels like the queen'.[2] The Duke of Longueville was likely a more attractive prospect than Louis to Mary, who resented the match and was famously careful to extract a promise from her brother that should Louis XII die before her and that if she were still childless, that she could then marry a man of her own choice. There is some speculation that she was in fact already in love with Henry VIII's closest friend, the handsome and chivalric Charles Brandon. If so perhaps the rumours reached the young Seymour's ears as he travelled with the princess.

In France Mary was married with splendour which surpassed even the events in London. She was accompanied by the Dukes of Norfolk, Dorset, Surrey, Lord Monteagle and the Bishop of Durham. These were followed by other noblemen and twenty-four ladies dressed in cloth of gold. Lastly, thirteen of Mary's closest women closed the procession. These would have included Mary Boleyn, although her sister Anne most likely missed the wedding as despite the fact that she had been chosen to join her sister in serving Queen Mary it was only on 14 August that Thomas Boleyn had written to recall Anne from the court of Margaret of Austria and it is therefore unlikely that she had caught up with the royal party by the time of the wedding, denying Edward Seymour his first glimpse of her. There is no record of where Edward Seymour was during the procession or ceremony but most likely he and the other pages were somewhere close by in order that they might carry trains, fetch water or run messages.[3] He would also have witnessed Mary's crowning as Queen of France which took place on the 5 November 1514 at the Cathedral of St Denis. Following their marriage Louis XII sent the majority of Mary's English household home, but Edward Seymour and the other pages were permitted to remain. Mary's marriage was the fulfilment of her brother's political ambitions but not her own. Louis XII was 52 years old, said to be riddled with gout and unattractive. Edward and Mary's time in France was cut short though by the death of Louis who died on the 1 January 1515.[4] Some blamed gout, others that he had been worn out by his exertions in the bedchamber with his new wife.[5] Either way, Mary was quickly shrouded in white, the traditional colour of French mourning and plans were made for her return to England.

Perhaps Edward was also keen to come home because just prior to his departure he and Catherine Fillol had married. We know nothing about the wedding itself, nor the celebrations that may have accompanied it; even the date itself is uncertain. As we have seen, because of their young ages, it seems most likely that the marriage at this stage was on paper which perhaps explains why there is no concrete reference to it. For Catherine, though, their marriage would have brought about a major change in that she was sent to live at Wulfhall with her new husband's family. The young couple were to live at Wulfhall until Edward reached the age of 21. For a young woman to be sent to live with her husband's family was not unusual, as upon her marriage Catherine's status now 'depended entirely on that of her husband and his family'.[6] She would have lived alongside Edward's sisters – Jane, who was born at Wulfhall sometime between October 1507 and October 1508, Elizabeth and Dorothy.[7] Given their difference in age it seems unlikely that Catherine and the Seymour girls grew particularly close but no doubt affection grew as the young Seymour sisters showed their sister-in-law around the house and together they may have enjoyed exploring the surrounding farmland and Savernake forest. They almost certainly already knew each other fairly well having lived close by for many years. The house that Catherine would have known no longer exists but we know that she and the Seymour daughters had a chaplain to minister to them, a separate chamber and servants to attend to them. Under her mother-in-law's supervision, Catherine's day-to-day life would have, in reality, changed very little. Women's lives all over Tudor England followed a general pattern. Together the women of the household would have learnt music, read the scriptures and spent a good deal of their time at their needlework. Jane would later become very accomplished at this under her mother's instruction, suggesting that Catherine might have received a similar level of tuition from Margery. She would also have enjoyed the outdoor pursuits considered very suitable for young women. The Seymour daughters were very good horsewomen, and again it seems logical to assume that even if Catherine could not ride well before joining the household, she soon learnt. John Seymour kept a pack of hounds and the young Seymour women often took part in the bloody chase.

While Catherine was settling into life at Wulfhall, Edward's marriage proved no barrier to either his appointment as page or his career, and upon his return from France he resumed or began a degree of further education. The evidence is contradictory but it seems that he went to study at Oxford University.[8] This meant that his education prior to this must have equipped him with a knowledge of Latin, the classics, theology and philosophy. At the time access to university was just opening up to members of the nobility, having been traditionally reserved for members of the clergy. In the medieval period there were 65 Benedictine Priories in England and 38 of these sent monks to Oxford University and more to Cambridge where they primarily studied theology and canon law.[9] By now, though, it was becoming usual for aspiring young men to complete a few years of education at a university to equip them for life in a royal court where both the monarch and his wife appreciated learning and the arts. To this end, he would not have taken a degree as we understand it; there is no evidence that he ever earned one, but rather received a high level of general education in subjects such as theology, philosophy, mathematics, astronomy, rhetoric and geometry. Rhetoric was the ability to express and defend oneself in a debate and was increasingly becoming an important and valued skill. These universities were still at this date firmly rooted in Roman Catholicism and the teachings of the Catholic Church; they had not yet become Cromwell's 'universities of England' in the manner that the Church would become itself 'of England'.[10] To this end, nearly all of his lectures would have been given in Latin and his textbooks written in that language.

By 1516 he is listed as being an attendant in the king's privy chamber, suggesting that he had left university by this date. He almost certainly joined the periphery of the young king's circle of athletic jousting companions which included men such as Charles Brandon, by now married to Mary Tudor, Henry Bourchier, Henry Clifford and Edward Stafford, Duke of Buckingham. The court records the details of the 'feats of arms' that these young men took part in. One such 1516 record, tells us that Brandon, conveniently on the king's team, did not lose a single duel and achieved the highest score during one jousting tournament, which saw him also break seventeen lances compared to Henry's twelve on the second day. There is no specific mention of Edward Seymour suggesting that he was not directly part of this group, likely on account of his young age, and that he was not athletically skilled enough to be an asset to the teams. Historian, David Loades, suggests that the fact that young Edward Seymour does not appear to have caught the king's attention might have been behind the fact that in 1517 his father, John Seymour, took pains to secure for himself and Edward jointly the constableship of Bristol castle, something which would have secured his eldest son's future and helped to 'strengthen his position in royal favour'.[11] Perhaps it was something that caught the eye of the latest man on the rise – the king's great friend, Cardinal Wolsey. The famously red-draped Cardinal, whose coat of arms was surmounted by a red cardinal's hat, was the son of an Ipswich butcher. He had attended Cambridge university and by 1520 was right at the pinnacle of his influence and success, having that year stage managed the Field of the Cloth of Gold at which Henry VIII and Francis I of France met, and arm wrestled in a display of male testosterone.

By early 1521, Edward Seymour was employed in the Cardinal's household and he was sent to the Hapsburg court.[12] He was sent to be the Cardinal's eyes and ears to the household of the Holy Roman Emperor, Charles V, when he presided over the Imperial Diet at Worms. Charles V took him on as a gentleman on the recommendation of, according to a letter written by Cuthbert Tunstall to Wolsey, 'the king and Wolsey ... with the entertainment of a gentleman's room'.[13] This event is particularly significant in Edward Seymour's life as it would have been the first occasion where he seriously encountered the views of the new Protestant/Lutheran religion.

The Diet was held from 28 January to 25 May at the Heylshof Gardens. Martin Luther himself was summoned to speak under guarantee of Imperial safe conduct, his teachings having already been condemned by both Rome and Pope Leo X. Luther famously made his declaration which states, amongst other things, that his books were 'written against the papacy and papal scheming and action, that is against those who through evil teaching and example have ruined Christendom laying it waste with the evils of spirit and of soul... [I have written] against certain private individuals who attempted to defend such Roman tyranny and denounce my pious doctrine ... I am come not to send peace but a sword to set a man against his father etc ...we condemn the Word of God if we do away with our factions and dissension'.[14] His words were to serve as a battle cry for the oncoming Protestant Reformation. Unsurprisingly his words were met with outrage across Christendom and by May the Emperor had issued his response which declared that anyone who sold, reproduced or even discussed Luther's works was a heretic. Necessarily Edward Seymour must have become aware of the issues and debates surrounding Martin Luther and his views during his time at Worms; perhaps he also began to realise that the touch paper which had been lit when Luther, a 33-year-old Augustine Friar, hammered his Ninety-Five Theses to the doors of the Castle Church of Wittenberg in Saxony, was not going to be easily extinguished. The Emperor and council were 'well pleased' with Seymour, perhaps implying that they struck up a friendship or agreed, for now at least, on religious grounds.[15] In England, meanwhile, the idea of Lutheranism was widely condemned with Cardinal Campeggio writing on 30 March to Cardinal Wolsey, congratulating him on his appointment to the See of Lincoln and asked him to urge Henry to 'write to the Emperor as the Pope had done to crush this pestilence entirely'. Henry did so and wrote to Pope Leo X that 'ever since [I] knew about Luther's heresy in Germany [he had] made it his study how to extirpate it'.[16] Wolsey himself was to write to Chievres to the same effect, and that same month complained that the powers he had from Rome did not allow him to 'burn books of Lutheran depravity'.[17]

Edward Seymour returned to England that same year and presumably continued in the king's service, returning to visit his wife and family at Wulfhall when his duties permitted. He next firmly appears in the historical record in 1523 when he, alongside his father, were named as part of the force which was to accompany Charles Brandon into France. He is listed in between Lord Monteagle and Sir William Kingston in a record of the men who accompanied him.[18] Relations had soured between France and England since the Field of the Cloth of Gold as the Treaty of Universal Peace began to fracture. By the middle of 1521 France and the Emperor, Charles V, were once again at war with each other following Francis' foray into north-east France and Navarre. Charles predictably made a retaliatory attack on French territory and England was inevitably drawn into the conflict. Wolsey and Henry quickly realised that the larger scale of the Emperor's resources would surely mean he would be on the winning side, so England agreed a secret alliance – declaring war on France in 1522. The expedition, led by Charles Brandon, was intended to be a joint one alongside the forces of Charles V and Charles, Duke of Bourbon. The force numbered approximately 14,000 Englishmen, 700 men from the Low Countries under the command of Floris d'Egmont, Count of Burn, and 10,000 from what is now Germany. The latter of which were to march into France from the east in an attempt to force Francis into fighting a war on two fronts. For a young man like Edward Seymour this was a chance to 'win his spurs' and gain some valuable military experience in an age when military prowess was still a crucially important attribute. Brandon and his English forces soon found themselves more or less on their own as Charles V hesitated to act and Bourbon's action never really got off the ground; it was 'the boldest and most penetrating invasion of France by the English since the reign of Henry V'.[19] They had to abandon their plan to take Boulogne and instead marched towards Paris, where they won a victory at Montdidier, fifty miles from the city, on 28 October but it was simply too late in the season for them to proceed any further. Winter was closing in, the weather was turning and men began to desert. The expedition was a failure; the English had to retreat and they lost any towns they had taken as they did not have the men, supplies or money to properly garrison them. Edward Seymour, however, had distinguished himself at some point and was knighted by Brandon 'in the field' at Roye, to the north side of the town, on 1 November, alongside 13 others.[20] By December, Seymour, along with the rest of the English forces, was back in England and soon afterwards could be found, once again, serving in the king's household, although exactly what his duties were is unclear.[21] Perhaps he would have witnessed the infamous pageant held on Shrove Tuesday 1522 at Wolsey's Palace of York Place, where a Chateau vert had been installed with three towers and battlements shining with green foil, hence the name. In each tower were eight court ladies dazzlingly dressed in satin and jewels. Each embodied a virtue including Anne Boleyn as Perseverance, although to what extent the king took notice of her at this early date has been open to debate then and ever since.[22] The castle was defended by eight boys of the Chapel Royal who were dressed 'like women of India', and would have been something the young man from Wiltshire was unlikely to ever forget.[23]

Seymour's next appointment was one which would have had an impact on Catherine's standing locally and the way in which she was regarded. He was made a Justice of the Peace in Wiltshire in 1525.[24] In Tudor times the role of Justice of the Peace was an important one having superseded the role of sheriff during the reign of Henry VII, who also greatly increased their numbers.[25] It did not require attendance at court, which perhaps indicates that Seymour began to spend more time at Wulfhall with his wife during this period. Seymour was now responsible for the maintenance of public order in Wiltshire and for implementing any legislation which had been introduced by the king and government in London. He was also responsible for raising men to fight should the king command it, maintaining roads and the system of fire beacons which could be used to raise the alarm in the event of invasion, attack or disturbance. They were in short 'the most useful tool of local government'.[26] This appointment, which presumably was carried out successfully both in Wiltshire and London, led to Seymour's most significant appointment to date when in 1525 he was made Master of the King's Horse to Henry VIII's bastard son, Henry Fitzroy, with a wage of sixty pounds a year.[27]

Henry Fitzroy had been born in 1519, the son of the king by his then mistress Elizabeth Blount, known as Bessie. He had been born at the Priory of St Lawrence at Blackmore in Essex, all of the arrangements for which had been handled by Wolsey.[28] Henry VIII had acknowledged the boy and in June 1525 had decided to ennoble him, infuriating his wife Queen Katherine. This action was not without precedent – in 1196 William Longspee, the illegitimate son of Henry II by Ida de Tosny, had married Ela of Salisbury and William was granted the earldom by his half-brother Richard I – but it was not a common occurrence.[29] Henry Fitzroy was created 1st Earl of Nottingham and then Duke of Richmond and Somerset. at the royal palace of Bridewell on 18 June 1525.[30] This action made him, at a stroke, the premier duke in the land, following Buckingham's execution and henceforth he was addressed as the 'right high and noble prince Henry, Duke of Richmond and Somerset'.[31] He was endowed with lands which were particularly significant to the Tudor dynasty, most of which had been held by Henry VIII's grandmother, Margaret Beaufort, as Countess of Richmond and inheritrix to her father, John Beaufort's lands. The granting of the Beaufort/Somerset lands were particularly significant. John Beaufort had been a royal bastard, the eldest son of John of Gaunt, Duke of Lancaster, and his mistress, later wife, Kathryn Swynford.[32] All this led to speculation that Henry VIII was planning to make the 6-year-old Fitzroy his heir, as his only legitimate child was a solitary daughter, Princess Mary; but this was not necessarily the case. Mary was sent at about this time to Ludlow castle in the Welsh Marches, to head the council there, as many a Prince of Wales had done previously. Her uncle, Henry VIII's elder brother, had been there when he sickened and died. Her household was presided over by John Dudley as her chamberlain and the Countess of Salisbury as her Lady Mistress. Fitzroy, meanwhile, was to be sent to Sheriff Hutton in Yorkshire, the traditional seat of the royal Council of the North. Within his household was Edward Seymour. The post of Master of the Horse might seem an insignificant one today but in the Tudor period it was a high status and valued one. He would have been responsible for all aspects of the household travel and he would also have had to run, manage the finances of and ensure that the stables were well maintained and stocked. Horses were needed for riding, pulling the baggage trains, jousting, and hunting. Mares had to be sourced for the ladies of the household, and litters had to be assembled and maintained. Even horses for working the lands around the Richmond and Somerset estates came under Seymour's remit. William Coffin, who was Master of the Horse to two of Henry VIII's queens, was in his role expected to be 'a professional household administrator, actively concerned with the staffing of his department'.[33] Fitzroy travelled north initially in a litter but then he 'hath ridden upon his hobby (pony) and hath been very well at ease'.[34] Seymour would also have been expected to ride with Fitzroy and ensure his personal safety when out and about, especially when hunting. Fitzroy it appears was a good hunter, felling a buck himself at only 6 years of age, suggesting that this was something Seymour had to give serious consideration to on a regular basis. This view is supported by the fact that Seymour's bill to Fitzroy's Clerk Comptroller for the necessities of his responsibility came to ninety-one pounds.[35] The necessity of being with Fitzroy frequently in person gave him the chance to build a personal relationship with the young royal, which considering Fitzroy seemed destined for a glittering future could only be advantageous, especially as on 16 July he was granted the additional appointment of Lord High Admiral of England.

It also brought Edward Seymour into the orbit of many other young men on the rise, amongst whom were Henry Grey (who would later become the father of Jane Grey), William Parr, Henry Clifford, Thomas Fines and Richard Page, Anne Stanhope's future stepfather, giving us a clear example of just how small and interconnected the world of the Tudor nobility was.

Seymour's new role would not have rid him of his obligation to attend the court entirely though and he must have frequently visited London, as he was still a squire of the king's household. He must also have visited Wulfhall and his wife whenever possible because we know that by 1526/7 Catherine Fillol was pregnant. Perhaps he went home early in 1527, just before he was sent to France as a member of Wolsey's vast retinue when the Cardinal was sent to meet with Francis I in place of the king. Wolsey was at the height of his power at this time and was preceded in his regal cavalcade by Seymour and other gentlemen dressed in black velvet and wearing heavy gold chains. But it was not to last because in 1527 Henry VIII began his quest for an annulment of his marriage to Katherine of Aragon so that he could marry Anne Boleyn. Together Wolsey, Henry and Francis planned to take advantage of the fact that Pope Clement VII was imprisoned in Rome and set up a temporary Church government. Wolsey intended to be appointed its head and then he would have the authority to annul his master's marriage, in defiance of Clement. The plan failed, but Seymour had now been exposed to the realities of extremely complex international diplomacy.

Chapter 3

Catherine

Back in Wiltshire, Catherine Fillol was by now in her mid-twenties and of prime age for childbearing. The fact that the child Catherine carried would be heir to all the Seymour lands and properties must have meant that a good deal of the family's hopes and dreams were invested in her pregnancy. There is, however, clear evidence that all was not right in Catherine's world. At some point Catherine and her husband quarrelled seriously with her father. William Fillol died in 1527 and in his will he went to great lengths to disinherit his daughter, her husband and their heirs. This was, the will states, for 'many diverse causes and considerations my moving, that neither my daughter dame Kateryn Seymour nor her heirs of her body nor Edward Seymour her husband in any ways shall have any parts or parcel of my said manors, lands, tenements and other premises'.[1] Her father left her instead forty pounds if she would 'live virtuously and abide in some house of religion of women'.[2]

It is not clear exactly when Catherine's child was born but I think it's safe to say that her last days of pregnancy and first as a new mother could hardly have been tranquil with the rooms of Wulfhall no doubt alive with speculation, rumour or outrage. William, after all, did not just disinherit Catherine but also Edward Seymour, and there is no way in which that could have been interpreted as anything other than an insult, a slur on the Seymour honour.

Pregnancy was already, in the words of historian, Elizabeth Norton, 'just about the most dangerous time in a woman's life'.[3] Without adequate medical knowledge or pain relief women only had their faith and the knowledge of countless women passed down from generation to generation to depend upon. On the other hand pregnancy and childbirth was also considered the culmination of a woman's destiny and it was the means by which they could yield power. Their husbands were told by the

Church to abstain from their beds at this time and pregnant noble women, women who were not physically required to work, such as Catherine, would have withdrawn into a private chamber as the time of her labour drew to a close, to be attended exclusively by women and kept warm, fed and rested. If the outcome of their confinement was a healthy son, their future was also secure. Henry VIII could never have divorced Katherine, or indeed killed Anne Boleyn even if he wished to, if either had borne him a son. Given that, as we have seen, the Fillol and Seymour families both had a history of female devotion, perhaps a religious relic was sent from one of the religious houses they subsidised, from which she could draw strength. It was common for holy relics to be sent for and held or pressed to the body during childbirth, as with Elizabeth of York who had sent for the girdle of Our Lady to be brought from Westminster Abbey for her confinements.

Catherine would have been attended by her sisters and mother-in-law. It would have been usual for a woman's mother to travel to be with her also, but given the family rift I think this can be discounted as a possibility. Denied the support of her husband, parents or her sister it is impossible to escape the idea that however attached she was by now to the Seymour family, Catherine must have felt isolated and very much alone.

Nevertheless Catherine did give birth in the warmth and security of Wulfhall, which gave her a decided advantage over many Tudor women, and there is no evidence that she suffered any long term consequences from her first childbed and her baby, a son, was healthy. He would most likely have been suckled by a wet nurse, probably a local woman or member of the family who had borne a child at a similar time. As the eldest son the baby, who was named John for his grandfather, would have eventually been expected to follow in his father's footsteps and forge a career based on education and patronage, but for now it is clear that he was left in the care of his mother at Wulfhall, to grow up surrounded by woods and fields. Catherine would have supervised his care and been involved in his day-to-day life as befitted a gentile noblewoman. Despite the wording of William Fillol's will, there is no evidence that there was any marital discord between Catherine and Edward. She did not retreat to a religious house as her father had requested, and certainly was still sleeping, in the fullest sense of the word, with her husband when he could be spared from his duties at court. By 1529, Edward had been granted the manors of Henstage and Charlecote, possibly with a view to living in one whilst his father lived and Catherine was once again pregnant. But something, both at court and within their marriage, was changing.

By autumn 1529 Cardinal Wolsey's fall from power was complete. He had failed to secure Henry VIII the annulment that he wanted and had paid the price. His lands and titles were forfeit to the Crown, although the extent to which Henry VIII intended to punish him remains unclear, as he was initially allowed to remain as Archbishop of York and to travel north to Cawood Castle. It was whilst he was there that he was accused of treason and ordered to return to London. He died on 29 November at Leicester before he reached the Capital.

Back at Wulfhall, however, equally serious discord was also brewing. Catherine's second pregnancy appears to have proceeded uneventfully and she gave birth to a second healthy son, this one named Edward for his father. However shortly after her Edward's birth, Edward Seymour repudiated his wife. Later historians have suggested, almost uniformly, that Catherine was unfaithful and that was why she was cast aside. She is called a wicked woman, of no virtue, and it is even suggested that she had had an affair with her own father-in-law, John Seymour. Historian, Alison Weir, claims that Catherine's misconduct was a 'scandal that shocked even Henry VIII's courtiers', whilst historian, Joanna Denny, also suggests that there was a 'great scandal [now] attached to the Seymour name'.[4] There is, however, no real evidence for this, the accusation of adultery with her own father-in-law comes from a far later date. It is not until the seventeenth century that Peter Heylyn firmly accuses Catherine of adultery. He writes that whilst he was in France, Edward Seymour 'did acquaint himself there with a learned man, supposed to have great skills in magics of whom he obtained, by great rewards and importunities, to let him see, by the help of some magical perspective, in what estate all his relations stood at home. In which impertinence he was so far satisfied as to behold a Gentleman of his acquaintance in a more familiar posture with his wife than was agreeable to the honour of either party. To which diabolical illusion he is said to have given so much credit that he did not only estrange himself from her society at his coming home but furnished his next wife with an excellent opportunity for pressing him to the disinheriting of his former children'. Later these rumours would take an even more unpleasant turn and in the margin of Vincent's baronage, there is a note which claims that Catherine was 'repudiata quia pater ejus post nuptias eam cognovit', that is repudiated because she had carnal knowledge of her father-in-law. There is also another nineteenth-century book which claims to have uncovered love letters written by John Seymour to Catherine, but no source is cited and if such letters exist they have not surfaced to date. The fact that John Seymour was friends with the poet, John Skelton, in his youth when, as we have seen, Skelton was an admirer of Margery's, has often been cited in support of the idea that John Seymour was a skilled poet, but again this doesn't stand up to scrutiny. If this was so, none of John Seymour's poems have ever turned up, nor is he referred to as a poet at court, which would be unusual if he was known for it in a society where such a skill was highly prized.

None of these sources are anywhere near contemporary though and they speak of a general historical trend to blame the woman for anything which transgressed the social norm; and Edward Seymour's repudiation of his wife definitely transgressed the social norm. There is, however, no evidence that Seymour's reputation suffered or was tainted by such a scandal. The Seymours certainly weren't shunned at the royal court, as one might expect if such a scandal touched them. As we have seen, Seymour was something of a rising star at the court on his own merit, long before his sister came to Henry VIII's attention. Henry VIII, with his curiously paradoxical brand of morality, would be unlikely to associate with a scandalous family, much less pursue a member to be his wife. He, after all, almost certainly shared the contemporary belief that immorality had a genetic component and would later be horrified at the manufactured allegation that Anne Boleyn had carnally known her brother.

Something, however, had certainly occurred to incur William Fillol's wrath, and whilst Catherine has traditionally been blamed, the fact that Edward was also barred from the will suggests that perhaps the quarrel was over money, land or something more practical. If Catherine had supported her husband over her father in the dispute, this might explain the wording of the will. It would also explain the fact that Henry VIII and the rest of the court took little notice of this 'scandal'. Traditionally the will and Catherine's later repudiation have been linked but there is actually no evidence to prove this and they might have been two different, unrelated issues.

Despite the fact that women lacked legal power in general it was actually very difficult for a man to repudiate his legitimate wife, especially if he had children with her; we need look no further than Henry VIII to be aware of that fact. Catherine Fillol, however, was no Katherine of Aragon, with the resources to fight a long and vicious battle against her husband. Catherine would have been entirely isolated, if indeed she had even wished to oppose the separation, and we must remember that we have no evidence either way. If she did try to oppose her husband, it could only have been a brief rebellion, as she soon retired to a nunnery.

A sixteenth-century nunnery could be a career, a vocation, a prison, a hospital or a refuge; which of these it was to Catherine we simply don't know, but we can speculate. In the early 1500s there were 138 nunneries in England, but relatively few women actually became nuns. By Catherine's time the women were almost exclusively from the upper classes which saw them become 'essentially aristocratic institutions, the refuge of the gentry born'.[5] We have seen that several women from both the Fillol and Seymour families chose to retire to nunneries in their widowhood, so there was a clear precedent for the action, albeit in different circumstances.

Catherine was too old by now to dream of using a nunnery to forge herself a career; such women were usually those who had grown up in a religious order or who brought enormous wealth, neither of which applied to Catherine Seymour. We cannot be certain though that Catherine had no desire as a child to retire to a nunnery, and that her retirement was simply of her own choosing, having harboured a lifelong vocation to be a nun. There is evidence of instances where women were allowed to leave their husbands in order to take the veil, having expressed a wish to do so. This required the husband's consent and, theoretically for him to remain celibate along with her while she lived.[6] For this reason few actually entered a nunnery this way, but it remains a possibility.

In Catherine's case, the nunnery is largely seen to take on the role of a prison, based on the assumption that some indiscretion had taken place. Religious houses had long been places to hide away inconvenient women. At Langland's nunnery, for example, we know that Johanne, a noble bastard, had been sent there, and that the rather too outspoken mistress of Peter de Montfort in the 1360s was packed off to be a nun at Pinley.[7] A theory here being that Edward wished to be rid of his adulterous wife and this was the best and easiest option open to him.

That Catherine was essentially sent to a hospital is also an intriguing option. If Catherine had been seriously ill with a long-standing condition, then by sending her to a nunnery Edward Seymour would have been ensuring that she had access to the best medical care available. Again there is precedent for this. Elizabeth Woodville is now believed to have died of plague during her retirement at Bermondsey Abbey, where she, already in poor health, was sent to receive the best spiritual and medical care. The issue with this is that if this was the case then surely it would have been common knowledge and it also does not explain William Fillol's disinheriting of her and Seymour. Likewise we know that Catherine recently gave birth and came through the rigours of childbirth alive, if not unscathed, which at least suggests a good level of baseline heath.

The idea that the religious order was her refuge allies closely with the idea that it was a prison; the two need not have been mutually exclusive and one tentative interpretation is that Catherine had been seduced or assaulted by someone and that she and Edward both felt that a religious refuge for Catherine and separation from Edward was the best way to move forward. With there being no evidence of familial discord between Edward and his father, he can safely be discounted as Catherine's seducer if adultery was involved, but that does not discount the possibility that she had otherwise either had an affair or been assaulted.

The question of where Catherine was sent is another which has no clear answer. The two wealthiest and most powerful nunneries in Dorset and Wiltshire were those of Shaftesbury and Wilton. Shaftesbury Abbey had, according to tradition, been founded in around 888 by Alfred the Great and presided over by his daughter, AEthelgifu, as abbess. It was rich and powerful; in 1539 at the Dissolution its income was assessed as a huge one thousand three hundred and twenty nine pounds, one shilling and sixpence.[8] Wilton, meanwhile, also had royal connections having been the home of two daughters of King Edward the Elder, Eadflaed and AEthelhild respectively, and then of Wulfthryth of Wilton, the wife or mistress of the Saxon King Edgar, who was abbess there. If there had been a huge scandal it is unlikely that any house with lofty connections would have been overjoyed at the idea of accepting Catherine into their fold, but the money she had been left might have been a powerful inducement. The forty pounds her father left her should she retire to a religious life might seem a small sum to us today but in the sixteenth century it was double the Prioress of Shaftesbury's pension.[9] In addition, Wilton in particular was no stranger to scandal with numerous nuns there being guilty of misconduct, notably in 1284 and 1302; it was a reputation which it found hard to shake off.[10] A new abbess was appointed in 1528, Isabel Jourdayne, which might have coincided with Catherine's own arrival there if it was to Wilton she was sent. Unfortunately no documentation has yet come to light which proves conclusively where Catherine was sent. Although both these nunneries would befit her rank, there were also, unfortunately, dozens of small daughter houses of those or of different orders where she could have lived, we simply don't know.

We do, however, know a little about what her life would have been like wherever she lived. Life for sixteenth-century nuns, to a large extent regardless of the order to which they belonged, followed a similar pattern, although it was largely dependent on the wealth of the woman and convent concerned.

By the 1500s convent life was not so austere as we might imagine it today. There was a 'growing practice of nuns receiving an annual monetary allowance … to buy clothing and treats', and servants were employed for much of the physical labour.[11] At Polsloe nunnery for example, maids were engaged to cook food for the nuns, which would not have been out of place at a noble table and featured fish, meat, sugar and other treats.[12] Nor were they necessarily insular, in the mid-1400s we know the nuns of St Radigunds in Cambridge took a river trip together to buy salt fish. One noblewoman turned nun, Joan Lancaster, and her sisters bargained in the market for smelts and stock fish at Kings Lynn.[13] We also know they took a trip to Ely's annual fayre.[14] Such trips were becoming increasingly widespread, suggesting that in general nuns were far from confined within convent walls. We also know that some nuns visited their families, exchanging gifts and foodstuffs. At Goring convent in 1530, the prioress explicitly complained that 'the nuns persist in sending messages (and goods) to their family friends'.[15] The fact that in 1489 Archbishop Rotherham sought to issue an injunction to limit the number of visitors to a nunnery, and how often nuns could journey out, demonstrates just how widespread this practice was.[16] Catherine may have been able to journey out and perhaps even visit her sons, although again I must stress this is only speculation. To date there is no evidence that Catherine ever saw her sons again; equally of course there is no evidence that she did not. I merely wish to show the possibilities and make it clear that there was at this time in general a 'steady intercourse between a convent and the outside world'.[17]

To this end, many convents adopted a more 'open door' policy with the nuns at Sheppey in 1511 complaining that closing the cloister immediately after the bell tolls for vespers and keeping it shut until prime was 'too strict especially in summertime and [they often] left it open until after supper'.[18]

This sort of environment would have been Catherine's reality. Inside a religious order her rank would almost certainly have ensured that she had access to accommodation almost in keeping with that which she would have experienced at Wulfhall. By this time communal dormitories were a thing of the past and the dorters were now divided to afford each woman a degree of privacy should she wish it. There were also riches to be viewed and used if not owned. A hundred years before Catherine's time the Prioress of Swine, Joan, describes how she received a 'gilded cup with a cover and round foot and in the bottom a chaplet of white and red roses and a hind carved in the midst and all around the outside carved with eagles, lions, crows and other ingenious devices'. She also wore a 'robe of murray cloth, mantle with furred hood "of budge, and other hood furred with ermine" as well as a series of "a very fair long robe"'. She also slept in a tester bed complete with white colter coverings and curtains. Catherine probably did not have access to such riches but she could have had a degree of comfort and privacy. If she had been sent away in disgrace it is unlikely that the Seymours would have furnished her with extra money or goods, but the forty pounds she did have was more than enough to ensure her comfortable accommodation.

Life would inevitably have changed for her though. Her life would now have been dominated by the religious services of the day and she would have been encouraged to spend time in contemplation and prayer. We have no way of knowing Catherine's own religious views, outside basic Catholicism, or how devout she was, but at the nunnery she would have had access to more devotional works than previously. By the 1500s religious houses were very much repositories of books and learning and volumes were regularly left to nunneries for the use of the nuns. For example, Eleanor Roos, a noble woman, left Joan Courtney, abbess in York, 'unum librum vocatum Mauldebuke' for this purpose in her will.[19] Catherine would also have been expected to work in the convent garden and still room, both of which would no doubt have been familiar tasks to her. Perhaps as a woman of noble birth her knowledge was sought after, or perhaps she brought with her family cures and preferences for the treatment of ailments? It seems likely, but we cannot be certain.

Although the rules for religious life were more relaxed than they had been 200 years earlier, obedience to the abbess and adherence to God was still expected and there were serious consequences for transgressions. One instance, in January 1527 at Romsey Abbey, saw a nun, Lady Alice Gorsyn, forced to wear a red tongue made of cloth beneath her chin for a month as a punishment for using bad language and 'spreading reproachful and defamatory words'.[20] The fact that Catherine's name fails to date to appear in any records suggests that she settled into religious life and made no ripples in the life of whichever convent she was sent to.

If Edward Seymour felt any grief at the events of 1529, he has left no trace. His and Catherine's sons remained in the care of his family at Wulfhall whilst he continued to navigate his career at court. At this point their legitimacy was not questioned nor were they excluded from inheriting Edward's lands and titles should he die. This suggests, at least, that he believed that he was their father. Court life had become increasingly complex with the rise of Anne Boleyn, and Henry VIII's seemingly endless quest to marry her. Seymour seems to have taken a middle course; he was not implicated in the fall of Wolsey, nor was he a member of the Boleyn 'faction' but neither was he opposed to them. Following Wolsey's fall he was granted, on 14 June 1530, lands to the value of one hundred and twenty three pounds twelve shillings and eight pence.[21] This was followed in September with an appointment as Esquire of the Body to the king, for which he would be paid fifty marks a year.[22] Edward had been joined at court by his sister, Jane. Continuing the veil of silence that had been drawn over the events of 1529, we have no idea what Jane felt about her sister-in-law's actions or Catherine's current situation. We do know that Jane was sent to serve in the household of Queen Katherine, as a maid of honour, and that she both knew Anne Boleyn and was with Queen Katherine on 11 July 1531 when Henry made the final break and simply rode away from Windsor and his wife of twenty years, in the company of Anne.

If not an avid supporter of Anne Boleyn, Edward Seymour was not her enemy either and he had a first-hand view of the burgeoning relationship between her and the king as 1531 progressed. He was now often physically close to the king and riding sufficiently high in rank and favour to present the king with a New Year's gift, the nature of which he must have given thought to. Gift giving, which took place at New Year during the Tudor period rather than on Christmas Day, was an important way to show both honour and regard for one's patron and monarch. Seymour gifted Henry a sword with an engraved gilt handle and in return received money from his sovereign.

Chapter 4

Anne

Another woman who was at court in 1529 was the now teenage Anne Stanhope. A painting of her hanging in Syon House, which may have been commissioned for the occasion, shows her to be a modest, pretty girl, with a smooth round face, plain, stylish dress, white hood and steady gaze. Almost certainly thanks to her stepfather, Richard Page's influence, she was given a position at court in the household of Katherine of Aragon as maid-in-waiting.[1] Page had been knighted in 1529 and was now in a position to make such a request. Places at the court were much sought after, not just because it afforded women riches and respect but because it granted them status independent of their husbands, an independent income, pension and personal access to the queen. Katherine of Aragon had eight ladies-in-waiting. She also had thirty maids-in-waiting. As a maid-in-waiting Anne was required to have impeccable society skills and an understanding of how the court worked. They attended the queen and her ladies and in the same way that a lady-in-waiting was required to 'have a vigilant and reverent respect and eye [so that they] ... would notice by their look or countenance what lacketh of is her pleasure to be had or be done', a maid was required to perform this duty for the queen and her ladies-in-waiting. Anne would also have been required to perform and entertain. Singing, dancing, music and other pastimes such as cards were all accomplishments that she was required to possess. Needlework was an essential skill and one which she would have learnt since early childhood. Beauty was also a requirement, and had been since the late 1400s when it was felt that beautiful young girls would grow into beautiful women and enhance the queen's household. Anne also had to be virtuous and completely chaste, for any scandal would reflect badly on the queen. Any hint of misconduct would mean instant dismissal, at least that was the theory. In practise the English court was felt by many to be a place of easy virtue, and Chapuys in 1536 was especially sceptical about the idea that Jane Seymour would have lasted so long at court with her virginity intact. Anne Boleyn had begun her career at court as a maid of honour or maid-in-waiting, and others whom Anne Stanhope would have known and spent her time alongside include Jane Popyncort, Mary Zouche, Anne Weston, Mary Norris, Bridget Fogge, Elizabeth Darrell, Joan Champernowne, Dorothy Bradby and her future sister-in-law, Jane Seymour. It is worth mentioning, given their later relationship, that one of Katherine's ladies-in-waiting at this time, one whom Anne would certainly have known well, was Maud Green, the widow of Sir Thomas Parr and mother of Katherine Parr. Anne and Katherine would barely have known each other at this time, as at the time Anne joined the court Katherine was being married to Edward Borough of Gainsborough, but they certainly knew of each other.[2] Whilst at court Anne also met and got to know very well the queen's daughter, Mary, who was of a similar age, a connection that would also have future implications. But for now, surely the most direct impact on the young Anne was made as she witnessed the king's treatment of his queen.

Whilst Anne Stanhope was in England serving the queen, Edward Seymour had a first-hand view of the rise of Anne Boleyn. He was probably present when on 1 September 1532, Anne was created Marquess of Pembroke in her own right in an elaborate ceremony at Windsor castle. This event was of huge significance as it granted Anne a suitable rank to accompany Henry to a meeting with the King of France. She was also the first woman to be granted the title, which was one with significant royal connections having previously been held by Henry VIII's great uncle, the ever loyal Jasper Tudor.[3] Anne was now the most high ranking woman in England, other than the king's sisters. Edward Seymour was part of Henry VIII's entourage, amongst his 'great number of gentlemen', when he and Anne Boleyn travelled to meet King Francis I of France at Calais in October 1532. Edward Hall, in his chronicle, reported that there were 300 of the king's gentleman who 'honourably received the French Lords at the English Pale and so brought them to the king's presence in Calais which stood under a rich cloth of estate of such value that they mused at the riches. The king received the French lord's very lovingly and amiable and with them took a day and place of meeting. These lords were highly feasted'. Historically this meeting is of great significance, not because of the diplomacy which took place but because it was during this visit that Anne Boleyn, in the words of Anne Boleyn authority Eric Ives, 'spent ten days living like a queen [with Henry] escorted by him everywhere and lodging with him in the Exchequer' and finally felt secure enough in her position to give in and sleep with Henry.[4] The chronicler, Edward Hall, also records that a secret marriage took place between Anne and Henry on 14 November – St Erkenwald's day – 'which marriage was kept so secret that very few knew of, til she was great with child at Easter after', that might also have prompted Anne's decision.[5] Chapuys then records that Anne and Henry spent something of a honeymoon back near Dover, not returning to Eltham Palace until 24 November, although Henry officially gave the reason for his delay as being 'for the purpose of having harbours constructed in the said town or at least of creating a spacious plea for asking money from his subject for the said works'.[6]

We do not know if Edward was with them or if he was privy to the change in their relationship. He next appears clearly in the historical record the following June when he was present at Anne's coronation where he served as a carver for the Archbishop of Canterbury. Edward Seymour clearly had no qualms about serving the new queen. The coronation took place on Whit Sunday, 1 June 1533. Both Edward and Anne Stanhope would have also witnessed the bustle in the city which had been 'ordered to make preparation as well as to fetch her grace from Greenwich to the Tower by water [and] to see the city ordered and garnished with pageants in places accustomed for the honour of her grace'.[7] At the banquet Edward Seymour was among the 120 support staff who were on hand to serve the nobles present. This was a great honour and required a high level of skill; carving a peacock neatly for example requires a good deal of dexterity and practice. He was joined on this occasion by his younger brother, Henry, who was subsequently called upon for his talent in carving at the dining table, despite preferring a life in the countryside. The opening course was escorted in by the Dukes of Suffolk and Norfolk, which included twenty-eight dishes for the queen and the archbishop. This was followed by a twenty-four dish second course and a thirty dish third course; the arrival of each one was heralded by trumpets.[8] The noise must have been deafening and it is remarkable that one of the centrepieces, a series of intricate wax ships, did not melt in the stifling atmosphere. Anne Boleyn was now England's new queen and, in a rather tense atmosphere, it was now punishable to accord anyone but Anne royal honours.[9] Despite this, Anne's chamberlain wrote that 'the pastime in the [new] queen's chamber was never more happy'.[10]

Anne Stanhope possibly attended the celebrations as part of Anne Boleyn's new entourage. Most ladies and maids-in-waiting simply remained in position and changed allegiance when the king changed his queen, although for many there was nothing simple or basic about it. For Anne Stanhope, her affection for Henry and Katherine's daughter, now Lady Mary, would surely have complicated her feelings. We know that Anne and Mary exchanged letters and gifts all throughout their lives and during the early 1530s they exchanged many of both. Mary later felt that Anne had been one of those loyal to her and her mother and they were 'assured friends'.[11] Mary also refers to Anne as 'her good Nann' or 'my good gossip', suggesting that the two young women shared confidences and updated each other on court gossip. The fact that they remained friends even after Anne Stanhope served Anne Boleyn and when they differed in matters of religion speaks volumes as to the depth of their affection.[12] It is almost certain that it was as part of Anne Boleyn's household that Anne Stanhope first encountered the reformed religion and its teachings. In 1533, Henry VIII declared himself Supreme Head of the Church Of England in order that he might grant his own divorce and marry Anne Boleyn, with Thomas Cromwell planning and later spearheading the Dissolution of the Monasteries. Anne Boleyn herself played a key role in personally and theologically pushing Henry towards this end. She supported the reformed Church and in the words of Eric Ives 'did so from the throne itself'.[13] Anne appointed reformist bishops and scholars who 'favoured the purer form of the gospel' including Cranmer, Latimer, Shaxton and Goodrich.[14] She also was personally devout and likely had been influenced by and exposed to reform prior to her return to England and her meeting with Henry. Anne's personal faith would have been of immediate relevance and importance to her maids and ladies. She read widely and collected a vast library of books, especially *The Pauline Epistles*.[15] These were books that her ladies would have had access to and been encouraged, within reason, to read from. Anne's faith should also be particularly noted for the importance it placed on charity and the responsibility that the rich had towards the poor. Anne ordered that relief be given to the poor, and that she would personally intervene if she felt petitioners were not being dealt with promptly or fairly. The maundy money handed out during her queenship was greatly increased and her ladies were required to sew clothes for the poor, which would be distributed on progress by priests who would also give each person a shilling, and give additional aid to any pregnant women.[16] Wyatt claims that her regular charity amounted to 1500 pounds a year, an enormous sum but one which Ives feels is 'just about credible'.[17] Anne Stanhope would have seen Anne's actions in this regard, and no doubt sat sewing many shirts to further her purpose. Given her later reformist faith, I would suggest that the seeds of it were sown in Anne Boleyn's household, in the same way as Edward's probably was on the Continent.

It is impossible to be certain when Anne Stanhope met Edward Seymour, but traditionally they are believed to have first encountered each other when Anne was serving Katherine of Aragon and were often in each other's company when she served Anne Boleyn. Edward, of course, was already married but Anne Stanhope, young, intelligent and with a serious position and connections, was the ideal wife for a young courtier on the rise. Evidence suggesting that he was planning a marriage is potentially offered by the fact that at this time he enters into a series of financial transactions to expand his land and property. His family connections were enough to make him an excellent match for Catherine Fillol, but he would need more to impress the Stanhope family. He had gained lands, as we have seen, following the downfall of Cardinal Wolsey, and now he began to acquire more. In 1532 he entered into a business relationship with Lord Lisle, Arthur Plantagenet, an illegitimate son of Edward IV, to purchase some land in Somerset and the reversion of Cheddar Norton. It proved to be a long, drawn out saga which demonstrates the lengths and complications Seymour was willing to endure to gain the outcome he desired. Arthur Plantagenet possessed the lands through his first wife, Elizabeth Grey, and as such he only had a life interest in them. Elizabeth Grey had been married before to Edmund Dudley, who had been treasurer to Henry VII and executed in 1510 by Henry VIII. By him she had a son, John Dudley, and when Elizabeth Grey died her inheritance was to pass to her son, not to Lord Lisle. It became complicated when John Dudley agreed to sell his claim to Edward Seymour if he paid Lisle 140 pounds a year as rent during Lisle's lifetime. Not happy with this, Seymour wanted the land without restrictions and the case drew a good deal of attention. Cromwell became involved and it was referred to in numerous letters as the 'Seymour matter'.[18] When, in 1536, Lisle required a loan, he secured it upon the land. He was not apparently aware that the land was in fact secured by Seymour, so that when it was due and he could not repay it, he was in Seymour's debt. Thomas Cromwell was forced to intervene and tried to mediate but Seymour would not give in and when Lisle again missed an extended deadline, he refused the money (which was sent late) and took full possession of the lands.[19] Edward's star continued to rise and in 1533 Seymour again exchanged New Year's gifts with the king. Catherine, in her convent, must have felt very far away. We know nothing more of Edward's first wife, except for the fact that she must have died before 9 March 1535. This means that she almost certainly lived long enough to know of, but not directly experience the king's schism with Rome and hear rumours of the Dissolution of the Monasteries, which would have ended her way of life had she lived long enough. Despite later hints of murder or poison designed to discredit Anne Stanhope when she was in a later, more powerful position, Catherine Fillol almost certainly simply died of disease. There would have been no need to kill her, Edward had already repudiated her, in one way or another, and even if he had pledged to remain celibate while Catherine lived, nobody would have held him to that. He could also have sought legal methods to remarry had he so wished under the circumstances. The most likely cause of death for Catherine should perhaps be regarded as the sweating sickness, which often became a regional epidemic throughout the early 1500s. Some historians today believe that it was likely brought to England with the mercenaries of Henry Tudor in 1485, and the king's printer, Richard Grafton, wrote that it was a 'new kind of sickness … which was so sore, so painful and so sharp that the like was never heard of to any man's remembrance before that time'.[20] Henry VIII and his nobles were paranoid about the disease which broke out periodically from the late 1480s until 1551, including in Somerset and Wiltshire. Today some think it was a strain of hantavirus, others a rare disease such as Seoul virus or more simply an influenza variant, but we simply cannot be certain.[21] We do know that sweating sickness affected convents and monasteries, where often the sick went to seek treatment and spiritual guidance. In the confined buildings it could spread quickly and whatever the precise nature of the disease was, without antibiotics there was little defence against it except prayer. Whether she died of the sweating sickness or some other ailment, Catherine did die and her story, for now at least, ended silently.

Chapter 5

Anne and Edward

Catherine's death left Edward Seymour free to marry again. If Edward was attracted to Anne's beauty and connections for Anne Stanhope, Edward Seymour was also an attractive prospect. Ten years her senior, his position at court meant that she would have at least known of him and probably knew him personally. This was undoubtedly an advantage in a time when a bride and groom often didn't even meet properly prior to their marriage. It is not certain when the two married, only that they were married by 9 March 1535 when they received a grant of land.[1] The marriage was, in the words of Antonia Fraser, an ideal one uniting 'the combination of a calculating husband and a strong willed wife [making)] the Seymours a team to be reckoned with'.[2] Following their marriage Anne quickly fell pregnant, but she likely remained within Anne Boleyn's household where she would have begun to witness the fragmentation of Henry and Anne's marriage. The birth of a daughter, Elizabeth, to the king and queen on 7 September, had sowed the seeds of discord, although at first there is little evidence that Henry's predominant emotion was anything other than relief that both mother and child were healthy and Anne Boleyn was soon pregnant again. But the tension and passion of their long courtship had not transmuted well into married life. As early as 1534 there had been rumours, largely perpetrated by the ever-biased Chapuys, that Henry had another mistress, though he does not name her. This is not widely supported and the frequency with which Anne fell pregnant, though she was not to carry another child to term, is evidence that the king and queen were still sleeping together frequently. When precisely Anne Stanhope's sister-in-law, Jane, first caught Henry's eye is unclear. We do know that Henry and Anne Boleyn went on progress in 1535 to Hampshire for most of September and October where they had spent their time hunting and hawking with great pleasure. In fact they were having so much fun that they signed few documents and several important ones had ended up being signed in something of a rush in early September at the Seymour's house of Wulfhall. These documents included some relating to the consecration of three reformist bishops, Fox, Latimer and Hilsey, which were to soon take place. It is unlikely that this visit reflects anything more than Henry's trust in one of his older colleagues and in one of his court's rising young men; he had visited before in 1518, 1520, 1523 and 1526 using it as a convenient stopping point. But the visit would of course later take on more significance. The king and queen arrived from Bromham, where they had been staying with Anne Boleyn's chamberlain, Sir Edward Baynton. At the time of Henry and Anne's visit, Wulfhall was still the home of John Seymour, Edward would not inherit until his father's death four years later. We know little of the events of the visit but it does seem likely that Anne Stanhope was present as part of Anne Boleyn's entourage; the question of whether Jane Seymour remained in Anne Boleyn's household uninterrupted is open to debate. The king was back staying with the Seymours again in October when, as Sir William Paulet records, the death of a person 'three quarters of a mile from Guildford and of four persons at Farnham' forced him to stay a night at 'Seymours place at Elvetham' before he moved on to Hertfordbridge, East Hampstead, and arrived at Windsor.[3] Elvetham Hall had come into John Seymour's hands in 1427 upon the death of William Sturney and whilst it was a handsome property it wasn't large. In 1591 many alterations had to be undertaken in order to make the property both suitable and ready for a visit from Henry and Anne's daughter, Queen Elizabeth I. The Seymours would have had only five days to prepare for Henry's October visit; the panic in the household as it sought to source suitable food and accommodations for the king and his entourage can easily be imagined. Henry dined with the family that evening and everything went off without a hitch.

Although she likely did not know it, Anne Boleyn was pregnant at this time and so too possibly, was Anne Stanhope. Anne Boleyn's pregnancy ended in absolute disaster, she miscarried a son in early 1536. It is suggested by historian, Margaret Scard, that Anne Stanhope bore her first child in early 1536, however it is more widely accepted that her first child, a son was born in 1537, by which time both Anne's lives had been utterly transformed. Anne Boleyn's failure to bear a living son meant that her position was inevitably weakened. Her enemies began to move against her and by March Henry's eye had fallen on Edward's sister, Anne's sister-in-law, Jane Seymour. Anthony Martinsen claims that it was Anne Stanhope's ambition which drove her husband and his family forward and that she constantly encouraged Jane and put her in the king's way.[4] As we have seen, however, the Seymours were quite ambitious enough on their own.

Jane Seymour was described at this time by Chapuys as 'of middle stature and no great beauty, so fair that one would call her rather pale than otherwise'. Perhaps her lack of conventional beauty was the reason why, despite being a reasonable match for any courtier on account of her rising brother, she had remained unmarried well into her twenties. She also had little dowry; as one of the three Seymour sisters she could expect no great inheritance. Historian, Dr Elizabeth Norton suggests that as Jane's younger sister, Elizabeth, was married before her, to Sir Anthony Ughtred sometime before 1530, she was considered the least beautiful of the sisters.[5] There has also been the implication that the reason that Jane married relatively late was down to the fact that following Edward's divorce the Seymours were a family which others 'shied away' from.[6] As we have seen, however, the occurrence of a serious Seymour scandal does not, in my opinion, hold up to scrutiny. Further evidence for this can be found by the fact that marriage options were being explored for Jane during the early 1530s. The leading candidate was the son of Sir Robert Dormer, William Dormer, who she no doubt knew as he was from a neighbouring family. The Seymours seem to have been enthusiastic about the match, which was championed by Sir Francis Bryan, but the Dormers were far less so. Anxious not to offend the king through Bryan, Lady Dormer took matters into her own hands and personally made a match instead for her son with Lady Sidney and their hurried marriage took place on 11 January 1535. The Dormers rejected her, it is said, because she possessed no great dowry, 'nor the hopes of increase of honours, wealth or advancement', evidence that although they were on the rise the Seymours were simply not important or powerful enough for a family like the wealthy Dormers.

By March 1536 at the latest, Jane Seymour had seriously caught the king's attention and he sent her a purse of gold sovereigns. Taking a leaf out of Anne Boleyn's book, Jane demurred; she kissed the letter but returned it unopened with a message for the king. She stated that she was 'a gentlewoman of good and honourable parents without reproach … that she had no greater riches in the world than her honour, which she would not injure for a thousand deaths and that if he wished to make her some present of money she begged it might be when God enabled her to make some honourable match'.[7] It has long been suggested that Edward and Anne coached Jane as to how best to appeal to the king. Whilst there is no proof of this, both would have seen first-hand the king's disillusionment with his wife and known well how to appeal to him. Whether Jane was told what to say is unclear but by presenting herself as a plain, simple, virtuous maid, the antithesis of passionate and fiery Anne Boleyn, she could scarcely have made herself more appealing to the king. Henry was determined once again to play the virtuous prince and determined that he would not see Jane without a chaperone present. Anne and Edward were the obvious choice for the job and on 18 April the king swiftly moved Thomas Cromwell out of his apartments close to the king's at Greenwich Palace in order that Anne Stanhope and Edward could move in. Henry could therefore visit them, and by extension Jane, there away from the prying eyes of the court. The royal palace at Greenwich was a courtyard house with a principal facade facing the Thames. The king's bedchamber was located on the first floor at the heart of a series of rooms which included a guard chamber, presence chamber, withdrawing chamber, cabinet, gallery and other chambers both on the same floor or below and it would have been in this series of rooms that Anne and Edward Seymour now found themselves living. Greenwich had been the scene of a large number of improvements under Henry VIII, improvements which included a tiltyard that was 650 feet long and 250 feet wide and had two permanent grandstands, connected by a linking gallery, in which members of the court often took their exercise. Recent archaeology has also revealed tantalising glimpses into the Tudor world at Greenwich which Anne would have experienced. We now know, for example, that she would have walked over wooden floors or glazed leaded floor tiles, heavily patterned, and that honey would have been available to the residents there thanks to the presence of numerous bee hives and bee boles, used to keep skeps during the winter months when the bee colonies were hibernating. There can be no doubt that Edward and Anne encouraged Jane; if Henry were to marry her the reward for them and their family would be huge. Ambassador Chapuys believed that the Seymours were plotting Jane's rise and that they had plotted with her to keep the king's interest. Catholic members of the court, such as Nicholas Carew, also wanted Anne Boleyn gone and encouraged Jane to take her place.

Anne would have spent a good deal of time in these weeks with her sister-in-law and the king. Her duties here would have taken precedence over those she owed to Anne Boleyn, but she was probably not absent from the queen's court entirely. Unfortunately, there is no evidence to suggest what her personal feelings towards her mistress were during these months; did she still harbour a desire for revenge against her for her treatment of Katherine and Mary? Or did she appreciate both the educational and religious reforms that Anne had made possible for her and sought to bring about? Probably the answer is that she felt a mixture of both, but sitting each evening with Jane and the king surely cannot have been an easy experience for her or her conscience, whatever her ambitions may have been for her husband and family. Perhaps any unease she felt was soothed by the fact her husband was reaping the rewards of the king's affection for Jane. On 3 March 1536, Edward was made a gentleman of the privy chamber, meaning that he was almost constantly in company with the king and had access to him in his most intimate moments. He would have taken turns one night sleeping at the foot of Henry's bed, the next with his wife.

Whilst her husband was prospering, however, another of Anne's family members was about to become caught up in the downfall of Anne Boleyn: her stepfather Richard Page. By April, Cromwell was ready to move against the queen but Anne would not go without a fight and she remained powerful until her last moments. There is not the scope here to discuss the issues surrounding the downfall of Anne Boleyn but one of relevance to Anne Stanhope was the fact that on 8 May 1536 her stepfather, Page, was sent to the Tower, where Anne Boleyn herself was now being held. According to the lost journal of Antony Antony, parts of which survive today in the notes of Thomas Tourneur, Page was detained at the same time as Wyatt but not charged. Henry was clearly very angry with him however, as on 12 May John Hussey writes that Henry Norris, William Brereton, Francis Weston and Mark Smeaton were now condemned to die and that 'Mr Page [and Wyatt] are in the Tower but it is said without danger of death … Mr. Page is banished from the King's presence and court forever'. However the next day Hussey changed his mind and believed that 'Wyatt and Mr. Page are like to suffer as the others'. Following the execution of Anne Boleyn on 19 May, Page was still in the Tower 'what shall become of (him) God knoweth best'. It is not known why Page was sent to the Tower but he had long been a supporter of Anne Boleyn, having been appointed to the privy chamber in 1527 after publicly taking Anne's side in a dispute with Cardinal Wolsey.[8]

It was probably thanks to his Seymour connection that Page was released, although there is no direct evidence that either Anne or Edward interceded on his behalf. Another theory is that it was in fact Cromwell who interceded for him, the two men having been longtime political allies. The question as to why Page was arrested to start with is an interesting one and suggests that Anne Boleyn and those who shared her fate were, at least by some, considered to be genuinely guilty. If the trials were merely for show, why arrest such a close Seymour connection? Equally though he may have been included simply for Cromwell and the king to be able to refute charges of bias. Whatever the reason, by 18 July Page had been freed and he wrote to Lady Lisle that 'I do ascertain you that I am long ago at liberty and the king my good and gracious lord but hitherto I have not greatly used to be a daily courtier again. And the king being so much my good lord as to give me liberty I am more meat for the country than the court. And to such a poor cabin as I have there is no lady nor gentlewoman in England shall be more welcome than ye shall be …Written from London this XVIII TH Day of July, By yours most bound R.Page'.[9] Anne's mother and half-sister, Elizabeth, who would have been in her late teens at the time, were no doubt hugely relieved, but for Anne at court the death of Anne Boleyn now brought about material change in her life.

On 17 May Thomas Cranmer had declared that Henry VIII's marriage to Anne Boleyn was null and void. The king was therefore now free to marry Jane and the necessary dispensation was issued on 19th which stated that they could marry 'although in the third and third degrees of affinity without publication of the Banns'.[10] Henry and Jane were betrothed the next day; Anne Boleyn's body was barely cold. Jane remained in London at Greenwich, presumably with Anne at her side and it was from there that on 30 July she sailed towards Whitehall to marry the king. The ceremony took place in the queen's closet in Whitehall, in private. Edward was now the king's brother-in-law and Anne Stanhope was sister-in-law to the queen. It is hard to imagine that Anne was not fully involved in the preparations with her sister and new queen and although not mentioned by name, it is almost certain that she was with Jane on her barge when she made her first journey as queen down the River Thames on 3 June. As Sir John Russel wrote to Lord Lisle, she stood with 'the queen and her ladies in the great barge', whilst Edward Seymour watched his wife and sister alongside the king from the royal barge.[11] Perhaps Anne was wearing velvet for the occasion because we know that Edward Seymour around this time had paid a number of bills including one for a lady's velvet gown.[12] We also know a good deal about the sort of dress that Anne Seymour would have worn. Anne Boleyn had been famous for her sense of style and the French hood she favoured. In contrast, Jane chose to wear the more traditional English gabled hood which fully covered a woman's hair. Her gowns were also more traditional and her ladies were told that their dresses 'should be made as the queen's gowns were made'. We know that Anne followed this advice for she is specifically mentioned as being the example which other ladies should follow because she had every detail of her outfits made in 'the very fashion that the queen and all her ladies doth wear'.[13] This included wearing a very English cap and gable hood.

Two days after the pageant Edward Seymour was made Viscount Beauchamp and given a large grant of land. He was given 20 marks a year and the manors of Brodeton, Sherston and Ambresburye, Wiltshire and the hundred of Ambresburye, Wynterboune and Alleworthbury, Wilts and all lands in those places belonging to the said manors and hundred. These were 'to be held by the said Edward and the heirs male of his body by dame Anne his wife'.[14] The inclusion of the clause clarifying that the lands were to go to any child born to Anne is the first indication we have that Edward might have begun to consider that his sons by his first marriage were illegitimate. Equally, it might simply reflect the fact that by now Anne Stanhope, who from now on would be addressed as Viscountess, was pregnant. In July he also received the office of keeper, government and captain of Jersey.[15]

Anne Boleyn's brother, George, had been granted a similar rank upon her elevation to queen but Henry did not elevate John Seymour in the same way he had Thomas Boleyn. The subject of Henry's true feelings for Jane is a difficult one to address. Certainly his one surviving letter to her has nothing of the passion of those he wrote for Anne Boleyn; in fact it is both short and dull. Plus, even at the hour of her triumph Jane herself would not have been able to escape the knowledge of the fate met by her two predecessors. To what extent Jane shared her fears with her sister-in-law we can never know, but there is some evidence that Anne and Jane were close. Jane's biological sisters, Dorothy and Elizabeth, did not join her court so it would be natural for her to turn to her brother's wife. We also know that other courtiers and ladies recognised that Anne had some influence with the queen. Lady Lisle, the woman whose husband had been involved in the land grab saga with Edward Seymour, wished to place her daughter as maid of honour in the queen's household and to this end appealed to the Countess of Rutland, Eleanor Manners, who she knew was 'in hand with my Lady Beauchamp and other of [the queen's] friends'. It worked and Anne Bassett was permitted to join the women of the court. Lady Lisle clearly believed that this was thanks to Anne's influence and she sent her thanks to Lady Beauchamp 'for divers causes'.[16] We also know that Anne received from Jane many gifts, which implies her favour and perhaps a certain closeness between the two women. In just one instance Lady Beauchamp (Anne) received beads, rich girdles and beautifully decorated borders with which to trim her gown.[17] The two women also shared a common cause, they both wished to see the Lady Mary restored to the king's favour. Jane had promised the ever present Chapuys that she would do what she could for Katherine of Aragon's daughter. In the summer following Jane's marriage, the second Act of Succession was passed which made clear the legitimacy of Henry and Jane's marriage and it declared Elizabeth a bastard on account of the fact that Henry's marriage to Anne Boleyn 'should be taken reputed … [with)] ... no force, strength or virtue'. However, it also confirmed that Lady Mary was illegitimate and therefore not in the line of succession. The key consequence of the Act was that it allowed Henry to name his own heir, regardless of legitimacy should it prove necessary, leading people then and since to speculate that he was planning on making his illegitimate son, Henry Fitzroy, his heir should Jane not provide him with a son. Richmond was by now 17 years old and cut a splendid figure in his fine clothes which included satin, velvet, damask and six very fine pairs of velvet shoes. Whatever plans Henry had for his son however, they came to nothing for Richmond died on 23 July 1536. For Henry this was a tragedy and Edward Seymour must also have grieved for the young man he had served. For the supporters of Lady Mary, however, this 'was no bad thing'.[18] Henry had, by this time, not seen his recalcitrant daughter for nearly three years as she steadfastly refused to accept the Act of Supremacy or that her parents' marriage was invalid and that she herself was illegitimate. Jane, no doubt with Anne's support, addressed this issue repeatedly with Henry. According to Ambassador Chapuys, Jane petitioned Henry and asked him to restore Mary to her former place in the succession. Henry told her 'that she [was] out of her mind to think of such a thing, and that she ought to study the welfare and exaltation of her own children if she had any by him instead of looking out for the good of others … [Jane replied that] ... she was asking for the good, the repose and tranquillity of himself and of the kingdom in general'.[19] Henry eventually agreed to Mary's return to the court at least, but only if she would submit to his will. Something Mary misunderstood when she wrote to her father following Anne's execution, believing all was to be forgiven. Henry sent a commission to Hunsdon, under the Duke of Norfolk, to force Mary to submit; she refused and Henry was utterly furious. He sent Lady Hussey to the Tower, who was both a supporter of Mary's and a friend of the Seymours. In her husband's letters there are references to Lady Hussey and Anne Seymour being in contact, although sadly none of their letters survive. Lady Hussey was charged with having called Lady Mary princess. Whilst this might seem trivial today, this was considered treason at the time, a fact that Mary herself and all the women involved must have been painfully aware. Henry also attacked her servants, arresting one, and Cromwell himself even came under suspicion. The fragility of Jane's position and by extension the Seymours was hit home when Jane again tried to intercede in support of Mary, Henry was furious and Jane was angrily 'repulsed' by him; according to tradition he also reminded her of the fate of Anne Boleyn. Jane and Mary's other supporters realised quickly that the situation was very grave indeed and urged her to submit, Chapuys himself assuring her it was no sin if she submitted to save her life. Mary duly did so, and signed the documents she was given without even reading them. Her reward was Henry's forgiveness, and on 6 July Henry and Jane met with Mary. She had been allowed back into the royal household, although she was neither returned to the succession nor granted the title of princess. Anne Seymour must have been delighted, and no doubt she too was soon reunited with Mary in Jane's household.

With Mary back in the family fold, plans were made for Jane's coronation as queen which was to take place on 29 October. By autumn Henry seems to have had cause to believe that Jane was pregnant, but this proved not to be the case. Something that surely played on Jane's mind as Anne's stomach began to swell. Jane's coronation would never take place; it was cancelled after an outbreak of plague occurred at Westminster. The king and queen instead spent Christmas at Greenwich at which Seymour, and no doubt his wife was present. The court was forced to ride through the city and crowds on the river bank as the Thames was frozen that year and they were blessed and 'censed' by abbots and priests wearing gold and holding aloft crosses. John Hussey wrote that they rode 'very merry and triumphantly'.[20] We have to wonder what the Seymours, Anne in particular with her interest in the reformed faith, made of these solemn men, their faces reddened in the cold. While Jane it seems was very much of the old faith, Anne Seymour's own position is less clear. She would later prove an adherent to the reformed faith and a supporter of female education, but at this stage her views are uncertain. Henry VIII was now the Supreme Head of the Church of England, and the smaller monasteries had already begun to be targeted by the Dissolution. Holy days were being greatly reduced and the use of 'idolatrous' images was being clamped down upon. Edward Seymour was initially sympathetic to the plight of the monasteries (or at least allowed himself to appear so) and St Mary's convent at Winchester attempted to secure a reprieve by giving money to the king and a manor to Seymour in exchange for his support.[21] Perhaps he realised that the people of England were very attached to their religious faith, the rituals which Henry saw to abolish dominated their lives and the priests and monks he saw to dismiss held in their hands the prospect of eternal salvation. In August 1536 Henry published his 'Ten Articles' which made clear his comprehensive view of religion in England. They were heavily influenced by Luther whilst also maintaining several aspects of Catholicism, such as the cult of saints and the veneration of images. His approach was both confusing and alarming and it led to increased unrest in the court and the country. From January 1535, Henry had allowed Cromwell to carry out visitations on monasteries in order to report back on their conduct. Most of these men were reformers and lawyers who had no time for what they believed to be 'archaic' ecclesiastical institutions. At the same time preachers and railers were sent out to deliver sermons on three key themes: the sinful hypocrisy of monks and nuns; the fact that monks and nuns were a drain on England's economy; and that if the king were to have the lands and riches of the monasteries then he could reduce taxes. They also dug out extremely lurid tales about monastic misconduct designed to win over the people to Henry's new order. Rebellion however was on the horizon.

Chapter 6

Dynasty

In this context, and aside from their royal duties, we know that during this time Anne and Edward were also considering where they might establish their own household. As members of the royal family they were expected to lodge with the court but they also now had the means to establish their own household in which their child could be raised. Anne was by now heavily pregnant and she would have put preparations in hand for the birth of her first child. Or was it? It is worth considering at this point that Anne might already have given birth to a daughter in 1536. The evidence for this is scant, but historian Susan Higginbotham suggests that another Seymour girl, named Anne after the previous queen, was born before the Seymours great rise and therefore escaped the reach of the chronicles of the day. The evidence she cites for this includes the fact that in November 1537 it was said that two of Anne's daughters visited Lady Mary and that there is no evidence that she gave birth to any twins. I would argue that this does indeed seem to be the most likely scenario, given that Anne was deemed old enough to receive a primer by late 1539. Whether this was her first or second child, childbirth in Tudor England was the most dangerous time of a woman's life. Perhaps Anne was attended by her mother or half-sisters; it would have been usual for this to be the case and Edward Seymour no doubt spared no expense in preparing for the birth of his heir. By February 1537 the Seymours had obtained a grant of land at Chester Place, outside Temple Bar, on the Strand from the king and it was here that Anne set about establishing her withdrawing chamber. It was also there on 22 February 1537, in the chapel, that Anne's child was christened. The king personally lent the royal font to the Seymours for the occasion. There had been some confusion about the sex of the child but recent research has revealed that it was a girl, named Jane for the queen, and Jane Seymour and Lady Mary stood as godmothers with the Lord Privy Seal, Thomas Cromwell, as godfather.[1] We know that

Anne had been well cared for during her confinement by a nurse and in thanks Mary gave her 20 shillings. Through Mary's movements we can trace the timeline of Anne's movements in early 1537. We know that she was not churched by 11 March and that Mary travelled back from her churching that same month and paid the nurse another ten shillings.[2] Anne would not have been seen in public until after her churching, where she was blessed and purified after the travail of childbed, nor would Edward Seymour have returned to her bed until then.

Whilst Anne was having her child, rebellion had in fact broken out across England and it is impossible to separate her life going forward from these events because they would ultimately affect every aspect of her life. In October 1536 a series of revolts had broken out in Lincolnshire amongst people unhappy with the Dissolution of the Monasteries, in particular the monastery at Louth. On 1 October, Thomas Kendall had preached that the very religion of England was in danger. This was followed the next day by a group of people in Lincoln seizing John Heneage, the Bishops of Lincoln's registrar, who had in his possession a report for Cromwell. This was followed by the capture of other of the king's commissioners and the situation quickly escalated. By 8 October a lawyer by the name of Robert Aske up in Yorkshire learnt of the Lincolnshire rebellion and became the leader of a group who shared their feelings. The rebels dispatched a document to the king which listed their grievances. Henry VIII was less than impressed, and although the rebels took pains to stress that they were 'undyingly loyal to the king' they nevertheless questioned his 'recent measures of taxation, the dissolution of the monasteries and the changes to the church and their religion'.[3] Henry dispatched Charles Brandon north to deal with the rebels but as the rebellion spread he became uncertain as to what to do. Should he deal with the Lincolnshire rebels or ride north to deal with those now taking up arms in Yorkshire, where now the rebellion was being referred to as a 'pilgrimage' to preserve the Church and it now numbered around 30,000 men. Henry sent further support in the shape of Thomas Howard, Duke of Norfolk, and the Dukes of Suffolk and Exeter along with soldiers on foot and on horseback.[4] Nevertheless the king's men were seriously outnumbered and the Duke of Suffolk, Charles Brandon, was ordered to negotiate. The king also instructed him that if that were not possible he was to 'with your forces run upon them with all extremity … destroy, burn and kill man, woman and child the terrible example of all others and specially the town of Louth because to this rebellion took his beginning in the same'.[5] On 26 November the rebels met with Norfolk at Scawsby Leys where Robert Aske, despite martial superiority, negotiated and it was determined that Sir Robert Bowes and Sir Ralph Ellerker would represent the pilgrims and take their grievances to the king. A truce was declared and the rebel forces disbanded with a promise of royal pardon. Robert Aske himself met the king who treated him well, but he did not address his complaints despite his earlier promises to do so.

For Anne Seymour, the most important fact during these months was that Queen Jane sided, at least in part, with the rebels and we know that Jane was actively engaged in trying to save some religious houses, specifically a house at Catesby, whose prioress wrote to Cromwell stating that: 'Pleaseth it your mastership to call to your remembrance that doctor Gwent informed you yesterday that the queen's grace hath moved his majesty for me and hath offered his highness two thousand marks in recompense for that house of Catesby and hath as yet no perfect answer … my trust is in God and you to help forward that the queens grace may obtain her request'.[6] During the period of the Pilgrimage of Grace, Jane went one step further and on one occasion she threw herself on her knees before Henry and begged that he restore the abbeys, arguing that 'perhaps God permitted this rebellion for the ruining of so many churches'. Henry was furious and coldly ordered her to her feet telling her that he had reminded her on numerous occasions 'not to meddle in his affairs' and that she should 'remember Anne Boleyn'. This was more than enough to, in the words of one observer, 'frighten a woman who [was] not very secure'.[7] The Seymours' position must suddenly have felt very precarious indeed. Henry VIII would ultimately break his word and when stirrings of rebellion occurred in early 1537 they were crushed; over 200 were executed despite the king's promise of pardon, including Aske himself.

Soon after Anne emerged following her churching, Jane Seymour realised that she was pregnant, something that must have been a huge relief to all the Seymours. Perhaps it was to Anne that Jane turned to discuss symptoms. By 23 May in a Lisle letter it is recorded that Jane was 'great with child' and that she made sure everyone knew of her pregnancy by leaving her gowns unlaced at the front to accommodate her growing belly.[8] The baby 'quickened in the womb' – that is Jane felt her baby move – on 27 May and Henry VIII ordered that a Te Deum be sung in St Paul's cathedral in celebration. Bonfires were lit and food and wine was distributed to the people of London so that they could join in the celebrations. Everyone prayed that the baby Jane was carrying would be a prince; it was a lot of pressure on the queen and the ladies who were ordered to tend her 'with great diligence'. As a result of Jane's pregnancy, Edward Seymour was appointed to the king's council on 22 May; the timing suggesting that Henry had learnt of the pregnancy shortly before that point. The Seymours were riding high and Anne's sister-in-law, Elizabeth, also now made a match with Gregory Cromwell, son of Thomas, something which was politically advantageous to both parties. The whole world was waiting with bated breath to see what the outcome of the queen's pregnancy would be. During that summer there was an outbreak of sweating sickness and in July a member of Cromwell's household contracted it. Jane was, as Sir John Russell reported to Henry VIII, 'very afraid'. She withdrew to Windsor with a reduced household by late August. We have no evidence that Anne was with her but it seems logical to assume that she was.

Jane Seymour took to her chamber in early September; the previous month Anne herself had fallen pregnant again. It had been decided that Jane would go to Hampton Court to await the birth of her child whilst the king waited at Esher Place; he is known to have been there by 30 September.[9] Jane went into labour on 10 October and the following day a procession took place which prayed for the queen.[10] The queen's labour was long and difficult and if Anne was indeed with her she must have felt the tension rising in the hot and foetid birthing chamber. Finally, at about two in the morning on 12 October, Jane gave birth to a healthy baby boy; the relief must have been indescribable. Edward Seymour was thrilled and he paid Robert Mousley who brought him the good news the large sum of 20 shillings as a reward.[11]

Despite her gruelling labour, Jane was well enough to announce the birth of her son as was traditional and joyously and proudly wrote:

> Right Trusty and well beloved, we greet you well, and for as much as by the inestimable goodness and grace of Almighty God we be delivered and brought in childbed for a Prince, conceived in most lawful matrimony between my lord the kings majesty and us … [to] ... the honour of God, joy and pleasure of my lord the king and us and the universal wealth, quiet and tranquillity of the whole realm.

By 8 o'clock the next morning the bells of England were pounding out a Te Deum and Edward surely felt a thrill of pleasure at the boy's name, Edward.

Not named for him of course, the baby had been born on the eve of The Feast of the Translation of Edward the Confessor and was named for that saint, but nevertheless he must have been proud to share a name with his royal nephew. He was also well rewarded for his sister's triumph as on 18 October he was created the Earl of Hertford, in the presence chamber at Hampton Court.[12] Edward Seymour was 'presented to the king first being preceded by the officers of arms, and Garter King bearing his patent of creation which was then presented by the Earl of Oxford, Great Chamberlain, to the king, who delivered it to lord Thomas Cromwell Secretary … Cromwell read the patent aloud and at the words concturam gladii the king girt the sword about his left shoulder. Then the lord secretary read out the letters patent and delivered them to the king who gave them to the Earl of Hertford who thanked the king'.[13]

Tragedy, both political and personal however, was just around the corner for Anne. Jane Seymour had at first seemed well. Prince Edward had been christened on 15 October in the chapel at Hampton Court in an elaborate court ceremony which had seen a great torch-lit procession take place from the prince's apartments through Hampton Court and down to the chapel. Anne's husband, Edward, had taken part in the ceremony carrying Lady Elizabeth, the king's daughter, and her brother-in-law, Thomas, helped to support the canopy over the Marchioness of Exeter as she carried the prince. Anne Seymour is not specifically listed as one of the attendants, although she may have been present, following Lady Mary as one of the queen's ladies who processed 'in their degrees'.[14] Alternatively she may have remained with the queen and been one of her attendants who wrapped the queen in velvet and furs to keep her warm whilst she awaited her son's return. In the queen's chamber the child was then brought to receive the blessing of his parents.[15]

Soon afterwards, however, Jane sickened. On the afternoon of 16 October she suffered 'a natural lax by reason whereof she began to lighten and to mend and so continued til towards night. All this night she had been very sick'. Lax in this context likely meant an episode of diarrhoea, not uncommon following childbirth.[16] Three days later, however, she was reported to be in grave danger and by 24 October she was dead. The cause of her death has been debated ever since; traditionally it has been attributed to puerperal fever but most today regard this as unlikely. At the time the fault was laid at the door of attendants who encouraged her to 'eat things which the fantasy in her sickness called for'. Historian, Alison Weir, argues that there were two illnesses – an original bout of food poisoning from which she recovered, hence the episode of diarrhoea, and another more serious condition, likely an embolism. If Jane had developed a clot in her leg it could have dislodged at any time and travelled to her heart or lungs. Death is not always instant in the way we imagine but such a clot would have put an intolerable strain on her body. If this was the case she would have become breathless, oxygen deprived, confused, delirious and then lost consciousness.[17] Anne would have looked on as both her family's future security and more poignantly her sister-in-law and friend died, and been utterly helpless.

In the midst of death there is life however and at around this time Anne would have felt the babe in her own womb quicken.

Following Jane's death, Henry removed himself to Esher Place to mourn. Cromwell wrote to the Bishop of Winchester, Stephen Gardiner, to rebuke him for suggesting that Henry would enjoy his time there declaring that rather 'there is a grief' at Esher.[18] Meanwhile Jane was buried and as was custom, and at Jane's 'desire', her clothing, jewels and treasures were divided between her ladies.[19] Anne, along with the rest of the court, went into morning. John Hussey records in a letter to Lady Lisle that the court women, in this case a Mrs Anne, 'will need nothing til her mourning be cast off', and that for further guidance he will refer to the other 'gentlewomen'.[20] Tudor court mourning for a lady of Anne Seymour's station would have included the wearing of a mourning habit and, on certain occasion, veils. Anne's own dress may have had to be let out on account of her advancing pregnancy.

We don't know if Anne attended Jane's sumptuous funeral, although she does not appear in the lists of the ladies who accompanied the queen's body. Lady Mary had been due to participate and take the role of chief mourner but had to be replaced by Frances Grey when she was too distraught to attend. Given Anne's absence in the list of names it seems logical that perhaps the same was true of Anne Seymour.

With no queen now to serve, Anne and the other ladies of the court were to serve the Lady Mary. She is listed between Lady Baynton and Lady Kingston in the record which shows that Mary paid 53 shillings and 4 pence for her servants.[21] It would have been an appointment that suited both women well. We know in the immediate aftermath of Jane's death, however, that she went with her husband to Chester Place, where the king visited them in November. The same month she sent her daughter Jane to visit Mary, perhaps to lift her spirits. It was common for godchildren to stay with their godparents and Mary was famously very fond of children.[22]

Anne's pregnancy, meanwhile, was advancing, and she spent her time in mourning and sometimes playing cards with Lady Mary. Perhaps she also spent a good deal of time at her needlework. One New Year Anne gave the king a shirt, which was worth an enormous 100 shillings, suggesting that it had been worked very finely indeed.[23] She gave birth to her second child in March 1538. This time her child was a boy and on 20 March Henry VIII paid his goldsmith, a man by the name of Morgan Wolf, 'for a certain cup given at the christening of the Earl of Hertford's son'.[24] It seems likely that this baby was called Henry for the king. Lady Mary also paid, in April, money to Lady Kingston to reimburse her for money, around 45 shillings, she had given at the two christenings she had recently attended; the second of which was for Anne's son who was also her godchild. The king and Cromwell stood as godfathers. A bill issued on July 17 also proves that fabric or clothing had been ordered for Anne's young son. Traditionally it has been suggested that this child was the aforementioned daughter, Anne, but as we have seen, clearly this child was a boy, lending credence to the idea that the boy was, in fact, Anne's third child. Sadly the infant doesn't seem to have lived for very long. The death of a child was far from being unusual in the Tudor period but that doesn't mean that Anne would not have grieved deeply for him. She also fell pregnant again very quickly.

Jane's death meant that the Seymours' meteoric rise stalled somewhat, but they were still riding high in the king's favour. On 19 November the Seymours were at court, a court which was 'never merrier'. They attended, alongside Lady Lisle and other women who had served the queen, and there 'had banquets in the chambers and the king's servants to wait upon them and did not take leave until four o'clock after dinner the next day'.[25] Lady Lisle records that they were 'highly feasted and after dinner his Grace showed us all the commodities of his palace'.[26] Edward Seymour then accompanied the king to Greenwich with the rest of the men of the privy chamber. Of particular interest to Anne, one imagines, was the gossip surrounding who the king might next marry – the Duchess of Milan was at the time the leading candidate.[27] Perhaps in the wake of this visit, Lady Lisle petitioned Edward and Anne to allow her daughter, Katherine, to join their household. Anne and Edward discussed the matter at length and Anne agreed with him that it was an excellent idea. He wrote to Lady Lisle saying that Katherine would be 'as welcome both to me and to my wife as any of our own daughters'.[28] Whilst it would have been usual for a husband to defer to his wife on female appointments, the image of Edward and Anne discussing the logistics and political advantages of Katherine's placement strongly speaks to a relationship in which both parties' opinions were respected and valued. In the end Katherine did not join their household but we can safely dismiss the later twentieth-century claim by William Seymour that it was because she did not wish to be treated as a servant by Anne Seymour; there simply is no contemporary evidence at all for it.[29] Instead Lady Lisle rather cites the simple fact that Katherine expressed a wish to remain with Lord and Lady Rutland, where she had been living.[30]

On 22 May 1539 Anne went into labour. Her labour came on so suddenly that a messenger, John Smith, had to be sent out with money to open the Ludgate and Aldgate after curfew so that a midwife could be reached faster than if they had taken a longer route avoiding the inner gates.[31] Anne must have been terrified, but all was well and she gave birth to a healthy baby boy who they named Edward after his father and royal cousin. Once again Edward and Anne had a healthy male heir and the boy was baptised in the chapel at Beauchamp Place, with the Dukes of Norfolk and Suffolk as his godfathers.[32] Two days later Edward Seymour completed the purchase for the manors of Honyngton, Bayclyff, Ablyngton, Box, Brodehenton and Stapleford which were sold to him by the Duke of Suffolk, Charles Brandon, increasing the inheritance which his son would receive.[33] Anne and Edward's children seem to have been raised largely at Wulfhall, where five women and two nurses were employed to take care of them. The raising of their children was something which we shall later see Anne took extremely seriously, but for now they were growing up in the well-appointed Wulfhall where they would have had two gardens to walk, run and observe the changing seasons in.

Edward Seymour, however, began to realise that the house needed renovation as befitted his status and that renovations ahead of the king's visit in August 1539 would be needed imminently. He and Anne realised that the house would not be large enough to host the king and his court and so he renovated the barn, which was an enormous 172 foot long and 26 feet wide. Henry VIII himself would stay at Wulfhall, whilst Edward's mother and his children moved into another of his houses, Penham Lodge. The estate records state that, by Thomas Hethe, 'certain painters, joiners, carpenters, masons and others [were paid] their wages in preparing and trimming the Barn at Wulfhall where in my Lord lay and kept his house during the kings abode there and also for the ridding, cleansing and garnishing of the Manor of Wulfhall wherein the king lay, and also to Penham Lodge where my Lords mother and children lay'.[34] Anne would have been in charge of the preparations for the king's visit, especially the ordering of food and the women's accommodation which fell under her remit. Without a queen the latter was a less onerous undertaking than it had been previously, but there was still an enormous amount of preparation needed. The king arrived on Saturday 9 August and on the same day Seymour paid one pound twelve shillings and threepence for 240 loaves of bread which the royal bakers had prepared. On Sunday 400 people were present and they feasted upon dishes such as mutton, veal, oxen, cygnets, coupons, poulets, chicken, quail, egrets, brawn, swan, crane, storks, peasants, partridges, snipes and larks. All of which were seasoned with cloves, ginger, cinnamon and coloured using a Tudor food colouring called turnsole which created the colour purple.[35] Dishes such as spiced pears were also served along with gallons of wine and beer.

Of great interest to Anne would have been the fact that negotiations were already underway for Henry VIII's fourth marriage, and she would be expected to serve the new queen. She would also have had access to first-hand information about the king's options, Thomas Seymour had been part of the party who negotiated with Christina of Denmark, which ultimately came to nothing. The Seymours, however, likely favoured Anne of Cleves, who was championed by their friend and ally, Cromwell. There is evidence that the Seymours and Cromwells were on fairly intimate terms; as we have seen they together brokered a marriage alliance between Thomas's son and Edward's sister and Cromwell's records show that they had regular contact. At some point in 1538–9, Hertford lent Cromwell one hundred pounds which was then repaid, and Cromwell stood as godfather to baby Edward Seymour, for whom he bought a gold cup to the value of eighteen pounds three shillings and threepence.[36] Almost immediately Anne fell pregnant again with another son, Henry, who was born in early 1540. This was followed immediately by another pregnancy which resulted in the birth of a daughter, Margaret, whose date of birth is not recorded precisely.

All of this took place against the backdrop of Edward Seymour's political career. Following Jane's death his career stalled somewhat, but he still remained a very important figure at court and he was involved in many of the key events of these years. Throughout 1538 he continually signed council letters which proved that he was at numerous meetings and he became involved in Henry VIII's revenge against the Pole family, which is now called the Exeter conspiracy. Reginald Pole was the son of Margaret Pole, the daughter of George, Duke of Clarence and as such had undisputed Plantagenet blood running through his veins. He was a Cardinal who opposed the Church of England and viciously attacked the king's religious policy in 1536 and urged the deposition of Henry. For this he had been declared a traitor, and he went into exile. Henry now made it a crime to even remain in touch with this 'traitor' and Reginald's brother, Geoffrey, was arrested and under torture cast doubts on the loyalty of the Poles and their allies the Courtenays. Margaret, her eldest son Henry (Exeter), Geoffrey and Sir Edward Neville were all arrested and Edward Seymour was assigned to their trial on 3 December. A year previously Exeter, riding high, had supported Seymour when he was created Earl of Hertford. Despite any personal pangs he might have felt, all were found guilty. The king was pleased and Edward Seymour had yet again proved his loyalty. Geoffrey was pardoned, the rest executed; if Seymour had ever thought his position was secure this surely must have hit home how quickly the king's mood could change.

For now though, Edward was riding high but his loyalty would soon be tested again. The king, on Cromwell's urging, chose Anne of Cleves to be his fourth wife. Seymour agreed absolutely and felt that a Cleves alliance was the best thing for England, who would now have a Protestant queen instead of a Catholic one. Anne Seymour was appointed to serve the new queen and perhaps she welcomed the prospect of a potential return to the educational salons of Anne Boleyn's time. Or perhaps she felt nothing but sadness at the prospect of another woman stepping into Jane's shoes. It was likely a mix of both, but she was enough of a pragmatist to know that the king needed to marry again. Thomas Seymour and Gregory Cromwell had both been part of the party which welcomed Anne of Cleves to Calais so perhaps Anne got advanced information about the likes and personality of her new mistress. Anne and Edward were part of the party which accompanied the kings when he received Anne at Shooters Hill, Greenwich, on 3 January, but the match had already got off to the worst possible start when she had failed to recognise the now overweight monarch.[37] Henry, for his part, married her but their wedding night was a disaster when he failed to consummate their union blaming (it is after all always the woman's fault) her large breasts, soft flesh and the fact that he believed she was not a virgin. Anne, as a member of the queen's privy household, would have had a first-hand view of Henry's six-week marriage which saw Anne of Cleves apparently in complete ignorance of both the reality of marital relations and of her position. She would also likely have realised, having seen it all before, that the king's eye had fallen on the very young and very pretty Catherine Howard.

For Cromwell, the failure of the Cleves match coupled with the wave of Protestantism sweeping through London for which Henry blamed him, was an utter disaster. Seymour was almost certainly present when, on 10 June, Cromwell was arrested at a council meeting. He did nothing to save him and was not implicated in his supposed crimes. His lack of intervention was not unique but it does call into question, by modern standards at least, the moral character of a man who clearly was not prepared to risk it all in the defence of his friends. His sister, Elizabeth, meanwhile, who was serving with Anne in the household of Anne of Cleves, was terrified that Gregory and herself would be implicated in Cromwell's treason. Perhaps on Anne's advice she wrote to the king and asked for clemency, I suggest this was perhaps Anne's doing based on the fact that we know the two women were together during this period and that Anne had good reason to think that Henry would respond favourably as she had seen him do so before.

Anne, though, also had other matters on her mind. She wanted to be certain that it would be her children and not Edward's by Catherine Fillol who inherited the Seymour lands. For Anne Stanhope, Edward's agreement to her demand was the highest possible honour and by Act of Parliament in 1540 all the Seymour lands were settled on 'the heirs male of himself and lady Anne, his wife'.[38] This disinherited his sons by Catherine. Anne was, by the standards of Tudor England, the perfect wife; she had proven her fertility by bearing her husband male heirs and daughters and served multiple queens. She was the highest woman in the land, successfully and without incident, and matched her husband's political ambitions. Edward now proved to his wife, and to the world, that he valued her.

Anne and Edward took the education of their children very seriously, in particular the education of their daughters who were given 'identical instruction in the Bible and classics by humanist tutors'.[39] Giving one's daughters an advanced, humanist education was extremely fashionable at the time and they engaged leading tutors of the day such as Thomas Becon and William Samuel to teach their sons and daughters. Later, as we shall see, their children excelled and could read and write in English, Latin, Greek and French. Another leading tutor, Nicholas Denisot, was engaged to teach them French.[40] Becon, in particular, praised Anne Stanhope for her progressive attitude and he strongly believed, as Anne herself clearly did, that 'women are the intellectual equals of men'.[41] When he later dedicated one of his works, *The Governance of Virtue*, to Anne and Edward's daughter, Jane, he went even further and said of Anne and Edward that 'there are no parents more godly last that deserved better of the Christian public weal that they which through God's gift having children, employ all their endeavours to train them up even from their very cradles in good letters and in the knowledge of God's most blessed will'.[42]

Chapter 7

Anne

With their children cared for, Anne Seymour continued her career at court. What she thought of Henry VIII's next choice of bride remains unrecorded but she seamlessly transferred to her household along with the majority of the queen's ladies.[1] Catherine was young, pert and pretty and perhaps Anne foresaw that it would all end in disaster for she and Edward distanced themselves subtly as events unfolded. For example, they did not join the king and queen when they went on progress to York from August to October 1541. Anne's absence could have been due to the fact she was once again expecting a child, but Seymour's certainly was a deliberate and well calculated move. He requested to be one of the nobles who remained behind in order to administer the business of government. Anne's absence, in particular, was fortuitous, as in October Cranmer was informed that Catherine had had sexual relations with two men – Francis Dereham and Henry Manox – before she married the king. This was not treason, but it came very close and the concerned Cranmer asked Seymour for his advice. He suggested that the king be informed carefully in a letter. Henry was devastated and Seymour was one of the men put in charge of questioning Catherine, her household and servants regarding the matter. It was soon revealed that she had had a relationship with Thomas Culpeper after her marriage to the king. This had occurred during their northern progress and the women of her household thought to be complicit were questioned under threat of loss of position or worse. Seymour must have been mightily relieved that Anne had been well out of the way at the time in question. These threats were not idle ones. Having survived the downfall of her husband and sister-in-law, Jane Boleyn, Lady Rochford would share her mistresses fate. An inventory of Jane Boleyn's possessions at this time give us a glimpse into the sort of possessions Anne Seymour also undoubtedly owned. These included flagons of silver, a silver and gilt basin, and a silver gilded bottle.

In terms of dress she owned 'a kirtle of black velvet, a kirtle of black satin, an nightgown of black taffeta, a gown of black damask, a gown of black satin' along with jewels such as 'A fair brooch black enamelled with six diamonds, a castkey with a purse and forty pounds in it, pearls and certain pieces of broken gold in a box and small pearls … a flower with a ruby and a great emerald with a pearl pendant, a tablet of gold with black green and white enamelled, a pair of bracelet of red cornelyns, a pair of bead of gold and stones, a brooch of gold with an adieu head and a white face'.[2] It is not known whether Jane Boleyn wore black as mourning for her husband or because it was fashionable to show off such an expensive colour. If the latter, perhaps Anne also wore black which had the advantage of also showing off any jewels she owned to their best effect; Edward Seymour could certainly afford to bedeck his wife in the latest trends. Seymour was responsible for questioning the dowager Duchess of Norfolk, who had been responsible for Catherine during her youth and in whose house her early affairs were said to have taken place. As those involved were tired and charged, Seymour was one of the men who tried Culpeper and Dereham. The result was a forgone conclusion for all accused. The men were executed and in February, Catherine Howard and Jane Boleyn also went to the block.

Edward Seymour's star now began to rise again, as, in a final Henrician burst of masculine vigour, England went to war with both Scotland and France. In June 1542, Henry committed himself to war with France by signing a treaty with the Emperor but the Scots presented a more pressing issue. Norfolk was sent north with instructions to find a reason to show English military strength and raid the lowland river country. On 13 October, Norfolk asked for a replacement for the ailing William Fitzwilliam, Earl of Southampton. He particularly asked for Edward Seymour because he valued him as 'my near kinsman'.[3] Seymour was duly at Berwick by 21 October. Norfolk had made demands which the Scots could not possibly agree to and so sent 10,000 men across the border under the command of Edward Seymour. They burnt their way through toward Kelso, destroying property and crops in appallingly bad conditions. For his success Edward was made Warden General of the Marches, a position which he felt uneasy about and in the end he was willingly replaced by John Dudley who was a more experienced soldier.

This time which Anne and Edward spent apart gives us a touching glimpse into the reality of their marriage, which appears to have been loving, supportive and mutually beneficial. They corresponded frequently, with Sir Thomas Wriothesley sending Anne's letters with his own to Edward whilst he was in the north, telling Edward that he sent 'letters from my lady Anne along with his correspondence'.[4] He also entreated him to reply quickly as Anne made it clear that 'she will not be merry until she hears from him'.[5] It is easy to picture Anne pacing and worrying as she eagerly awaited news down in London. In other letters she can be found 'beseeching him for speedy answer', but Wriothesley's assistance it seems was not a foolproof communication method and some of their letters went astray. Edward did not hear from Anne as often as he wanted and begged that she be not 'slack in writing'.[6] She was right to worry – James V retaliated after Seymour's raid and launched 20,000 men into England. The threat was very real but the Scots were defeated by the English forces under the command of Sir Thomas Wharton at the Battle of Solway Moss. The death of James V a week later, who it is said simply turned his face to the wall and died, left the Scottish Crown in the hands of his newborn baby daughter, Mary Queen of Scots.

By 28 December Seymour had been appointed as Lord Admiral but he had been replaced by late January by John Dudley, Lord Lisle and instead he was appointed to the position of Lord Great Chamberlain.

Back in London, Anne was joined at court gatherings by Katherine Parr, now Lady Latimer. Her husband's actions during the Pilgrimage of Grace had led to a downturn in her fortunes but Lady Mary remembered her warmly and welcomed her into her household, where she and Anne would have often met. Anne would also have been considering the possibility that they might soon be more closely related, for Katherine Parr had fallen in love with Thomas Seymour, Anne's brother-in-law. He cut a stunning figure at the court and could sing, write poetry, and dressed magnificently; his fondness for such clothing was one that Katherine shared. He also could boast of military prowess and excellent connections in the shape of Edward and Anne. For Katherine's part she was slim, elegant, and educated, with warm, burnished gold hair and an exemplary reputation.[7] Nothing is known of their courtship, but Katherine apparently 'handled their feelings with wisdom and discretion'.[8] However when Henry's eye fell on Katherine Parr, Thomas Seymour's feelings for Katherine could have become something of a problem, but he had the good sense to back off when it became clear that Henry was pursuing her. It was widely noted that Henry began to visit the ladies, in the words of Chapuys 'with curious frequency'.[9] Katherine was not keen to marry Henry, he was no longer the dashing prince he still claimed to be – rather he was, in the words of historian Alison Weir, 'already an old man, with an old man's set ways and uncertain temper. His bad leg sometimes rendered him immobile and needed constant redressing; on occasions it stank'.[10] Nevertheless, Katherine knew in reality that she had very little choice and she prayed upon the matter. One of her later letters which she wrote to Thomas Seymour explaining her decision to marry the king offers us a glimpse into Katherine's thought process at the time. She assured Seymour that her 'mind was fully bent the other time I was at liberty to marry you before any other man I knew. Howbeit God withstood my will therein most vehemently for a time and through his grace and goodness made that possible which seem to me impossible, that was made me renounce utterly mine own will and to follow his will most willingly. It were too long to write all the process of the matter. If I live I shall declare it to you myself I can say nothing but as my Lady Suffolk saith God is a marvellous man… Katherine the Queen'.[11] She expresses similar sentiments to her brother after her marriage in which she makes it clear that it was God's will which was behind her marriage and as such she regarded it as 'the greatest joy and comfort that could happen to her'.[12]

Later historians have Anne Seymour and Katherine Parr as implacable enemies, and whilst there is no doubt that they did have some later disagreements, for now they were friends and religious allies. They were of a similar age and both enjoyed the favour of Lady Mary. They had also known each other and of each other for a long time. Anne would also have realised that Katherine was an eminently suitable wife for the ailing king being naturally patient, kind and generous. The dedicated care and nursing which she had shown towards her stepdaughter, Mary, from an earlier marriage, until her early death was something of which the court was well aware.

Anne and Edward Seymour were present when Henry married Katherine Parr on 12 June 1544 in the queen's closet at Hampton Court.[13] Lady Mary and Lady Elizabeth were also present and it would have been something of a cramped occasion with several other people present, as the room is only around 24 metres square.[14] 'Anne countess of Hertford' is clearly listed as an attendee alongside Margaret Douglas, Katherine, Duchess of Suffolk and Jane, Lady Dudley by Richard Watkins, the king's protonotary or chief clerk.

Anne now found herself serving yet another queen but this one had a circle of ladies who were not only related by blood and friendship but who also shared 'an interest in scholarly pursuits and a missionary zeal to define and disseminate the tenets of new religion'.[15] Despite universal approval of Katherine, initially Anne Stanhope soon became suspected, alongside the Duchess of Suffolk and Lady Dudley, of 'infecting' Katherine with their advanced reformist views.[16] Anne Seymour was very clearly by now of the 'new' faith. Traditionally her reformist views have been attributed to her desire for political advancements and contrasted with Katherine Willoughby's hard fought and tortured conversion which saw her change from devout Catholic daughter to Charles Brandon's wife and a leading member of Katherine's reformist circle, going so far as to appoint leading reformers such as William Paget, Anthony Denny and John Gates as sponsors for her son's wardship.[17] Latterly she would go even further and give refuge to Hugh Latimer when his reformist views made him a target of Henry VIII's 'heresy hunt' of the mid 1540s, an act the Seymours themselves would repeat in 1549.[18] It can, however, be argued that Anne's appointment of similar reformists to educate her own daughters is ample evidence that she shared Katherine Willoughby's fervour. There is also evidence for the existence of a personal friendship between Katherine and Anne. Soon after Katherine Parr's marriage to the king, Anne was once again with child and she spent time away from the court at Sheen. Katherine visited her there often and when they were not together the two women exchanged many letters which discussed everything from their children to the court gossip and religion.[19] Katherine also felt comfortable enough to gift Edward Seymour a horse in 1544. All of which suggests the two women were both good friends and equally fervent and progressive in matters of religion.

Whilst Anne was helping Katherine Parr settle into her new role, she had after all been at court for twenty years by now and served five queens already whilst Katherine Parr lived in the country, Edward Seymour was dealing with further political upheaval. On 1 July, shortly after his sixth marriage, Henry concluded a marriage treaty with Scotland: Prince Edward was to marry the infant Mary, Queen of Scots uniting the two countries forever. However the treaty collapsed and by the end of the year the deal was off and Henry was considering sending Seymour to deal with the situation. He was by now considered to be an able soldier, excellent statesman and member of the reformist faction. Ambassador Chapuys was right to fear their power and influence on the king. Seymour was considered to be the ringleader alongside Thomas Cranmer, Archbishop of Canterbury, Anthony Denny and John Dudley. The wives of the latter two also lived, prayed and studied alongside Anne Stanhope in the queen's household. They were opposed by the conservative faction who were led by the Bishop of Winchester, Stephen Gardiner, Thomas Wriothesley, and the Duke of Norfolk, Thomas Howard. These men feared the influence that Anne Stanhope and the other women had upon the queen, and through her, on the king.

Chapuys also did not underestimate, and nor should we, the amount of influence and power which Anne Seymour wielded as both Edward's wife and one of the queen's ladies. Women of the queen's household had the independent power to distribute patronage, influence the queen and control access to her. Anne Seymour was petitioned on several occasions to grant her favour or recommend a daughter of the nobility to the queen, as she had been during Queen Jane's tenure. She also had regular and personal access to the queen and frequently attended, along with the other ladies, Katherine's 'salons' where together they heard theological works and sermons being preached which 'oftimes touched such abuses as in the church that were rife'.[20] They were exposed to preachers who attacked the Catholic Church and participated in 'a daily regime that included prayer, scripture, study and theological training'.[21] All of which was in violation of the 1543 Act for the Advancement of the True Religion which banned 'women, artificers, apprentices etc' from reading the Bible. It later clarified that noble women could read it in private but they could not read it aloud or debate it – something that Katherine and her women chose to ignore. The queen's household wasn't all about study though, the queen and her women often rode out hawking and hunting. The queen's accounts for this year are littered with references to such activities, for example Morrice Ludlow rode at the 'Master of the Horses command with a cast of falcons from Eltham for the master of the Queens hawks'.[22] A more personal matter for Anne at this time was the birth of her child and her husband's absence. At some point she had spoken to Katherine about her fears and Katherine had promised to use her influence with the king to try to bring Edward home from the north where he was still serving as Warden of the Scottish Marches. This personal appeal is further evidence that Anne and Katherine shared a warm relationship at this time and Katherine took pains to reassure Anne that:

> My lord your husbands coming hither is not altered, for he shall come home before the king's majesty taketh his journey over the seas, as it pleased His Majesty to declare to me of late. You may be right assured I would not have forgotten my

> promise to you in a matter of less effect than that, and so I pray you most heartily to think. And thus with my very hearty commendations to you I end, wishing you so well as far as I would myself. Your Assured friend Katherine the Queen.[23]

It also seems certain that she stood as godmother to Anne and Edward's child at the christening in August. In addition we also know that she paid for a servant to row her to 'the Earl of Hertford's house' so that she could pay a personal visit on Anne and her child.[24]

Whether due to Katherine's influence or not Seymour was soon back in London in order to advise Katherine when she was left as Regent during Henry's expedition to France. This appointment also included responsibility for establishing Prince Edward's household. Eighteen boys were appointed to keep the now 7-year-old prince company and Anne's son, Edward, was amongst them where he is described as being the 'image of his father'.[25] Whilst Anne recovered from childbirth, Edward was once again sent abroad, Henry's great expedition had failed and he now required skilled negotiators. To this end, Seymour and Stephen Gardiner were ordered to Boulogne to sue for peace. They were quickly joined by Suffolk, Rich and Paget for the lengthy negotiations. Boulogne surrendered on 14 September but this good news was cancelled out by the news that the Emperor and France had now made peace and were allied against England. By 30 September, Seymour was sailing home with the king leaving Boulogne garrisoned, but on the 18 October Seymour was back in Calais to try to reach a resolution over the thorny issue of Boulogne. The Emperor's men attempted to mediate but would not take sides meaning that the meeting ended without agreement. Seymour was then dispatched to Brussels to speak with the Emperor, with whom they were to forge an alliance against France if an agreement could not be reached to English advantage. The meeting was once again tortuously long and Seymour and Gardiner were forced to ask for more money to sustain them.[26] By Christmas they were back in London having failed to reach an agreement, to deal with their somewhat disgruntled king.

For Anne though, one thing which was celebrated at Christmas would have pleased her immensely and that was Lady Mary's restoration to the succession. The act had been passed in March restoring both Mary and Elizabeth to the succession after their brother but it was at Christmas that the full reality of this resolution could be felt. Ambassador Chapuys took time to thank Katherine Parr that Christmas on behalf of the Emperor for all she had done for Mary. In 1543, for the first time, all of Henry's children had celebrated Christmas at court together but by 1544 all were much more settled in their positions and the court was calm and merry under Queen Katherine's influence in a way it had not been for years.

As the new year dawned, however, the queen's world, and by extension that of her ladies, was to soon come under serious threat. The views and minds of these women were beginning to attract a lot of attention. In 1545 Katherine Parr published her own book called *Prayers or Meditations*, with the king's consent of course. The same year Nicholas Udall dedicated his translation of Erasmus' work *Paraphrases* to Katherine, hoping that she could persuade Henry to be more radical in his reforms. John Parkhurst, who was chaplain to both Katherine Parr and Katherine Willoughby, was a supporter of reform and he wrote epigrams praising their conduct as mistresses of such virtuous households.[27] However, whilst Katherine's views were becoming more publicised and reformist, Henry's were stalling. On Christmas Eve 1545, Henry VIII addressed the issue of religious reform in his last speech to Parliament. In it he chastised Parliament for their division and debate regarding religion and beseeched them to 'study and take pains to amend one thing; which is surely amiss, and far out of order, to which I most heartily require you; which is that charity and discord is not amongst you, but discord and dissension beareth rule in every place. St Paul saieth to the Corinthians, the thirteenth chapter, charity is gentle, charity is not envious, charity is not proud, and so forth in the said chapter. Behold then what love and charity is amongst you when the one calleth the other heretic and anabaptist and he calleth him again papist, hypocrite and pharisee. Be these tokens of charity amongst you? Are these the signs of fraternal love between you? No, no. I assure you, that this lack of charity amongst yourselves will be the hindrance and assuaging of the fervent love between us'. He finished his speech with a warning that the men of the Lords and Commons must 'Amend these crimes I exhort you and set forth God's word both by true preaching and good example-giving or else I, whom God hath appointed his vicar and high minister here, will see these divisions extinct and their enormity corrected according to my very duty'.[28] Henry is making his position clear, abide by the doctrine he endorsed and stop arguing or he will take steps to force such an agreement.

Such an accord, however, would prove to be impossible; the genie was out of the bottle and it could not be put back in. The conservatives at court felt they had the upper hand and that this was confirmed by the passing of the Act of Six Articles but slowly this began to change. Of particular concern to many was Katherine Parr's influence on the young prince, who was receiving a humanist education under Katherine's careful watch. Prince Edward called Katherine his 'dearest mother' and the two were in constant communication.[29] They also began to fear that Katherine, through her secretary Richard Butler, was seeking 'to solicit the German princes to form a [Lutheran] league against King Henry'.[30] Slowly the uneasy conservatives began to move against the reformists. Their ultimate target was Thomas Cranmer, and as early as 1543 conservatives at court had been complaining that the archbishop was giving treasonous heretics his personal support and protection. Henry, however, charged Cranmer with investigating and naturally the matter came to an end. By 1545, Cranmer was under threat of arrest again but Henry saved him and his accusers remained helpless when Cranmer showed them irrefutable proof of Henry's favour: the royal ring. With Cranmer seemingly out of reach the conservatives turned to what they felt to be an easier target: the queen and her ladies.

Chapter 8

The Queen's Lady

Bringing down Anne Seymour with the queen would have the added bonus of taking down Edward Seymour as well. It was a very clever plan and demonstrates again the influence that women like Anne wielded. She was no 'consort'; she and Edward Seymour were regarded as operating as one – take out either and the other would also fall. The same was true of many of Katherine's other ladies with powerful husbands at court. In the words of historian, Micheline White 'the conservative plot against Katherine Parr also had the potential to destroy those reformers closest to the king'.[1]

In June 1546 a woman by the name of Anne Askew, a Protestant, was arrested and charged with denying the doctrine of transubstantiation – the key Catholic belief that during Mass the bread and wine are transformed into the actual substance of the body and blood of Christ, with only the appearance of bread and wine still remaining. Protestants on the other hand were beginning to argue that the bread and wine was only representative of Christ's body and blood, it did not take on the actual substance of it itself. This belief was heresy at the time.

Anne Askew was an educated woman from Lincolnshire and a fervent Protestant, whom her Catholic husband, Thomas Kyme, had thrown out of the house. Anne had travelled south where she had met the Anabaptist, Joan Bocher. The two women smuggled into the queen's royal household Tyndale's version of the New Testament. Tyndale had been called the 'most dangerous man in England' in the early 1500s and his work was considered so incendiary that Henry VIII had bought 3000 copies earlier in his reign only to have them burnt in an attempt to prevent them reaching the general population. Tyndale had been strangled to death and then burnt in 1536 and his last words were reported to be 'Lord, open the king of England's eyes!'[2] Anne Askew had previously been arrested in March 1545 on the insistence of her husband who wanted her to return to Lincolnshire and live quietly.

She was interrogated by the Bishop of London, and conservative Edmund Bonner but Anne escaped and had continued to preach in London. The question of to what extent Anne Askew knew Anne Seymour, Katherine Parr and other ladies of the court has been a subject of debate ever since Anne's arrest. Historian, Derek Wilson, argues that 'Anne [Askew] was something of a celebrity in the world of London's religious radicals and her views were more extreme than Katherine's. It would have in any case been unwise for Katherine to be seen as openly offering her patronage. This does not mean that the two ladies never met, just that there is no firm evidence for such a meeting'.[3] Anne Askew was taken to the Tower of London where she was tortured on the rack, something which was technically illegal and she is the only woman ever recorded to have suffered such torture. She was asked again and again to name 'like-minded women' in the queen's household but she steadfastly refused. Eventually the Constable of the Tower, Sir Anthony Knyvett, refused to continue to torture Anne but it continued under Thomas Wriothesley, the Lord Chancellor, and Sir Richard Rich until 'both her arms and legs became disjointed'.[4] Despite the pain, her screams could be heard in the garden of the lower ward, Anne Askew refused to give up any names or renounce her beliefs.[5] The only two women she mentioned were Anne Seymour herself, and Joan Denny (sometimes called Joan Champernowne) whom she said sent her money, but even then she was careful with her phrasing. She would only say that two men had brought her money claiming that it was from Anne and Joan, but she could not say for certain.[6] Specifically, in relation to Anne Seymour it was, Anne Askew said, 'a man in a blue coat who delivered me ten shillings and said that my lady Hertford sent it'.[7] Anne Askew's nephew would later claim that Anne was captured when a letter she was trying to send to the queen as part of an 'organised letter writing campaign' was intercepted, a network of which Anne Seymour was a part.[8] In addition Nicholas Throckmorton, a cousin of Katherine's, also visited her in the Tower.[9] It must be remembered that Anne Askew also had a perfectly respectable connection with the royal court – her brother, Edward, had served in Cranmer's household and her sister, Jane, was married to a lawyer who worked for Katherine Willoughby and her husband.[10] Taken together most historians today consider that there was some sort of clandestine relationship, or at least trade in books, between some of the queen's ladies and Anne Askew, if not specifically the queen herself and the scant evidence does seem to imply that it was Anne Seymour and Joan Denny who facilitated this arrangement, but this simply cannot be proven beyond reasonable doubt. If Anne Seymour did send money to Anne Askew or communicate with her, she was running a terrible risk and for her to undertake such an action surely speaks to the depth of her reformist convictions and her dedication to the members of her network. Perhaps she felt her position secure enough to associate with such a figure, but it was an awful chance to take.

If Anne had in fact staked her safety on Anne Askew's loyalty, she was right to do so, Askew gave up no one and the interrogators did not have enough evidence to move against the queen, or as James argues even to fabricate such a coup. Despite this, Anne Askew's refusal to renounce her beliefs was heresy and she was sentenced to death. After the torture she was unable to walk and so she was carried to her execution and burnt at the stake on 16 July 1546. Eight days earlier a proclamation had been made which dealt with the issue of heretical books and it was made clear that 'from henceforth no man, woman or other person, of what estate, condition or degree she or they may be, shall, after the last day of August next ensuing, receive, have, take or keep in his or their possession the text of the New testament of Tyndales or Coverdales'.[11] The ladies of Katherine's circle certainly possessed such books. They almost certainly also had access to works such as Luther's writings or those of Melanchthon and texts such as Calvin's *Institutions of the Christian Religion*, of which Princess Elizabeth also had a copy. The discovery of any one of these texts would incur the king's wrath.

The crisis may have passed for now but none of the ladies of the court were safe. Katherine seems to have grown bolder in her discussions with the king and irritated Henry. This gave Gardiner an opening. He called Katherine 'a serpent within [Henry's] own bosom' and suggested that she and her ladies, including Anne Seymour, should be arrested and questioned on their religious beliefs. Henry agreed to move against the queen and signed her arrest warrant but, whether by design or good fortune, Katherine was made aware of the threat. Foxe's *Book of Martyrs* had it that the warrant was dropped and found its way into the queen's hands.[12] Others that one of Katherine's ladies was told and then informed the queen. If so we do not know which of Katherine's ladies was informed and passed the message onto the queen but all of her ladies would have been well aware that it was their lives on the line as well. If Katherine fell, so did they all this time. Katherine initially became hysterical but then steadied herself. She went to Henry and begged his pardon. Fearing that he had utterly forsaken her, she assured him that she had only ever meant to divert him from the pain in his leg by virtue of the religious debate which he had always enjoyed. The king was not convinced and 'tried to lure Katherine into another compromising religious argument' but she remained steadfast, explaining that she was 'only a woman' and that she had only ever wanted to learn from Henry.[13] She acknowledged him as the 'supreme head and governor here on earth next unto God' and that as such he was the only authority she was subject to and wished to learn from.[14] Henry forgave her utterly and declared that they were as perfect friends as ever they had been.[15] Katherine was safe, and when Wriothesley came to arrest her the king was furious and ordered him away, calling him an errant knave and a fool. But Katherine had been badly frightened and ordered her ladies to get rid of all the incriminating books they possessed. Whether Anne and others obeyed entirely or merely squirrelled them away remains unclear.

Katherine had survived and when Anne's husband returned to England in autumn the reformist faction was firmly in the ascendancy. That same month he joined the king on progress and on 31 August he was named as one of the men who were granted the 'authority to sign on the king's behalf and name during his pleasure warrants, bills, grants, leases, pardons, letters missive, commission and all other writings and minutes from this date until the 10 May 1547 … with a drie stampe made at the king's command to make an impression without blackening'.[16] Seymour was requested to leave for Boulogne and before departing he saw Ambassador Selve on 17 September. Selve complained that England was making 'war preparations' but Seymour said that such rumours 'displeased him' as they were simply reinforcements against the Scots, whose ships were 'pillaging the English'.[17] He left Anne in London and departed on 21 September and had a pleasant crossing, and he was soon deep in negotiations.[18] The fact that he was sent on such an embassy with, in the words of David Loades, a good deal of independence, speaks volumes about the high regard in which he was now held. Further to this it was noted that soon Edward Seymour was back at court, after which the persecution of reformers all but stopped and that, according to the new Imperial Ambassador, Francis Van der Delft, 'the meetings of the council are mostly held at the Earl of Hertford's house'.[19] It was also noted that the Privy Council were 'much inclined to please and entertain the Earl (of Hertford) and Admiral', the position of admiral having been given to Edward's brother, Thomas, shortly beforehand.[20]

The Hertford faction, as it was now termed, soon felt powerful enough to move against the conservatives. Henry VIII himself was, by now, aware he was dying and he feared that the Norfolk conservative faction was planning a Catholic coup. In October, Lord Lisle was exiled from the council after he punched Gardiner in anger. This was soon followed by the exclusion of Gardiner himself, ostensibly because he refused to swap some lands with the king but in reality because he opposed the ascendant reformist party. By 4 December Henry demanded that Gardiner 'should not molest us further' and the disgraced bishop was forced away from the court.[21] Thomas Howard, Duke of Norfolk was the next target. In June he had sensed which way the wind was blowing and despite his Catholic faith he sought an alliance with the Seymours. An earlier proposed marriage between Thomas Seymour and Norfolk's daughter, Mary Howard, had not taken place but again it is testament to just how high the Seymours had risen that such a match between them and one of the 'great-blooded' families of England was something which was not only possible but which they did not have to scramble to ensure took place. Seymour blood was, after all, about to sit on the throne of England; what need had Edward or Anne for a Norfolk alliance? They clearly did not favour one, possibly on grounds of faith, and when Norfolk again suggested in 1546 that two of his grandchildren by Henry Howard, Earl of Surrey should marry two of the Seymour children, the proposal was rejected by them. It was also rejected firmly by Surrey who stated that he 'would never agree to his family being allied with men whom he considered were not truly noble'.[22] Surrey was well noted for his rash and violent behaviour which had landed him in prison previously, and until now, however, the king had chosen to turn a blind eye. Now, though, he moved swiftly, Surrey was accused of having 'questionable loyalties to the king'.[23] Wriothesley questioned him and on 12 December he was arrested and sent to the Tower. Norfolk's arrest the same day left the reformers triumphant and the conservatives in total disarray. Crucially, Surrey now confessed to bearing the arms of Edward the Confessor, which technically he was allowed to do, but he also used 'three labels silver' which was only allowed to be used by the royal heir. Henry saw this as proof of his ambition and that he was a viable threat to Edward's succession. Surrey was found guilty and executed on 19 January 1547. Norfolk was also found guilty but spared execution by the death of the king.

Henry's health had been failing for a long time and his last Christmas was spent quietly with the queen away at Greenwich at Henry's command.

During this time Henry made his final decision regarding the makeup of his son's regency council, Edward was deemed too young to rule alone by contemporary standards. Sixteen men were appointed to a council which was to see that Henry's will was carried out after his death. The men named were Edward Seymour, Thomas Cranmer, John Dudley, Anthony Denny, and other reformers. A couple of key conservatives, however, were also named, including Thomas Wriothesley and William Paget, both of whom Seymour now allied himself with. Paget, he knew, 'was now of the utmost importance for interpreting [the king's] will, for the distribution of dignities in the new reign was to be determined solely by what Paget declared had been Henry's intentions'.[24] Between themselves they now plotted to essentially undo Henry's wishes and create a Protectorate with Edward Seymour at its head who, for his part, promised to be guided always by Paget.[25] Physical evidence of their alliance can be seen in the number of times Paget can be found at Hertford's house. For example, on 4 January Selve and La Garde write to Francis I that 'Paget spoke with La Garde in Hertford's House'.[26] Henry appears to have been unaware of this and he demonstrated his confidence in Seymour once again by appointing him as Earl Marshall, a hereditary title of the Duke of Norfolk, and Lord Treasurer.[27] Anne Seymour, for her part, would have been well aware that Katherine Parr was hoping that Henry might appoint her as Regent to her young stepson; it was no secret. At home and abroad speculation was rife as to who would assume power, but most were pleased that at least 'the queen and the Earl of Hertford, Uncle to the Prince are well disposed to pious doctrine'.[28]

Henry VIII died on the evening of Friday 28 January 1547 at his palace of Whitehall. His exact cause of death is unclear but historian, Alison Weir, suggests that it might have been a pulmonary embolism.[29] Just three days later Selve and La Garde, when writing to Francis I, reported that the king had named 'twenty commissioners and governors for his son and this realm of whom Hertford is chief … confirmed to La Garde by an English physician formerly in his service and now in that of the said king'.[30] This was not Henry's intention but it was a reality which Edward Seymour now strove to bring about.

Chapter 9

Fight the Good Fight

Henry's death changed the Seymour's world. Although Henry had honoured Edward Seymour he had not given him pre-eminence during Prince Edward's regency. Now though, Edward Seymour moved fast to secure such a position. He and Paget agreed that the news of the king's death must be kept secret, ostensibly to allow time for Edward to be brought to London, in reality so that Edward could assume power with Paget as his chief advisor. Two years later Paget would remind Seymour about their discussions and urged him to 'remember what you promised me in the gallery at Westminster before the breath was out of the body of the king that dead is. Remember what you promised immediately after devising with me concerning the place which you now occupy … and that was to follow mine advice in all your proceedings more than any other man's'.[1] Once this had been decided, Seymour rode quickly to Hertford to the young prince and he took him to his sister, Elizabeth, at Enfield so the two children were together when the news of the king's death was broken to them.[2] On 31 January the news of the king's death was broken and Seymour was back in London where Edward was lodged in the Tower until his coronation. They arrived by 3 pm and were greeted by the firing of the guns from ships along the Thames and the Tower itself. On Monday evening, the first meeting of the new Privy Council took place with only three minor absentees. Henry VIII's will was read out and the men present agreed to 'maintain every part and article of the same to the uttermost of our powers'. However, it took them no time at all to reverse this decision; only Wriothesley continued in his objections. They decided that for the sake of the good governance of England that 'some special man … must be preferred in name and place before others' and would be best placed to oversee all the others by virtue of their 'grace, wisdom and experience'.[3] They were in agreement that Edward Seymour should be this man.

The next day, February 1, Prince Edward was brought from the Tower to Westminster where the will was read again and it was revealed that Edward Seymour had been appointed as Lord Protector and Governor. Edward gave his consent to this decision and a commission under the Great Seal was issued which made the appointment legal.[4] Seymour also well rewarded his supporters – John Dudley was made the Earl of Warwick, Sir Philip Hoby became Master of the Ordnance and Edward's brother, Thomas, became Lord High Admiral and Baron Seymour of Sudeley, which might sound like impressive titles but in reality he was largely excluded from holding real power. The Imperial ambassador, Van der Delft, remarked that despite the Seymour family unity heretofore being unchallenged, the two brothers were in fact 'widely different in character', something which would soon become apparent.[5] It was also decided in the early days of the reign that Edward Seymour would take the title Duke of Somerset, which was a senior royal title traditionally held by the king's Beaufort ancestors and also by Henry Fitzroy in the more recent past. He was also given land with a yearly value of eight hundred pounds and which, by July, included the sites of Glastonbury and Syon Abbey as well as the castle at Marlborough.

Edward Seymour now gave a speech which stated that he would trust God to help him carry out his new role and tellingly letters were dispatched across Europe to the Emperor, to Francis I and to Flanders to inform them of the peaceful succession of King Edward VI and the appointment of Seymour as Lord Protector. New ambassadors such as Sir Richard Morysine, who was sent to the Danish king, were dispatched in the name of King Edward but rather tellingly such documents were only signed by 'the Earl of Hertford', and not the king himself.[6] Likewise, when letters were written in reply they were often addressed, as one dated February 8 at Valenciennes by Edward Carne is, to 'the most noble Lord the Earl of Hertford, Governor of the King's Majesty most excellent person during his minority, and to the Lords of his majesty's most honourable council'.[7]

Edward Seymour's elevation meant that Anne's position at court now changed. Up until now she had served the queen, Katherine Parr, but now it was she who was married to the power behind the throne. Anne was now a Duchess and she had more political influence than any other woman in England. Previously it had been Katherine who guided her women, now it was Anne who would set the time of the court. Traditionally this has been seen as the beginning of the enmity which would develop between the two women; there is in fact little evidence for this at this time but there were certainly tensions developing. Katherine had hoped to assume the Regency during Edward's minority herself and resented that the position had gone to Seymour. She was, however, still the highest ranking woman in England as queen dowager, after the king's daughters. After the king's death, Katherine Parr was left very well provided for. She was left three thousand pounds worth of jewels, plate and household goods, one thousand pounds in simple cash and the rights and use of all her lands. Although Henry's decision to exclude her might seem harsh, he was likely considering that she would wish to remarry.

Seymour was occupied by now with the arrangements for the king's coronation. The streets of London were to be swept and cleaned; tapestries, gold and other decorations were hung from buildings on the route of the coronation procession. Seymour was to have the honour of carrying the king's crown, the magnificent crown of St Edward, his namesake. He also had a smaller crown made for the young king, which he would be able to wear for longer. At nine o'clock on the morning of 20 February 1547, King Edward was accompanied by Seymour along with 'certain others of his Privy chamber' to Whitehall where the court of Augmentations was 'richly hung with cloth of Arras and cloth of estate'. The king was dressed in his robe of crimson velvet and ermine 'wearing on his head a cap of black velvet'. Edward Seymour then led the king in procession, carrying the crown. The Duke of Suffolk carried the orb and Dorset the sceptre. Then came Edward, flanked by the Earl of Shrewsbury and the Bishop of Durham. Behind them walked John Dudley, William Parr and Thomas Seymour, all of whom bore the king's train. A scaffold structure had been built on which the throne sat so that everyone could see the small figure of the king. The coronation then followed the pattern of all since 1375 when the ceremonies of coronation had been laid down, but there was one crucial difference. Edward's coronation oath now stated that 'reform of the church could now be enabled by royal prerogative, the king's as law maker'.[8] Archbishop Thomas Cranmer also gave a coronation speech which opened with the words: 'Most dread and royal sovereign. The promises your highness hath made here at your coronation, to forsake the devil and all his works, are not to be taken in the bishop of Rome's sense'; anyone harbouring hopes of a return to Rome could be under no illusion that this new king or his government would tolerate such thoughts. He went on to liken Edward to Josiah who would see 'idolatry destroyed [and] the tyranny of the bishops of Rome banished from your subjects'. Seymour was the first to pay homage to his new king and he vowed that he was his 'liege man for life and limb and of earthly worship, and faith and truth I shall bear unto you against all manner of folks, as I am bound by my allegiance and by the laws and statues of this realm, so help us God and Allhallows'.[9] The new reformist order it seemed was here to stay.

With Edward VI safely crowned, everyone now moved to Westminster Hall for the great coronation banquet. Edward Seymour was granted the honour of washing immediately after the king and he sat to the right of the king at the high table. Together they and the court enjoyed a feast which included numerous dishes including those of mutton, swan and poulet.

Following Edward's coronation, Katherine Parr retired to the Old Manor at Chelsea, which had once belonged to Thomas More but which had reverted to the Crown after his execution. It was a lovely red brick building in Chelsea, which had water piped into it and stunning gardens where peach and cherry trees were grown.[10] There she was taught by the scholars Roger Ascham and later Miles Coverdale.[11]

Katherine's retirement to Chelsea meant that, for now at least, Anne Seymour was left as the first lady of the court. This left her in a position of power and it is clear that while her husband turned his mind to governing England, Anne used her new position to establish herself as a patron of Protestantism and she was frequently asked to patronise religious publications. Over the next few years many books would be dedicated to her, the examination of which we shall come back to later. This mirrored Edwards Seymour's own patronage of Protestantism and in 1548 Calvin himself would dedicate his *Commentary on the Epistles to Timothy* to him in which he acknowledged Seymour's 'distinguished piety'.[12]

When Edward Seymour came to power as Lord Protector, England was still essentially a Catholic country; for all the reformers campaigning and cajoling of the old king, he had remained in essence a Catholic at heart. However the Catholic Church's hold on the people of England was no doubt weakening, as many of those such as the Seymours and Willoughbys felt that change was necessary. Seymour explicitly stated that he wished to bequeath to Edward, when he came of age, an England which was 'flourishing in men, possessions, wealth, learning, wisdom and in God's religion and doctrine … and Gods will then we found it'.[13] London, which had ever been a hotbed of radicalism, saw some churches desecrated. In February 1547 the church of St Martins removed and destroyed the crucifix on the rood screen and replaced the colourful saints with religious texts and a painted coat of arms of the king. This violence caused Gardiner to beg Seymour to oppose this iconoclasm and make no changes to the religion of England until Edward was of age and could decide for himself. Gardiner had been excluded from the new group of ruling men. Seymour, however, was not an extremist and he wished more to reform the Church rather than create a new Church all together. He asked the Church, in this instance, to replace the crucifix but did not otherwise persecute those committing iconoclasm. Soon he and the council went one step further and began to debate the removal of all 'idolatrous' images. By March, Van der Delft reported that Edward VI's ministers derided Catholicism when speaking or preaching to the new king and that those in the council previously known to be reformists now openly opposed Catholicism.[14]

Soon though, both Anne and Edward Seymour's attention would be diverted by more personal matters. Thomas Seymour was a difficult brother to have – he was ambitious and resentful of his present exclusion from power. Edward, for his part, was equally ambitious and an incident in May 1547 clearly demonstrates this. When Van der Delft's wife had a son, he invited Edward Seymour and the king to be his godfathers and Mary to be his godmother. The rite was held by proxy and it was determined that John Dudley would be the proxy for Somerset, whilst Seymour himself would stand in for the king, thus ensuring he took precedence over everyone else. Van der Delft wrote that he was 'determined to take first place on every occasion'.

Thomas Seymour was still, at not yet 40 years old, dashing and handsome. Excluded from real power by his brother, as he perceived it, Thomas Seymour now sought power and influence by another means. He sought to marry the king's daughter, Elizabeth. Kate Astley later acknowledged that if Thomas Seymour had been able to act as he wished he would have married Elizabeth before turning his attention elsewhere.[15] He also explored the option of marrying Mary but both options were blocked by Edward Seymour who stated plainly that 'neither of them was born to be King, nor to marry king's daughters'.[16] It is unlikely that either woman was tempted; it was an extraordinary idea and both would lose their dowry and right to the crown should they have accepted his proposal in defiance of the council's will.

Katherine Parr probably did not know that Thomas had considered such an option when he once again turned his attention to her. Katherine had been in love with him before she had married King Henry, now she saw an opportunity for happiness on a more personal level. One of Katherine's letters to Seymour gives us a powerful insight into her thought process at this time. She writes to Thomas that 'I would not have you to think that this mine honest good will towards you to proceed of any sudden motion or passion; for as truly as God is God my mind was fully bent the other time I was at liberty to marry you before any man I know. Howbeit God withstood my will therein most vehemently for a time, and through His grace and goodness made that possible which seemeth impossible to me: that was made to me renounce utterly my own will and to follow his most willingly'. She had married Henry willing to please God, but now she would please herself. Knowing that Katherine was eager, Thomas quickly began his pursuit in earnest, but the whole affair had to be shrouded in secrecy given that Katherine was the king's widow. Thomas' barge was often seen travelling early in the morning down river to Chelsea and was usually gone by seven at Katherine's insistence.[17] Historian, Nicola Tallis, suggests that Anne Herbert, Katherine's sister at court, soon became aware of what was going on and soon rumours were rife.[18] These rumours must have reached the ears of Anne and Edward but, by the time they were so well-established that foreign ambassadors were reporting them, Thomas and Katherine were already married. Susan James suggests that the wedding took place in May at Baynard's castle – Anne Herbert's London home.[19] Katherine knew that Edward would disapprove of the marriage but perhaps she hoped that Anne would be more understanding, likely on the basis of the fact the two women had had a perfectly amicable and even friendly relationship up to this point, as is evidenced by letters they exchanged in the wake of Henry's death and following the break-up of Katherine's household as queen. If so, she was to be disappointed. Sometime in March Thomas Seymour spoke with Anne and told her of his and Katherine's relationship, asking her to see Katherine the next day. Anne had a prior engagement at Sheen and after their meeting he wrote to Katherine and told her that 'My Lady Somerset [Anne] told me on Friday night that she would to Sheen the next day, and at her return on Tuesday she would see your highness … I pray if ye see yourself in good credit with her, to desire her grace to be my good lady. And if I see myself more in favour than you I shall make the like request for you'.[20] This letter also has the effect of giving us a brief insight into Anne Seymour's relationship. Thomas and Katherine clearly felt that she had the power to influence her husband in their favour, should she so wish. It seems, though, that Anne did not wish to help the couple, nor get involved, by May 17 she still had not had the promised talk with Katherine. Katherine blamed Anne for not coming when she promised but for Anne's part she said that the day was on account of the fact she was unwell, and now intended only to travel with her husband. It is unlikely that Anne feared her husband's disapproval but perhaps the disapproval of the king's children, particularly Mary to whom she remained close to despite their differing views on matters of religion. If so, Anne was correct in her thinking. When Thomas tried to enlist the help of Mary, Mary quickly made it clear that she would not be helping them writing 'I perceive strange news concerning a suit you have in hand to the Queen for marriage. For the sooner obtaining whereof you seem to think my letters might do you pleasure … [she refused] ... to be a meddler in this matter considering whose wife her grace was of late'.[21] Mary went so far as to criticise Katherine and she ended that she 'will not suffer her to grant your suit. I am nothing able to persuade her to forget the loss of him, who is as yet very ripe in mine own remembrances'.[22] Anne and Mary remained close at this time and in April Mary wrote to Anne teasing her gently by addressing her 'as my good gossip' and calling herself 'your loving friend during my life'. Like Katherine she was also seeking Anne's assistance in bringing a matter to her husband's attention, in this instance petitioning for assistance for two men, including Richard Wood who had been her mother's servant when Anne was maiden of honour to Katherine of Aragon. She asked Anne to mention it to 'my lord your husband, for I shall conspire that it is in manner impossible for him to remember all such matters, having such a heap of business as he hath'. She speaks of Anne in the most affectionate terms calling her 'my good Nann' and thanking her for all her previous assistance. This clearly was not the first time that she had sought Anne's assistance and she thanked her again for 'all my suits hitherto'.[23] Nor was Mary the only woman whom Anne aided – Dorothy Wingfield sought her assistance regarding her husband's lands at a Suffolk priory, and this must be the tip of the iceberg. It is hard to imagine that Anne was not inundated with such petitioners, many of whom later expressed gratitude for her assistance. On a more personal level we know that Anne and Mary were still close and were exchanging gifts at the end of January 1547, when Mary sent Anne a 'ring of gold with a diamond in it' which she often wore.[24]

Whatever her reasons, be they personal or political, it is clear that Anne was not willing to intercede on Katherine's behalf and Katherine was becoming increasingly irritated. In February, when Katherine's lands were being settled, there was some delay and Katherine squarely laid the blame at Anne's door. She had evidently spoken with Seymour before about receiving her dower lands and she wrote to Thomas complaining that 'my Lord your brother hath deferred answer concerning such request as I made to him til his coming hither. This is not his first promise I have received of his coming and yet unperformed. I think my lady [Anne] hath taught him that lesson, for it is her custom to promise many comings to her friends and to perform none. I trust in greater matters she is more circumspect.'[25] It was entirely natural for Anne to side with her husband but Katherine clearly felt that Anne, who had been her lady-in -waiting barely two months before, should have taken her part. The relationship between the two women took a downward turn again in May when Katherine met with Edward Seymour and then Anne. Anne sided with her husband in what could not have been an easy meeting and in a letter afterwards Katherine famously called Anne 'that hell'.[26] This portrayal of Anne is in stark contrast to the one we have evidence for heretofore. The Anne we know from Lady Mary's letters, Lady Lisle and other petitioners was kind, gossipy, loyal, generous and subject to many warm words. In fact it is notable that no evidence at all, other than Katherine's angry words, suggests that Anne Seymour was either power hungry, disloyal or imperious. Nothing existed prior to her husband's arrest in 1549.[27] Given this, it is hard to believe that Katherine's words and accusations were anything other than those of a woman who was angry that Anne did not agree with her actions.

Ironically it is possible that Anne, and even Edward, could in fact have supported Katherine and Thomas' marriage as a means of 'political strategy aimed at strengthening the power of the Seymour family', had they waited but the speed with which the two protagonists acted made it an utterly unacceptable act, and one that they could not endorse.[28] As queen dowager Katherine should have waited two years before considering a remarriage and then only undertaken one at the council's approval.

When Katherine did finally meet directly with Edward Seymour in May 1547 it did not go well. Katherine wrote to Thomas afterwards that 'my lord your brother hath this afternoon a little made me warm. It was fortunate we were so much distant, for I suppose else I should have bitten him. What cause have they to fear you having such a wife? Tomorrow or else upon Saturday afternoon about 3 o'clock I will see the king where I intend to utter my choler to my lord your brother, if you shall now give me advice to the contrary'.[29] After failing to gain support from either Edward, Anne, or the council, Thomas and Katherine went behind their backs and went straight to the king. Thomas asked Edward for help in persuading Katherine to marry him, the king unaware that their marriage had, in fact, already taken place. Edward seems to have been supportive and wrote that they 'need not fear of any grief to come … I will provide for you both that hereafter if any grief shall befall, I shall be sufficient succour'.[30] This was enough for the council to reluctantly sanction the marriage by the end of June 1547, despite Edward Seymour being 'much offended by it', and Thomas Seymour was given permission to live with Katherine at Chelsea alongside the young princess Elizabeth. Katherine, by bringing Thomas into the household, was unwittingly creating a recipe for disaster.[31]

Chapter 10

Anne

Shortly after the sanctioning of Katherine and Thomas' marriage, in July 1547, Edward Seymour was leading England in its preparations for war against Scotland in an attempt to force it to ratify the marriage treaty which would bring about the union of England and Scotland through the marriage of Mary, Queen of Scots to Prince Edward. He hoped to avoid open confrontation and to this end sent men to meet with the Scottish commissioners on 8 July to make a final stab at diplomacy. One which failed when the Scots refused to attend. Seymour had spent a good deal of the past six months preparing for the violence that was now inevitable, and he intended to lead the invasion force himself, being on 11 August confirmed as Lieutenant and Captain General at land and at sea.[1] He issued a proclamation from Sheen, in his own name not the king's, in which he claimed he only would be coming to Scotland as a friend to chastise rebels and to bring about the marriage which would 'unite both realms … preserve the laws of Scotland and abolish the jurisdiction of the Bishop of Rome'.[2] The Scots were not convinced but the proclamation was nailed to many prominent buildings.

Details of his invasion force survive in the Calendar of State Papers which reveal that it consisted of around 18,000 men and that initially the invasion was intended to be 30 days long. Each man would receive 2lbs of meat, 1lb of bread and drink a day so long as they got the job done in that time frame; any longer and there would be biscuits and beer to fall back on. Amongst the men assembled to fight was Edward Seymour's son, Edward, by Catherine Fillol. He was to be the captain of his father's 'personal band'.[3] The English fleet, which as well as taking military action would also help to supply the land forces, consisted of eighty warships, galleys and merchant ships.[4] The army mustered at Berwick with a smaller force of 2500 at Carlisle, which would be a diversionary tactic.[5]

Throughout this period Anne was almost constantly pregnant, literal proof that she and Edward were sleeping together regularly. The dates of Anne's later pregnancies are even harder to pin down than her earlier ones and so it is not possible to determine for certain whether or not she was pregnant when her husband marched north this time. She would no doubt have been anxious regardless, as we have seen that she was when her husband had previously fought in the north. Almost certainly one of her husband's final acts before he matched north would have pleased her though. He made her stepfather, Richard Page, who was chamberlain of Edward VI's household and had been since 1537, Governor of England during his absence. This had the effect of further alienating Thomas Seymour who, although he was given control of lands in southern England and English holdings in France, was excluded from the council and the governorship.

By 27 August Seymour was in Newcastle and the Mayor there ordered a gun volley to welcome him, before the English forces under his leadership began to move north.[6] The Scottish forces were mustering under the Earl of Arran at Edinburgh and at Falla, meaning they were able to respond should the threat come by sea or by land. James Hamilton, 2nd Earl of Arran was a great grandson of James II of Scotland who had periodically been heir presumptive to the Scottish throne. At this time he was Regent of Scotland on behalf of the infant Mary; something he had in common with Seymour. He was experienced, proud and a Scottish spy who was reporting to Englishman, Thomas Wharton. He reported that he had now assembled the 'strongest host and most numerous in the best order since Flodden'.[7] When it became clear that the English were moving north along the coast to maintain contact with the fleet, Arran moved to hold the Esk river crossing at Musselburgh. On 8 September, just east of Edinburgh, 600 Scottish horsemen appeared and were fired upon. They retreated but were back the next day when Seymour reluctantly sent out a cavalry force to attack them. In response Arran sent most of the Scottish cavalry and English victory deprived him of one of his most valuable assets.[8] 800 Scots were killed or captured. The Scots knew they were in trouble and they offered to negotiate or to settle the matter by single combat, both of which Seymour rejected.[9] He also prevented his friend and fellow nobleman, John Dudley, from accepting the challenge on his behalf.

On the morning of 10 September, Seymour moved the great artillery pieces that he had dragged north towards Inveresk; when they saw movement the Scots advanced to meet them. It has long been suggested that Arran mistakenly now thought that the English were seeking to retreat towards their ships and sought to cut them off. An alternative interpretation is that Arran knew he did not have the artillery to match Seymour and so sought to prevent the guns from being deployed.

Seymour sensed an advantage and stopped the English and ordered them to reform to face the fast approaching Scots, and to pull the guns into position behind them. The Scottish left wing now came under heavy fire from the English ships lying just offshore in the Firth of Forth. The fighting was fierce, and not as one-sided as the English chroniclers would have us believe. The marshy ground hampered their advance and Edward Seymour's son was lucky to escape one melee with his life when his horse was hacked down. Lord Grey, captain of the cavalry took a pike to the face and Sir Andrew Flammack, who held aloft the king's standard, was badly injured and only escaped death through the actions of Sir Ralph Coppinger who came to his rescue. He managed to hold onto the standard, though it was badly damaged.[10] The English held on though and ordered a hail of arrows down onto the Scottish forces; the line broke and the English pursued the retreating Scots, with many drowning in the Esk or slaughtered by the English. A violent and brutal description of the massacre survived in the account of William Patten who wrote that there were 'dead corpses lying disperse abroad, some their legs off, some but houghed and left lying half dead, some thrust quite through the body, there's the arms cut off diverse their necks half asunder many their head cloven of sundry their brains bashed out, some others again their head quite off, with other many kinds of killing … and thus with bloods and slaughter of the enemy this chase [of the English] was continued for five miles in length westward from the place of their standing which was in the fallow fields of Inveresk … dead bodies lay as thick as a man may note … the morality was so great as it was thought the like aforetime not to have been seen'.[11] At about 5pm Edward Seymour halted the slaughter when he recalled the cavalry and ordered that the trumpeters sound the retreat. The English had lost about 600 men, the Scots about 10,000 according to contemporary chroniclers. High profile casualties included Lord Fleming, James V's former chamberlain and the sons and heirs of the Lords Methven, Ruthven, Avondale, Odlivy, and Erskine. Robert Graham, the heir to the Earldom of Montrose, and John Stewart, heir to that of Buchan, also lay amongst the dead. The Earl of Arran survived the battle but was 'forced to abandon some of his clothing on the field'.[12] The news of her husband's great victory would have reached Anne in London by 19 September at the latest, and her relief can be imagined. The Imperial ambassador, Van der Delft, travelled to the king at Oatlands Palace to hear the news and he wrote to Mary that Seymour had already reached an accord with some of the defeated Scots.[13] Something which was true as many of the defeated Scots quickly chose to approach Seymour offering their loyalty to his regime in exchange for their lives and English protection – something that Seymour was happy to give. Seymour now marched his forces on to Leith unopposed, the Scots simply no longer had an army with which to stop him. His plan was now to garrison Scotland with English troops and to this end he set about inspecting and identifying suitable sites such as that of Inchcolm which was garrisoned with 150 men under Sir John Luttrell. It was chosen specifically because its location at the mouth of the Firth of Forth, meant that it could control ships coming in and out of the Forth. They built ramparts there and gun platforms and two ships were stationed there under Luttrell's command – the *Saker* and the *Double Rose*. Thanks to a contemporary illustration and notes which survives in the Anthony Roll, we know that the *Double Rose* had a crew of 39 and was armed with the same type of 'bastard culverin' guns that were aboard the *Mary Rose*.[14] He went on to sail to Broughty Castle which quickly surrendered without a shot being fired. A messenger from the castle, by the name of Ninian Cockburn, had already spoken with Seymour and came to this arrangement.[15] Like Inchcolm, Broughty Castle guarded the mouth of the Tay and in the words of William Patten it 'being gotten both Dundee and St Johns Town [Perth] and many other towns else shall become subject to this hold or be compelled to forgo the use of the river'.[16] Seymour saw to it that Leith was burnt and throughout the campaign there was a good deal of violence before the English turned south to take the surrender of Hume castle, Lauder, Kelso and Roxburgh where Seymour ordered that the defences be improved. Before he returned to England, Seymour knighted thirty of his commanders at Leith and forty-eight more of his men who had done 'noble service' during the battle – these included his son, Edward Seymour. Further evidence that despite what the legal record or gossip might suggest, he regarded his first-born son by Catherine Fillol to be his biological child.

By 8 October he was back in London where he was welcomed by the men of the city at Finsbury Field. He declined a military triumph but accepted as a reward the palace and lands of the Bishopric of Bath and Wells as well as other parcels of land scattered across the country which the king insisted on including.[17] Somerset was determined to end the Scottish issue once and for all and to this end he sent a messenger to Mary of Guise and the Earl of Arran asking them to reach terms and co-operate but neither was so inclined and they opted instead to plot with the French against England. The garrisons left behind were also struggling. Sir Andrew Dudley, in command at Broughty, wrote by November that he was struggling without warmth or adequate provisions. He also had a lack of gunners and the Scots were constantly hounding them. It was a similar story at Roxburgh where they were running out of beer to drink, a necessity rather than a luxury at a time when the water was more often than not disease-ridden and dangerous to drink. Meanwhile, at Norham, the soldiers were demanding their pay, something that Seymour was making them wait for.

Seymour was also making Bishop Gardiner wait. The irate bishop wrote to him no fewer than six times before he received a reply and he remained implacably opposed to religion reform. A further nineteen letters to Seymour that year alone were sent by him and the recalcitrant bishop was imprisoned in Fleet prison from 25 September 1547 to 7 January 1548.[18] Seymour was annoyed and told him so, which prompted Gardiner to somewhat backtrack and claim that he had misunderstood him and ask for permission to put his case before the council.

It is at around this time that later historians would have us believe that the relationship between Anne Seymour and Katherine Parr completely broke down as Anne sought to assert her right to be first lady in the land. There are numerous problems with this as we have seen, not least because none of these accusations predate the 1550s when Catholics were seeking to damage her reputation because she was a leading figure in the religious reformist movement. The most famous of these attacks comes from the pen of Peter Heylyn who was writing in the seventeenth century and who claims to be able to know Anne's thoughts. His hyperbolic prose accuses Anne of being 'a woman of most infinite pride and of a nature so imperious as to know no rule but her own will… For what she sayeth within herself "Am I not wife to the Protector who is king in power though not in title a Duke in order and degree, Lord Treasurer and Earl Marshall and what else he pleaseth and one who hath enobled his highest honours by his late great victory? And did not Henry marry Katherine Parr in his doting days when he had brought himself to such a condition by his lusts and cruelty that no lady who stood upon her honour would venture upon him? So not all knees bow before me and all hands pay the tribute of obedience to me and all eyes look upon me as the first in state through whose had the principal offices in the court and the chief preferments in the church are observed to pass? Have I so long commanded him who commands two kingdoms? And shall I now give place to her who in her former best estate was but Latimer's wife and is now fain to cast herself for support and countenance into the despised bed of a younger brother? If Mr Admiral teach his wife no better manners I am she that will and will choose rather to remove them both than be outshined in my own sphere and trampled on within the verge of my jurisdiction"'.[19] This is clearly a much later inventive and imagined speech written by a man well removed from Anne's own time and situation. Another source which references this 'quarrel' is the very dubious Spanish Chronicle which clearly is inaccurate as the writer has Edward Seymour engineering the match between Katherine and Thomas Seymour himself – something which the contemporary letter and documents clearly show was not the case. He also places the quarrel at a time when we know Katherine was not at court but at Sudeley.

In 1585 Nicolas Sander also references this 'battle for precedence' but his pro-Catholic bias is very apparent and he was seeking to discredit both Edward and Anne.[20] Likewise, John Heyward's accounts which were published in 1630 had a well-documented hatred of women, and educated women particularly, calling wives 'sweet poison, the most desired evil in the world [and she should not be] counsellor, much less a controller and director'.[21] There simply is no contemporary source which suggests that Anne Seymour and Katherine Parr battled for precedence.

As we have seen though, there was some discord between the two women. It is reported by John Foxe who spoke of a 'displeasure' which arose between them following Katherine's fourth marriage. John Foxe had been part of Katherine Willoughby's household for a time and was a friend of William Cecil who had been Edward's secretary, so he was well placed to observe that there was some discord within the Seymour family.[22] Nothing indicates this arose from more than Thomas and Katherine's marriage though.

As 1548 approached, Thomas and Katherine travelled to Seymour Place for the festive season.[23] Anne though was becoming increasingly concerned by reports of events occurring within the dowager queen's household.

In 1547, shortly after their marriage, Thomas and Katherine had taken into their household Lady Jane Grey, a great granddaughter of

Henry VII through his daughter, Mary Tudor. Jane Grey was the daughter of Frances Brandon and Henry Grey, 1st Duke of Suffolk. Katherine, Princess Elizabeth and Jane lived together in what was described as a learned household. Katherine Parr published her book *Lamentations of a Sinner* on 5 November 1547, which proves that she was by now a fully-fledged reformist, and in it she 'expressed some of the radical religious views [she] had kept under wraps during the reign of her late husband'.[24] Despite the apparent piety of the household, Anne Seymour was soon to become increasingly concerned by other rumours circulating concerning Thomas Seymour's relationship with the 13-year-old Elizabeth. We know that soon after Thomas moved into the household at Chelsea he started to enter Elizabeth's bed chamber, sometimes before she had even risen, and then would wish her good morning and 'strike her upon the back or on the buttocks familiarly and so forth'. Elizabeth learnt to retreat further into her bed 'so that he could not come at her'.[25] Soon he went further and one morning, according to the now horrified Kate Astley 'strove to have kissed her in bed'.[26] Kate now confronted him and angrily told him that he was endangering Elizabeth's reputation as she was being by now 'ill spoken of'. Anne Seymour certainly seems to have heard the rumours for she wrote to Kate Astley and rebuked her for allowing Elizabeth to travel by barge late at night 'for other light parts' and that she was not 'worthy to have governance of the king's daughter'.[27] From a modern perspective it is hard to disagree and even by contemporary standards Thomas Seymour's conduct was unacceptable. Later it would become evident that he had gone further, and that on a stroll in the gardens Seymour had cut Elizabeth's gown from her 'into a hundred pieces' whilst Elizabeth was held by Katherine. Katherine must have by now realised that her husband's actions were improper but as historian Elizabeth Norton points out, when she married Thomas, Katherine had vowed to obey him and stopped acting independently. She was also aware of his volatility.[28] Her suspicions were raised though and she confronted her husband who called it innocent horseplay. Katherine was not convinced and when Thomas tried to deflect attention from himself by telling Katherine a story about having seen Elizabeth with her arms about a man's neck in the gallery, she realised that this was fiction.[29] Perhaps Anne's sharp rebuke also influenced Katherine and Elizabeth was sent away to Hanworth.

Whilst in London these issues continued to plague the relationship between Thomas and Edward Seymour. Anne, meanwhile, was becoming increasingly concerned that Kate Astley was being 'too great a friend to Thomas' and not taking enough care of Elizabeth.[30] She had also been concerned by yet another scandal which had beset Katherine's household and which was causing more unfavourable gossip at the court. Katherine's brother was William Parr, the Marquis of Northampton who wished to remarry. His marriage to Anne Bourchier in 1527, when he was just 13, had not been a happy one. In 1542 Anne Bourchier had left him stating that she 'would live as she lusted' and gave birth to an illegitimate child who he strove to ensure would never inherit his lands and titles.[31] For Edward and Anne this must have been an uncomfortable echo of Edward's own chequered marital past. For his part, William Parr had a long term affection for Elizabeth Brooke, whose mother had been a lady-in-waiting to Anne Boleyn, and, as such, a woman Anne Seymour would have known well.[32] Elizabeth had also served, alongside Anne Seymour, in the household of Katherine Parr. Despite this affection William had had an affair with Elizabeth's aunt which had caused a huge scandal.[33] Unsurprisingly, Elizabeth kept Parr at arm's length until in early 1548 they married with Van der Delft writing that the two had married in secret 'by means of his sister the Queen and of the Duchess of Suffolk and that eight or nine days afterwards he was obliged by the command of the council to put her away and never speak to her again on pain of death in consequence of his having a wife living although he has long been separated from her'.[34] Edward Seymour was forced to create a commission to investigate whether or not William Parr was now a bigamist. Katherine's involvement was further evidence for Edward and Anne that the morality of her household was, by now, highly questionable.

Anne and Katherine did however have one thing in common as 1548 progressed and that was that both women were pregnant. For Anne this was likely her ninth pregnancy, for Katherine it was her first and she soon was suffering from morning sickness. For her health she retreated to her house at Hanworth where Elizabeth had previously been sent on ahead. Events in Katherine's household were about to come to a head. Soon after their arrival Katherine, having resolved to keep a closer eye upon her husband, came across Elizabeth and Thomas Seymour alone, 'he having her in his arms'.[35] Katherine was stunned by their betrayal and Elizabeth was sent away whilst Katherine retreated to Sudeley to await the birth of her child. To his brother's annoyance, Thomas Seymour had spent a huge one thousand pounds on making improvements to the castle and preparing a lavish nursery – maybe out of a sense of duty, maybe out of guilt.[36] Thomas, however, was not content to rest easy in the country, he now picked up again the campaign for his wife's jewels. There had long been a dispute between the brothers as to whether the queen's jewels belonged to Katherine 'or to the crown and should therefore be worn by the wife of the Lord Protector'.[37] Thomas felt they should belong to Katherine and as such would have added to his personal fortune; Edward Seymour was of the opposite view and had confiscated them upon the death of Henry VIII as the late king had not left them to his wife in his will.[38] Traditionally, this is when Anne and Katherine are said to have fought over the jewels but this is simply not the case. Katherine was in mourning and did not appear in public or even attend the only two great court events following Henry's death and prior to Katherine's. There could not have been any public showdown and the only evidence we have for Anne accessing the jewels dates to after Katherine's death, when she and her brother made an inventory at the Jewel Tower, an incident which we shall return to later.[39] Edward Seymour had catalogued them but there is no evidence of Anne using them.[40] We do, however, know that Katherine was annoyed at Edward's control of her jewels, and she asked him to return the pieces that had been her mother's.[41]

On 18 July 1548 Anne safely gave birth to a 'goodly boy, thanks be to God; and, I trust in almighty God the Queen's grace shall have another'.[42] We know nothing of her labour but she was well used to the ritual of childbirth by now and was quickly back at court. This latest Seymour son was named Edward, again after the king who stood as his godfather. Just over a month later, on 30 August 1548, Katherine gave birth to a daughter named Mary. Edward Seymour wrote to his brother to congratulate him on the birth of 'so pretty a daughter' and express his pleasure that Katherine had had a good delivery and seemed well.[43] Anne, too, must surely have breathed a sigh of relief, but all was not as well as another letter from Thomas relayed that Katherine had succumbed to puerperal fever, five days after Mary's birth. In her delirium she had accused Thomas of poisoning her, declaring that she 'was not well handled for those that be about me careth not for me but standeth laughing at my grief and the more good I will to them the less good they will to me'.[44] Two days after that she was dead leaving everything to her husband. The infant Mary was taken into her aunt Anne's care, whilst Thomas Seymour grieved and plans were made for the future.[45] Anne also quickly took over Katherine's sponsorship of John Olde's translation of

Paraphrases, perhaps as a tribute to her friend and former mistress, perhaps simply in the name of the religious reformist beliefs which both women shared. Anne also found Olde a vicarage, at the request of his friend Latimer, for which in thanks he dedicated the work to her.[46]

This was just the first of several works that Anne would have dedicated to her over the next two years.

Chapter 11

Edward

Whilst Anne and Katherine had been bearing their respective children, Edward Seymour had been dealing with affairs of state. His hopes of an enduring Scottish alliance were slowly falling apart. By 2 July, just prior to his son's birth, Edward Seymour received news that Haddington, which was now the largest and strongest of the English garrisons, was effectively under French control.[1] Henri II of France wanted Mary to marry his own son, uniting their two kingdoms and the French and Scots now joined forces and re-established a force of about 10,000 men with which to expel the English. Seymour planned to send another army north under the command of the Earl of Shrewsbury but Mary was smuggled out of Scotland and into France before he could take action. Shrewsbury was sent north, nonetheless, and forced a French withdrawal at Haddington where the newly replenished English garrison withstood an assault in October. Seymour, however, did not have the money available to continue the occupation of Scotland.

He had also set about more serious religious reform. He had authorised Gardiner's release and in June 1548 allowed him to preach in the privy garden at Whitehall, using a text he had provided. He hoped that he was winning the hearts and minds of such men through gentler means than William Cecil advocated for. Cecil would have seen him banished to the Tower long ago. Gardiner was required to preach in compliance with the recent ruling which had stated that no one could preach the theology of the Eucharist until it had been properly determined by the king and his council. Gardiner, however, refused to co-operate and instead spoke on the 'sacrifice of the Mass', and though he admitted that communion could be received in both manners and he attacked Papal authority, he went on to defend Catholic religious ceremonies on the basis that they helped 'to movement towards God'.[2] Crucially he also did not acknowledge the king and council's right to authority in matters of religion. Seymour was utterly furious and Gardiner was sent back to the Tower; however he did not deprive him of his Bishopric and still, it seems, he was holding out hope that he would come around. He treated the Bishop of London, Edward Bonner, in much the same way, first committing him to the Fleet in 1547, then releasing him before his further opposition saw him imprisoned in the Tower. Many of Seymour's reformist colleagues felt he was being rather too lenient.

The Seymours, at that time, welcomed a number of religious reformists into their personal household, or they came to England under their patronage. As the Seymour household fell under Anne's remit it is natural to assume that she, and her children, had daily contact with these men who supported her husband politically. For Anne, life under Edward would have been very different. She was no longer tied to the court as a lady-in-waiting to the queen; instead she was free to live where she pleased and devote herself to her family in a way which would not have previously been possible. We have firm evidence that Anne was personally very keen on receiving such men into her household and that she actively engaged with them, because she criticised one Thomas Smith for being 'too neutral in matters of religion' and encouraged him to do better.[3] Historian M. L Bush argues that the key to Seymour's religious beliefs 'lies in his protegees and associates rather than in his words and reputation. They reveal him [and his wife] to be much more pious and anticlerical, far from moderate or ambiguous in his religious affiliations'.[4]

One such reformer who was welcomed into the Seymour household, and gives us an indication as to the nature of the Seymours' evolving religious faith, was Thomas Becon who had studied under Hugh Latimer, Bishop of Worcester and been ordained in 1533. He was educated at St John's College in Cambridge following the ratification of the Six Articles in 1539 and had been arrested two years later for his Protestant faith with its 'evil and false doctrine'. He was forced to recant and went into hiding. When Edward VI came to the throne he was welcomed into the Seymour household and became their chaplain, where he was highly regarded and treated as their 'confidante and advisor'.[5] In 1548, Becon was one of only eighty priests who retained their right to preach, until the exact nature of religious doctrine was decided upon, demonstrating the regard in which he was held. Together both men debated such theological issues as to whether there was a requirement to kneel in the *Second Book of Common Prayer*.

Did kneeling signify respect or adoration? The former, it was agreed upon, was fine; the second was papist and clearly not.[6]

Another of Seymour's chaplains was William Turner who also served as the family physician. He was given charge of the gardens at Syon House where he oversaw the growing of pomegranates, figs and apricots, indicating that Anne, Edward and their children would have tasted such things. Whilst in their household he began work on his seminal work, *The New Herbal*, which listed and described in detail 238 English plants, and which, when it was eventually published, he would dedicate to Seymour. He too had come into the sphere of Hugh Latimer and he was ordained in 1536 and developed a reputation as a fiery Protestant preacher. He had come under increasing suspicion in the last years of Henry VIII's reign and went into exile.[7] Like Becon and others he extensively studied Calvin, Zwingli and Bullinger and debated religion with Seymour. On a more personal level we know that Turner used his herbalist knowledge to treat members of the Seymour household, perhaps educating Anne, whose role as lady of the household encompassed overseeing the still room and the health of the household.[8]

Both these men and others would have had daily contact with Anne and Edward's daughters. Becon, in particular, praised Anne for 'training their children in good literature' of the correct religious faith.[9] Their sons, Edward and Henry, were often taught alongside their cousin, Edward VI, by the king's tutors, but their daughters' education was truly remarkable and was undertaken at home with Anne's close supervision where they undertook 'fruitful studies'.[10] This included corresponding with other exiled reformers. Bucer and Phagius sent them books and the 11-year-old Jane Seymour would write a letter of thanks in which her capabilities as a scholar are clearly visible. She delightedly likens their letters to those of Cicero claiming that they have the 'same grace and eloquence'.[11] Calvin himself wrote to Anne's daughter, another Anne, praising her and stating that she was 'so conversant in the doctrines of Christ as to afford easy access to his ministers'.[12] This level of education was, again in the words of Calvin, 'liberal … and very unusual for a lady of such birth and station'.[13] He also expressed his personal regard for Anne, who in 1549 would send him a ring as a token of her personal esteem in return.[14] One of Jane Seymour's letters also offers a touching glimpse into the affectionate relationship which Anne had with her daughters. When Bucer and Phagius enquired about Anne's health, Jane replied with a heartfelt 'my mother thank God is in good health; she desires her best respects to you both and also thanks you for your salutation to her grace'.[15]

In addition to this impressive education, we know that the children of Anne and Edward would also have had fun. Whilst Edward VI's court had a later reputation for sobriety and piety, tightly regulated by Seymour, this was not always the case and we know that many court entertainments were held, many of which reflected the rise of the new Protestant order. Seymour knew how to have fun. At Christmas 1547 there was a masque of Prester John held and one featuring a Tower of Babylon – both subjects which had a Protestant bias. Edward also had inherited his father's fool, Will Somers, and musicians including trumpeters, drummers and minstrels. He also had his own troops of minstrels including Hugh Pallard, Edward Lake, Thomas Alee, Thomas Curson, Robert May, Allan Robinson and Thomas Paginton. We also know that he performed in the festivities himself and was almost certainly joined by the sons and daughters of Anne and Edward Seymour. At Shrovetide 1548, for example, Seymour and his family were at the celebrations where Edward appeared as a Moor and a priest in the theatrics.[16] At the same celebration John Stowe tells us that there was also a 'castle storming to shew the King the manner of Wars wherein he had great pleasure'.[17]

Edward Seymour managed such entertainments, which were designed to please his king, but the summer of 1548 also saw him looking to the future of England and he began to implement social reforms alongside religious ones. The issue of common land and land ownership/enclosure was an important one to Tudor men and women. The feudal system was by now in decline and rich noble landowners sought to breed animals such as sheep on their land to meet the demands of England's profitable wool trade. This meant that land was becoming increasingly enclosed, denying the ordinary men and women access to the pasture they traditionally had a right to use. This meant not only that England was being threatened by a very real shortage of grain and meat, but that people were increasingly moving into towns and leaving behind their smallholdings. This had the knock on effect that fewer men were available to be raised from the Shires should England require an army, as it had done to face the Scots most recently or may do in the future to face the growing French threat. Seymour set up a commission to gather information about these events, supported by John Hales who was one of England's most able administrators and who sought to 'redress the evil' of land enclosure through the commission. He was also a Protestant, in favour of reform and just the sort of man it was claimed that Anne Seymour favoured because she wanted him to influence her husband.[18] The reforms did not come about quickly enough for many and local riots broke out. In an attempt to address the issue, Seymour introduced a bill which improved the rights of land tenants and gave security of tenure to them, to a fairly minor degree. Ironically, at about the same time, he began to enclose the park at Wulfhall where he was planning to build a new house there, on Bedwyn Brail. He began correspondence with Sir John Thynne who was going to direct the project.[19] He did, however, make some provision for his tenants who were affected and he offered alternative fields to some; a pathway was also left open and a new pond was dug to replace access to the old one.[20] His willingness to compromise began to earn him friends amongst the people, whilst of course irritating noblemen who enjoyed the benefits of land enclosure.

Seymour's building of a new London residence was also continuing; Beauchamp House was now too small and he now wanted to build a great palace 'Somerset House' on the banks of the Thames. In order to do so he had to carve out the ideal location, which turned out to be on the south of the Strand and just down river from Whitehall. The new site consisted of six acres with a six hundred foot river frontage. To build his new palace he had to tear down other buildings, such as Strand Inn, the London house of the Bishop Worcester and the church of St Mary le Strand. Stone was taken from the destruction of the church of St John of Jerusalem and the cloisters of St Pauls which were being taken apart. Who was going to be the architect of this new house has long been a subject of debate and may have been either Sir John Thynne or John of Padua, the latter of whom is one of the most mysterious architects of the Tudor period with very little work being identified as having been definitely his. In the eighteenth century a historian and engraver, George Vertue, whilst studying the records held by the Office of Works, uncovered references to John of Padua and concluded that he had designed both Somerset House and Longleat House.[21] He had based his assumption on the buildings' similarities to the four gates of Keys College, but this was refuted by the poet, Thomas Gray, who was looking at the matter for Horace Walpole in the eighteenth century. Nevertheless, Walpole concluded that John of Padua was the likely architect, something which is still widely accepted as a possibility if not a certainty today.[22] Sir John Thynne is a more substantial historical figure with a proven association with Seymour. He was Seymour's steward and had accompanied him to Scotland where he had been knighted after the Battle of Pinkie.[23] Afterwards, he is reported to have 'managed all matters relating to the Seymours private household' making him a figure with whom Edward and Anne would both have been familiar on a day to day basis.[24] However whilst, as we have seen, there is evidence that he negotiated on Seymour's behalf regarding the building of a new mansion at Bedwyn Brail near Wulfhall, we have no proof that he dealt with the building of Somerset House.[25] He was a capable designer who has, like John of Padua, also been credited with the design of Longleat. As he would have been responsible for overseeing the construction of Somerset House, if he had such experience it would have made sense that he should design it himself.

Whoever designed it, we do not know exactly what the Seymour house looked like but we do know that it stood two storeys high and that its buildings were focused around two courtyards.[26] Its gardens stretched along the water edge and would have exploited the 'glorious setting just in the middle of the bow which the river forms between the bridge and Westminster, commanding the prospect both ways and looking directly onto the fine hills of Surrey'.[27] It would also have had a great hall, long gallery, privy and withdrawing chambers, and a presence chamber alongside the private and practical necessities of such a building. We know that Seymour often stayed at Somerset House whilst the building works were being undertaken, and that Anne was usually with him.[28] She also spent a good deal of her time at Syon House, granted to her husband in 1547, and that too underwent large scale renovations which cost, by one estimate, around seven thousand pounds. Edward and Anne transformed the former abbey complex into a Renaissance style private house, complete with the garden in which Turner grew his exotic fruit. The house was largely situated over what was the west end of the abbey church and the abbey's undercroft remains beneath the Great Hall. Sadly no plans exist for the house prior to 1593 so we cannot be certain of the layout of the Seymours' house but the Deputy House Manager of Syon House believes that 'much of the house looks the same as when it was built … it follows the footprint of the original house with the exception of the later northern wing'. Its long gallery is particularly fine, which measures 136 feet long and although Adam's ornate decoration is later, it is not difficult to imagine Anne and her female companions walking the length of the gallery deep in conversation. Legend would later claim that it was in the Seymour-built long gallery that Lady Jane Grey would be offered the crown in 1553.

Anne's status meant that she attracted many women who wished to seek positions for their husbands or children to her side, at Syon and elsewhere. We do know, however, that she also had close friends who had shared her life and faith prior to her rise and whom she now spent time with. One of these was Mildred Cooke, the wife of William Cecil, and although younger than Anne she was just the sort of educated woman who Anne liked to converse with. Mildred translated Basil the Great's sermon on the book of *Deuteronomy*, which she would dedicate to Anne, calling herself 'Your graces humble servant and debtor'. The antiquarian historian, John Strype, would report that Mildred could speak Greek as easily as she could English.[29] Mildred was devoted to Anne and called her a 'right good lady and mistress'.[30] The historian, Pauline Croft, suggests that Mildred was in fact educated in the Seymour's reformist household under Anne's supervision and that 'Mildred became a member of the feminine reformist circle of the 1540s'.[31] She also suggests that Mildred met her husband, Cecil, in Anne's household; the couple married in 1545 but we know she and Anne maintained their friendship throughout the 1540s.

Another of Anne's frequent companions was Jane Dudley, Duchess of Northumberland, whom she had known for many years, and who as we have seen, was her close friend and ally ever since their days together in Katherine Parr's reformist household. Her husband, John Dudley, had been made Earl of Warwick and fought alongside Edward Seymour in Scotland. Jane was another highly educated woman who, like Anne, was a devout reformist. Jane's conversion had likely occurred around the same time as Anne's and it was known that by 1547 no Mass was said in the Dudley household, something which both women championed.[32] The Dudleys, like the Seymours, had a happy marriage of both convenience, respect and cooperation, with John Dudley going so far as to neglect his court duties in order that he could be with his wife who suffered from bouts of ill health.[33] Jane, like Anne, maintained a reformist household and educated her and John's sons and daughters to a high degree. It is testament to the closeness of the two women that their friendship would survive that, and the lives of both their husbands.

Katherine Willoughby also provided companionship, again born out of their long association as discussed previously, although it was, at times, rather fraught. Others such as Mary Hill, the wife of John Cheke, and Elizabeth Carkeke, the wife of Thomas Smith were also her frequent companions during this period.[34] John Cheke would thank Anne profusely for her 'goodness and good mind towards him [and his wife and for her] singular favour towards him' which was 'one of his chief comforts'.[35] Edward Seymour was now considered by many in 1548, to be king in all but name. He began to use the royal 'we' in his letters, adopted the royal mace in his imagery, and spent lavishly on his building projects, all of which began to attract criticism.

Chapter 12

Edward Versus Thomas

Of more pressing concern, however, were the actions of Edward's brother, Thomas, who since the death of his wife had continued his plotting. Kate Astley was right when she had predicted to the teenage Elizabeth that with Katherine dead Thomas would now come 'to woo you'.[1]

Anne had sent her friend Mary Hill, the wife of John Cheke, to Thomas Seymour after the death of Katherine Parr to comfort him. Mary had known Elizabeth for years – she had been part of her household until her marriage to John Cheke and it was likely that Anne also wanted her to help keep an eye on what was happening.[2] Up until then we know that Mary had been staying at Syon with Anne Seymour, likely serving as one of her ladies-in-waiting. Mary later reported that Thomas had admitted to her that he wanted to visit Elizabeth but feared it would be said he came a wooing.[3] It is unclear whether Mary was spying for Anne or colluding with Seymour, which could be the cause of their later quarrel, with Haynes implying that she travelled to Chelsea not to meet with Lady Herbert and find out what was going on but to talk with Thomas Seymour.[4] Exactly what they discussed is unknown but Anne and Mary did quarrel soon afterwards.

Soon, however, there were more explicit rumours abounding, John Seymour had been asked by the admiral to enquire of Kate Astley whether or not Elizabeth's 'buttocks were grown any less or no'.[5] He wanted to visit Elizabeth but she refused although she wrote to him asking for his help with her business affairs.[6] Which has been interpreted then and since as her tactic for encouragement.

His potential courtship of Elizabeth was just one issue that Thomas was causing for his brother. It had long been reported that Anne and Edward were planning to marry Lady Jane Grey to their eldest son, Edward.[7] Thomas, it now became clear, intended to thwart this plan if he could. Following Katherine's death, he had initially planned to send Jane Grey back to her

Above left: 1. John Seymour — Edward's father and Catherine and Anne's father-in-law.

Above right: 2. Tomb brass in Great Bedywn Church of John Seymour, John and Margery's eldest son and Edward's brother. His premature death meant Edward became the Seymour heir.

Right: 3. Katherine of Aragon, the first wife of Henry VIII. Anne Stanhope entered the court as her maid-in-waiting. Anne had a first hand view of her treatment and the events leading to her divorce. Her daughter, Mary, was Anne's lifelong friend. This portrait is a copy of a lost work attributed to Jannes Corvus.

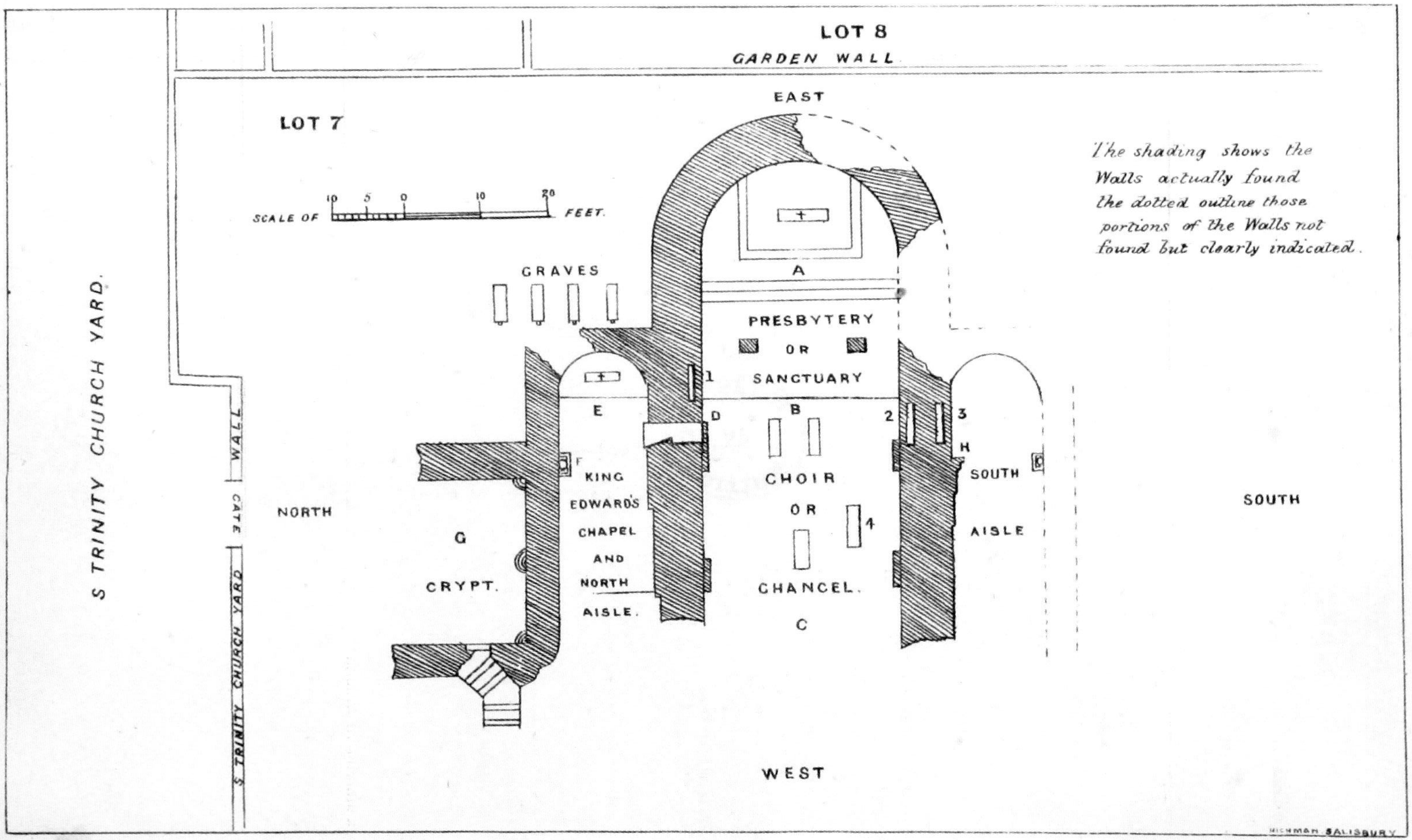

GROUND PLAN OF THE ABBEY CHURCH, EXCAVATED A.D. 1861.2. IN THE GARDEN MARKED LOT 7. IN THE

Opposite: 4. A plan of Shaftesbury Abbey. Catherine may have lived here or at an abbey very much like it.

Above: 5. The tomb of John Seymour, Edward's father.

Right: 6. Anne Stanhope at around age 16 when she entered the household of Katherine of Aragon.

7. A young Edward Seymour.

8. Previously identified as Catherine Howard, this is now thought to portray Elizabeth Seymour, sister to Edward, Thomas and Jane.

9. Jane Seymour, sister to Edward and third wife of Henry VIII. Anne Stanhope served as her lady-in-waiting and oversaw her courtship. Jane was the mother of King Edward VI.

10. Queen Mary I. She and Anne Stanhope, later Seymour, became friends when the latter served in the household of her mother. Despite their differences in matters of religion, they remained friends throughout their lives, writing letters and exchanging gifts. Mary was godmother to some of Anne's children and one of her first acts when becoming queen was to free Anne and ensure her future.

Right: 11. Anne Seymour nee Stanhope.

Below: 12. The death of William Tyndale. Anne would have access to his dangerous and illegal translation of the Bible whilst in Katherine Parr's household. Image taken from Foxe's Book of Martyrs.

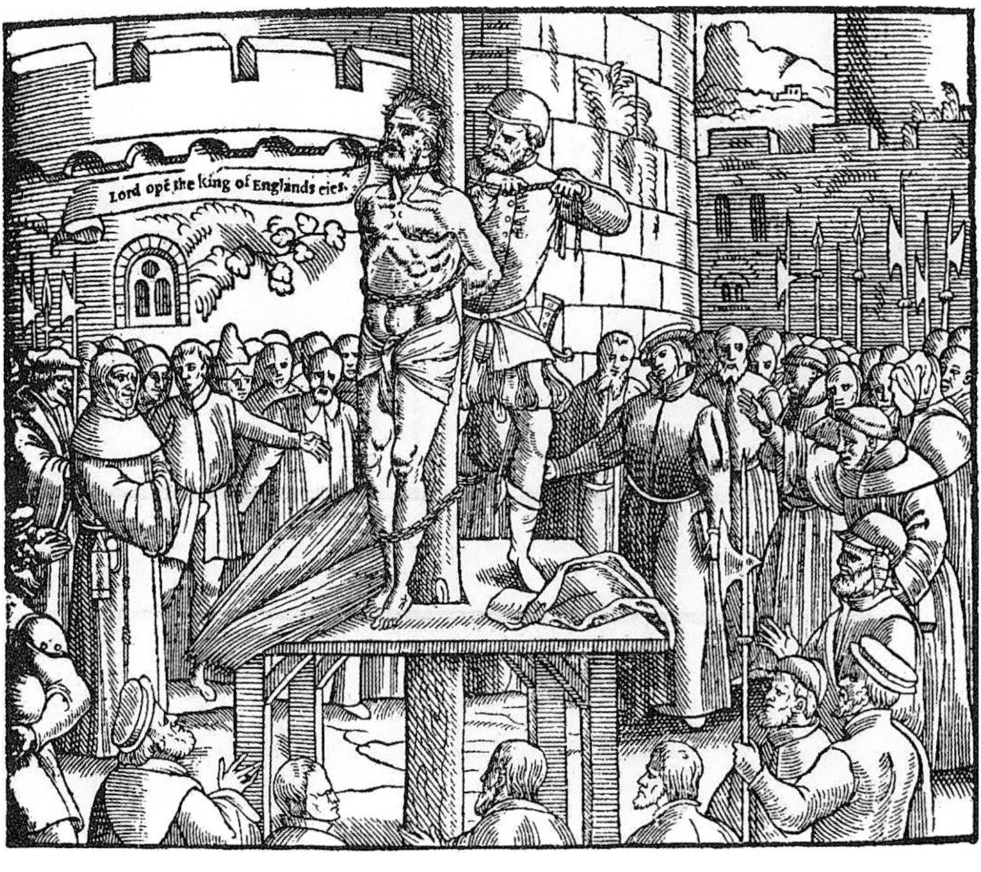

Above: 13. The execution of Anne Askew. The degree to which she was connected to Katherine Parr's reformist household is open to debate, but her steadfast refusal to name the queen or her ladies as complicit in her heresy saved Katherine and the others from persecution. Anne Seymour sent money to Anne Askew during her imprisonment. Image taken from *Foxe's Book of Martyrs*.

Left: 14. King Edward VI.

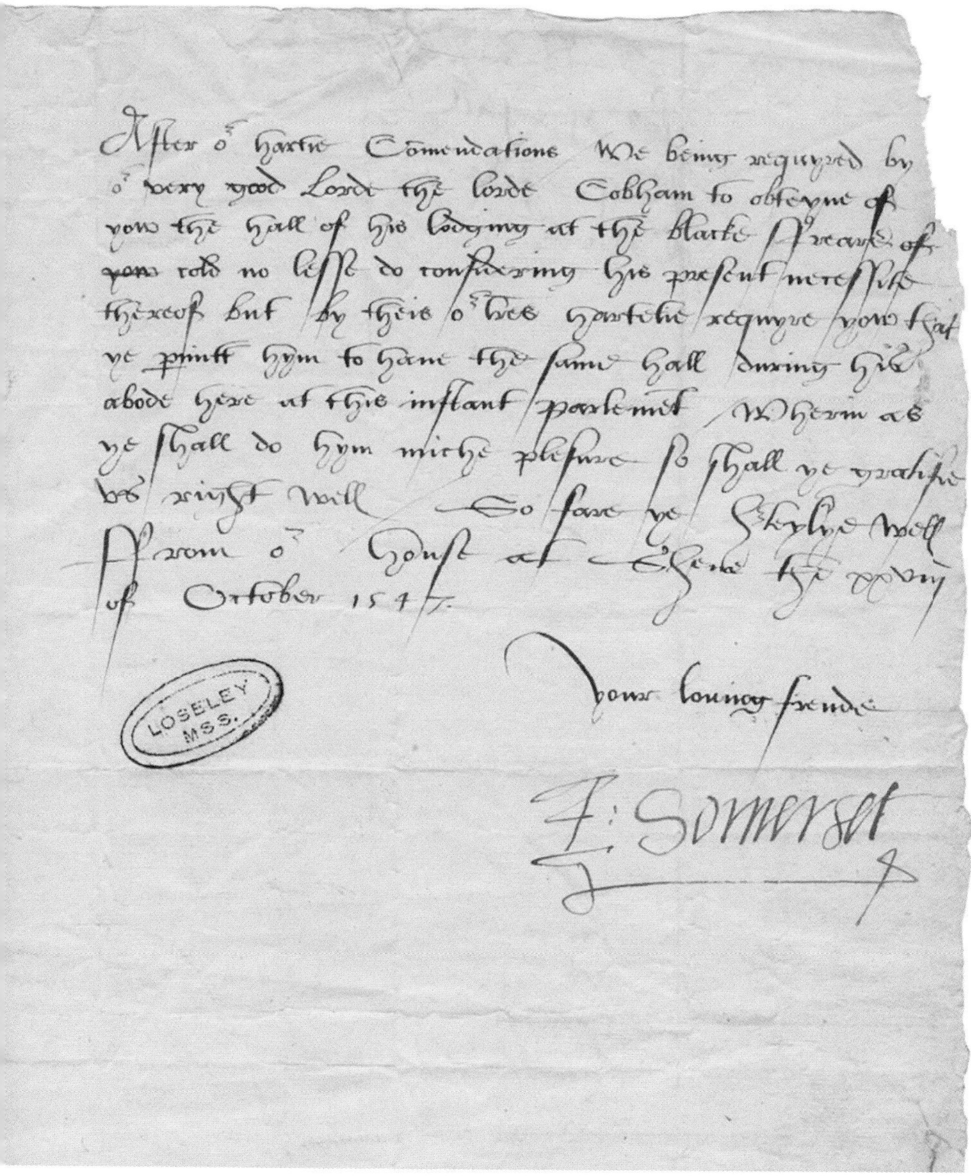

After or hartie Comendations We being requyred by
or very good Lorde the lorde Cobham to obteyne of
yow the hall of his lodging at the blacke ffreres of
yow cold no lesse do considering his present necessitie
thereof but by theis or lres hartelie requyre yow that
ye pmitt hym to have the same hall during his
abode here at this instant parlemnt Wherin as
ye shall do hym mich pleasure so shall ye gratifie
us right well So fare ye hartelie well
ffrom or house at Shene the xxvij
of October 1547.

Your loving frende

E. Somerset

15. Document bearing the signature of Edward Seymour.

Above: 16. Syon House, one of Edward and Anne's London homes. Anne would be granted continued use of the house after Edward's death.

Left: 17. King Edward VI, son of Henry VIII and Jane Seymour. He was the nephew of Edward and Anne Seymour and grew up alongside the Seymour children. Edward served as his Lord Protector during his minority. The king's premature death led to a short-lived succession crisis.

18. A coin minted by Edward VI, showing the young king in profile. The debasement of the English coinage was a major issue during his reign.

19. Modern day Somerset House sits on the site of the Seymours' great building project of the same name. Today only a few traces remain.

20. Painting of Beaudesert, one of the houses belonging to William Paget. William Paget, a one-time Seymour ally, lost patience with Edward over his refusal to listen to his advice.

21. John Dudley, Earl of Warwick and later Duke of Northumberland. He was Edward Seymour's friend and ally until he led the coup d'etat against him. His wife, Jane, was a close friend of Anne Seymour. After the death of Edward VI, Dudley tried to put his daughter-in-law, Lady Jane Grey, on the throne. This coup failed and he was executed on the orders of Queen Mary I.

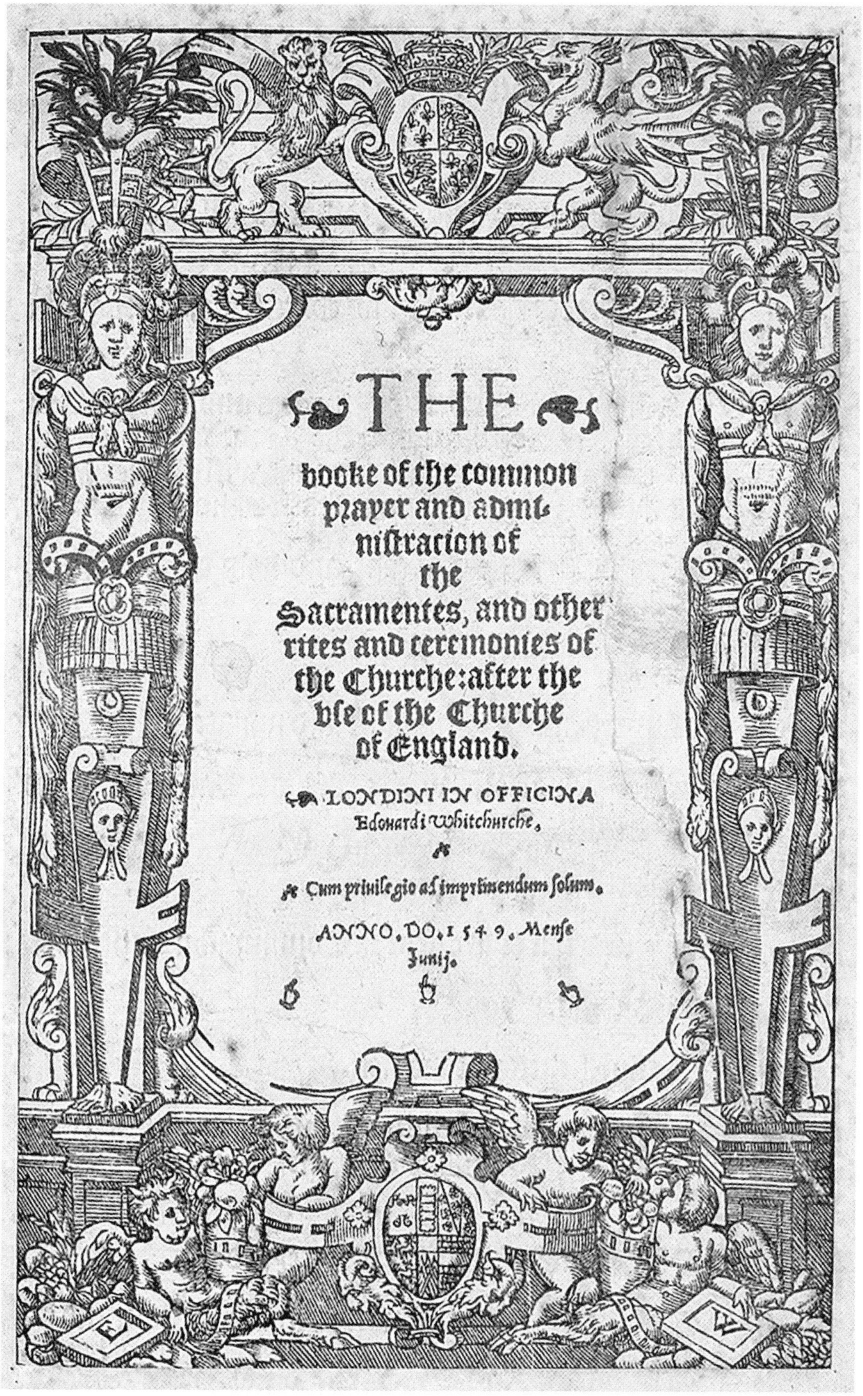

THE
booke of the common
prayer and admi-
nistracion of
the
Sacramentes, and other
rites and ceremonies of
the Churche: after the
vse of the Churche
of England.

LONDINI IN OFFICINA
Edouardi Whitchurche.

Cum privilegio ad imprimendum solum.

ANNO. DO. 1549. Mense
Junij.

22. Title page from Cranmer's 1549 *Book of Common Prayer*.

Left: 23. Anne's half-brother, Sir Michael Stanhope, with whom she was close. He would be executed a few days after Edward Seymour.

Below: 24. Tower Hill, where Edward Seymour met his death. His name is inscribed there alongside the other noblemen who suffered the same fate.

Above: 25. The magnificent tomb of Anne Seymour in Westminster Abbey.

Right: 26. Edward Seymour as 1st Earl of Hertford, a son of Edward and Catherine. His loyalty to his father as well as his chequered marital history saw him thrown into the Tower, but he lived to prosper under James I.

27. Sir Henry Unton, an Elizabethan diplomat and court figure. He was Edward and Anne's grandson through their daughter, Mary.

parents, but he changed his mind and with his mother, Margery Seymour, now in residence where she would 'be as dear unto the Lady Jane as though she were her own daughter', the arrangement was felt to be respectable.[8] He held her wardship and through it control of her marriage and he, instead of matching her with his nephew, Edward Seymour, intended that she would instead marry another Edward: the king. It was a plan that he knew Edward and Anne would oppose, writing that he would cause 'much ado' by pursuing the scheme.[9]

The discord between the brothers had long been recognised and generally the blame was laid at Thomas's door. Nicholas Throckmorton told him that 'the world beginneth to talk very unfavourably of him' and urged Thomas to be more humble in his manner, less argumentative and that even now this would allow him to 'become a new manner of man both in heart and in service'.[10]

Thomas paid no heed and he now turned his attention to his nephew himself. He hoped to encourage Edward to break away from Edward's Protectorate and assert his independence, and the young king would then of course favour Thomas. Rumours reached Thomas that the king was complaining that he did not have enough money to reward the men who served him. Thomas saw an opening and using John Fowler, one of Edward's grooms of the privy chamber as an intermediary, he passed money and messages to Edward.[11] Edward Seymour himself often used John Fowler to transmit messages to the king. When Edward had wished to hear news about the siege of Haddington in July 1548, Seymour had forwarded letters through Fowler to Edward, which must have made his involvement when everything came light particularly galling. For his part, Fowler knew that Edward Seymour would not approve and he begged Thomas to destroy his letters so that it could 'tell no tales' upon him.[12] Money started to slip from Thomas Seymour's pocket into Edward's; on one occasion Thomas sent twenty pounds for Edward to give to his servants as he saw fit, in addition to twenty pounds as a reward to Bishop Latimer for preaching a sermon which Edward particularly admired. Bishop Hugh Latimer was one of the most popular English reformers and he preached before Edward several times, suggesting that the young king could be counted among his admirers. Edward VI listened to him preach at St Paul's cross on 29 January, and later at his Palace of Westminster on several occasions. Seymour was long a supporter of Latimer's and encouraged this and we know that Latimer supported the Seymour regime because in 'the seven sermons which he preached before the king in the following lent are a curious combination of moral fervour and political partisanship, eloquently denouncing a series of current abuses and paying the warmest tribute to the government of Somerset'.[13]

Edward, for whom Thomas's attention likely was a fun novelty, enjoyed both the money and the attention. It has long been claimed that Edward Seymour kept Edward VI chronically short of money but in fact Edward himself admitted that his financial affairs were well managed by Sir Michael Stanhope, Anne's half-brother, who had been appointed as chief gentlemen of the privy chamber, keeper of the privy purse and controller of the king's coffers. The king told Thomas that 'Mr Stanhope had money for me', implying that it was perhaps more the attention than the money from Thomas which caught the king's attention.

Michael Stanhope's position was just one of many appointments to the king's household granted to Anne's relations. Her step father, Richard Page, had been chamberlain to Edward VI until his death in February 1548, upon which he had bequeathed Edward Seymour a 'silver and family cup enamelled after the antique fashion with five lions standing upon castles to bear up the foot'.[14] Richard Page's appointment had angered Thomas who had raged that he was nothing but a drunkard, hardly likely considering Henry VIII had entrusted his son into his care. Both Anne and Edward were close to Michael Stanhope, whom Edward addressed as 'my very loving brother-in-law'.[15] His own brother, meanwhile, continued his schemes, and he now went further and urged the king to remove his brother, but the king would not be party to any underhand plotting.

By November, his scheme to marry Elizabeth was also common knowledge and Lord Russell, the Lord Privy Seal, warned him to give up the plan. Instead he pressed on and through Thomas Parry, Elizabeth's cofferer, suggested that Elizabeth might spend Christmas with him at Seymour Place.[16] He was also criticising Edward Seymour at every opportunity at court to men such as Lord Dorset, Northampton, Rutland and Southampton.[17] He was clearly attempting to build his own power base and everyone was growing increasingly alarmed, with Wriothesley warning him 'for God's sake take heed what you do. You may say what you will that you mean well and mind all for the king but indeed you shall show yourself to be his greatest enemy … you being a faction and trouble but you cannot end it when you would'.[18] Dudley, meanwhile, warned him that 'neither the king nor I will be governed by you, nor would we be governed by your brother were it not that his virtues and loyalty towards the King and the kingdom make him the fittest man to administer the affairs of the country during the king's minority'. Edward Seymour, however, had put off taking any action, hoping that his threats, such as the one he made threatening that he would throw Thomas into the Tower if he visited Elizabeth, would be enough to discourage his brother.[19]

Christmas 1548 was looming and Edward Seymour wanted to focus on other things. The Scots issue again reared its head and Edward Seymour met with the French ambassador to assert the king's right to 'the supremacy of Scotland' and submitted documentary evidence to that effect which the French promised to examine, which he felt was good progress.[20] Despite this, Seymour must have been aware that he was coming under increasing criticism. On Christmas day his friend and longtime ally, Paget, sat down and wrote him a letter. Although it was never sent, it expresses the concerns which were growing about Seymour. He states that Seymour had failed to adequately support the nobility, had turned England into Scotland's number one enemy, and he stated that Seymour 'hear not all things nor all men', meaning that he had stopped listening to his and others' counsel. It reveals that he was beginning to oppose some of Seymour's policies and that Seymour's reformist position was by now diverging from his conservative outlook in which a successful government was required to satisfy the interests of the men who held political power and he felt that Seymour was leading the country awry. He concludes by suggesting that he felt that Seymour now regarded him as 'presumptuous, rash and unadvised'.[21] The truth of Seymour's feelings are hard to speculate about, and Paget never sent the letter suggesting that he did not feel strongly enough to do so, or simply that he wished to retain what influence he could.

The two men were, however, united along with most of the other council members, on the necessity of dealing properly with Thomas Seymour. It was now widely supposed that he had been making plans to raise an army to forcibly overthrow his brother, In January 1549 the vice-treasurer of the mint in Bristol, Sir William Sharington, a wealthy man and influential moneylender, admitted that he had been debasing the currency and working with Thomas Seymour with a plan to possibly create ten thousand coins which Thomas could then use to pay for an army of the same number of men.[22] It was a step too far and on 11 January Edward Seymour asked that Thomas meet with him. Thomas, who wanted witnesses to their discussion, asked that the meeting be postponed. Meanwhile, more and more men began to speak out against him, including Dudley and the Earl of Rutland, who claimed to have knowledge of Thomas Seymour's plans.

What exactly happened on the evening of 16 January is unclear but at the Palace of Whitehall, where the king was sleeping, the gentleman who slept in the king's bedchamber with him was startled by the 'barking of the dog which lies before the kings door'. By the time he reached the door the dog had been stabbed and in a panic he cried out 'Help! Murder!'[23] The king's guards came running and the blame soon fell on Thomas who had been seen at the palace and who had a key to the king's bedchamber. It was soon widely accepted that Thomas had tried to take charge of the person of his nephew but when the dog barked he panicked and killed it, before disappearing into the maze that was Whitehall Palace. The incident was soon the talk of the court, and of Europe with Van der Delft reporting that the 'Admiral had attempted to "outrage" the person of the king by night'.[24]

The next morning Thomas was summoned before Parliament and then arrested and sent to the Tower. Soon afterwards a whole flurry of other arrests followed including Sharington and Fowler. Both of them gave damning evidence, as did Wightman, a servant of the admiral's. At some point the king himself was also questioned and he revealed that Thomas had asked him 'why I did not bear rule as other kings do. I said I needed not for I was well enough. When he went into the country he desired me that if anything were said against him that I should not believe it until he came himself'.[25]

Then attention turned to proving that he had treasonously conspired against Elizabeth. Sir Anthony Denny and Lord St John were sent to her household at Hatfield to arrest Thomas Parry and Kate Astley and convey them to the Tower. Elizabeth herself would soon face questioning by Sir Robert Tyrwhitt who was sent, along with his wife, to take charge of Elizabeth's household. She was horrified by the rumours circulating that she was 'in the Tower and with child by my Lord Admiral', and wrote to Edward Seymour asking that she be allowed to come to court and show herself; Edward ignored the letter.[26]

Inside the Tower there was nothing Thomas Seymour could do but await his own interrogation which began on 25 January under Lord Russell, Southampton and Petre. In the meantime his goods and effects were seized.[27] The list of 'interrogatories for the Lord Admiral' was enormous, ranging from conspiring with Elizabeth to the forceful overthrow of the king, but all he would admit to was that he had encouraged the king to assume control of the council himself, before he reached his full majority.

It is clear that Edward Seymour felt the threat to both his regime and to the king was very real as he ordered that no one be allowed to wear armour or bear arms within three miles of the Capital.[28] It is hard to get a clear glimpse of Edward Seymour's thoughts at this time; later Anne would be accused of urging him to remove his brother but the contemporary evidence, systematically set out in the state papers reveals little more than a thorough and systematic examination of the evidence against Thomas by members of the council reporting to Edward Seymour. He also received numerous letters from everyone involved begging his pardon and asking for forgiveness, suggesting that there was a good deal of uncertainty over which direction the council would go when it sought to remove the threat Thomas Seymour posed.

Thomas Seymour himself seems to have felt that after a meeting on 18 February, when a delegation of noblemen visited him, that the situation might soon be resolved and that he would be released.[29] There is evidence to support this idea. Elizabeth in later life would recall that Edward felt that if he and Thomas had spoken properly then he need not have died, and for now Edward clearly felt that there was still ample opportunity for Thomas to save himself, discrediting the idea that Edward was personally driving events forward and intending Thomas's death.[30]

The evidence collected by the council was more than enough to charge Thomas with High Treason, the gravest offence in the land defined as 'Treason against the Crown' or 'against the monarch'. He was duly charged with 'sore charges of divers and sundry Articles of High Treason, great falsehoods and marvellous heinous misdemeanours against the Kings Majesties person and his Royal Crown'. The Privy Council Act also stated that the same was 'so manifestly proven against him by diverse ways that it appeared not able to be avoided but he should be guilty of them'.[31] On 23 February, members of the council, but notably not Edward Seymour, rode to the Tower to read out the thirty-three offences to Thomas with which he was charged. This took place in a 'chamber in the Tower of London which is in the side of the Kings Majesties Gallery there'.[32] The key focus was Thomas's plans concerning the king, the question of whether he had meant to seize and therefore endanger the king's person, or if he had sought to unduly influence him which was an insult to the royal majesty. The second tier of accusations concerned his garnering of support and money for a rebellion, the use of pirates and his intention to raise a private army.[33] The Privy Council Act also reveals that 'the King's Majestie by the advice of the Lord Protector and the rest of the council did determine to have him in any way heard what he could or would be able to say as to whether [the allegations] should be true'.[34] Unwisely Thomas again refused to respond to them properly and so Seymour had only the report of his councillors to listen to, which he did the next day, After a good dinner the council took the matter to the king before whom Rich read out the charges and each councillor was required to give their opinion. Edward Seymour spoke last and declared 'how sorrowful this case was to him, but said that he did yet regard himself as bound by his duty to the kings majesty and the crown of England [more so] than to his own son or brother … and as such he would not be against the Lords request [to charge Thomas] ... and if himself should commit such offences he could not think himself worthy of life … and therefore he could not refuse justice'.[35] After listening to the members of his council speak, the king agreed to proceed with charging Thomas, but all present agreed that, in accordance with usual procedure, the matter should now be referred to Parliament. Before this, a delegation again went to visit Thomas in the Tower, headed by Rich, Warwick, Shrewsbury and Southampton, to ask him again to speak in his own defence.

This time Thomas replied to the first three most serious charges pertaining to the threat he posed to the person of the king and the peace of the realm. He stated 'that about Eastertide [a year ago] he said to Fowler … that if he might have the king in his custody as Mr Page had he would be glad and that he thought a man might bring him through the Gallery to his chamber and so to his house, but this he said he spoke merely, meaning no hurt'. He also admitted that he 'gave money to the king … and divers times he sayeth the king hath sent to him for money and that he hath sent it [through Fowler]'.[36] Finally he admitted that he had drawn up a Bill and had planned to offer it to the king and suggest he write a letter asking that Thomas should have the 'governance of him as Mr Stanhope had'.[37] After saying this he stated that he 'could by no means be brought or persuaded to answer anymore of the said articles and therefore refused to hear them wherefore they were constrained with the answers to the three articles [to return with]'.[38]

The next day, 25 February, the Bill of Accusation was presented to Parliament and it was declared by the Lords to be a case of 'manifest treason'.[39] Edward Seymour sat in the chair of state as the evidence was read out; he was present the next day too, but on the third day he was notable for his absence despite the attendance of all the other Lords, because he had asked 'for natural pities sake' to be allowed to be absent when the final vote, which would likely condemn his brother, to death took place. Are these the actions of a man struggling with the desperate burden his oath of allegiance to the king had placed upon him, torn between his head and heart and under almost unimaginable anguish? Or is this the scheming action of a man who wished to distance himself from his brother's ultimate downfall having done nothing to save him? It is impossible for us to know the answer at a distance of five hundred years; common sense suggests that it was a mixture of both, but I would argue that there is little to prove that Seymour desired or wanted this outcome. That he could have done more to save his brother seems obvious by modern standards but the fact remains that all the evidence and indeed Thomas's own words proved that he plotted to whisk the king away to his house, and meant that he was guilty of treason by the standards of the day. In addition, if we level the charge that he should have done more for a man he, presumably at one point at least, loved as a brother then the same charge could be levelled at the king, who didn't lift a finger in the defence of the man he had once termed his favourite uncle. Or indeed at any other council member, all of which had once considered Thomas a colleague, ally and friend.

Thomas Seymour was now formally removed from Parliament and the case referred to the lower house 'where it was very much debated and argued'.[40] There was a good deal of support from those who owed their position to Thomas's patronage but it was not enough. The house was 'divers full' when the attainder of treason against Thomas Seymour was passed on 5 March; on 6 March it was passed by the Lords.[41] Four days later, on 10 March, Edward Seymour was at a council meeting held at the Palace of Westminster where the question of what should happen next was debated. Although both Edward and the king were present it was suggested by the Lords that the matter should now be left entirely in their hands 'without [the need of] further troubling of molesting in this heavy case either his highness or the Lord Protector'.[42] This might be seen as an indication that the other members of the council now feared that Edward Seymour might attempt to save his brother from the scaffold, and that he might be able to persuade the king to offer him a pardon. Indeed the council took pains now to keep Seymour as in the dark as they could about the upcoming events, and he was not present at the meeting which condemned Thomas to death. His signature is present in the document authorising his execution though, alongside the names of Cant, Rich, St John, Russel, Warwick, Shrewsbury, Southampton, Petre, Smith, Denny, Paget, Wingfield, North, Sadler, Baker and Monatagu.[43] Looking at the document it is obvious that Edward Seymour's signature was added at different time to the others, probably after theirs, again suggesting possible hesitancy on Edward's part or that he was persuaded to add his signature by the others after they had all signed, to demonstrate their determination and unity on the matter. Equally, however, the explanation might be simply practical, we can never be certain, but the fact that signing at separate times was unusual indicates to me one of the former explanations.

Edward's brother, Thomas Seymour, was executed on 20 March 1549. It was reported that he died bravely but that it took two blows of the axe to sever his head. Just prior to his execution he is said to have written the following words as he tried to make his peace with God:

> Forgetting God to love a king
> Hath been my rod or else nothing:
> In this frail life being a blast of care and strife
> till it be past.
> Yet God did call me in my pride
> lest I should fall and from him slide
> for whom loves he and not correct
> that they may be of his elect.
> The death haste thee
> thou shalt me gain
> Immortally with him to reign
> Who send the king
> Like years as new in governing His realm in joy
> And after this frail life such grace
> As in his bliss
> he may have place.[44]

History has long implicated Anne Seymour in her brother-in-law's downfall, but as we have seen there is no contemporary evidence for her own feelings or involvement, and no source definitively predates her husband's later arrest.[45] There is evidence though that following Thomas's arrest she intervened to protect Cheke and his wife. Anne, as we know, quarrelled with Mary concerning the latter's interactions with Seymour but her anger cannot have been severe. Cheke wrote to Anne, afraid that he would be implicated in Seymour's scheme and then thanked her for her unspecified 'favourable undeserved goodness'. He credited her for his political survival and the fact he had been able to 'pass the whole course of my danger and feel the less storme of causeless hap'.[46] Later evidence for Anne's supposed involvement in Thomas's downfall can be found in the words of Hugh Latimer who wrote that 'some think and say that I was hired to it [that is to preach his condemnation of Thomas Seymour's actions on 19 April 1549] or that my Lady of Somerset Grace hired me to it'.[47] Not only, however, is this written after Edward Seymour's downfall but Latimer does not state that the rumours are true, merely that they were circulating. By then Anne's vilification had well and truly begun. Foxe, likewise, would later claim that there were 'many … who reported that the Duchess of Somerset had wrought his death', but he offers no other evidence other than post-1549 gossip.[48]

Instead, the day following Thomas Seymour's execution we get a glimpse again into Anne's activities when Paget wrote to her. He was afraid that Edward was angry with him for pressing a suit against another petitioner, who it turned out was Anne herself. The particulars of the matter are unclear and the issue was soon cleared up when Anne replied to Paget and assured him that she had not discussed the issue with her husband and that he had therefore judged fairly. Paget was relieved and 'prayed that Somerset continue his good Lord'.[49] He went on to say that he loved both Seymour and Anne herself equally and that he maintained the greatest trust in her.

Upon his death, Thomas Seymour's daughter, Mary, was still in Anne's household, but he desired that she now be placed in the household of Katherine Brandon and that she should raise the child. Edward and Anne honoured his wishes and in July, following her father's execution, Mary was sent to her household. It wasn't a responsibility which Katherine wanted or which she could afford, and she tried instead to place Mary Seymour with William and Elizabeth Parr. But she was well aware that they 'hath as weak a back for such a burden as I have, and he would receive her [more willingly] if he might receive her with the appurtenances'.[50] Katherine did take in the child, but was annoyed when the promised money and furniture for her did not arrive. She wrote to Anne who spoke with her husband and replied to Katherine letting her know that 'my Lord's grace at her suit [that is her urging] had granted certain nursery plate [including cushions of cloth of gold and silver goblets] should be delivered to the child'.[51]

The delay in authorising funds for Mary can easily be explained by the fact that, for the Seymours, there was brewing unrest in both the council and the realm at large.

Chapter 13

I Predict a Riot

On 15 January 1549 the Act of Uniformity was passed in the House of Lords which abolished the Latin Mass. Six days before Thomas's death a Parliamentary meeting had also finally agreed on the form of the first English Prayer book, its basic contents, and that of the Act, having been approved the previous year at a lengthy and complex debate chaired by Seymour himself. Until now the council reforms had been piecemeal and gradual; now they were going to impose a new uniform religion throughout England under one clarified doctrine of faith. Catholicism was now to be erased from England. The book was largely the work of Thomas Cranmer, who had been working on its form for many years, but there is no doubt that Edward Seymour was both aware of and approved of its contents. It was based upon the *Sarum Use* but was also heavily influenced by Lutheran texts and services. Seymour did not have universal support; there were those who opposed both including Lords Derby, Dacre and Windsor, but it was a clear and decisive majority.

The publication of the *Book of Common Prayer* was the culmination of a mass of publication activity during the early years of Somerset's Protectorate. In 1548 alone, thirty-one widely published tracts were calling and debating the need for specific reforms relating to the issue of transubstantiation.[1] The Act of Uniformity sought to end this type of debate once and for all. The *Book of Common Prayer* prescribed a simpler service and eradicated what it termed Catholic superstition and Latin which the lay people could not fully understand. Such was Anne Seymour's reputation for faith, reform and learning that it was later said in the State Papers for September 1549, that Edward introduced the book 'at his wife's instigation'.[2] The idea that Anne was personally responsible is clearly hyperbolic but the fact that she is mentioned at all in association with the act suggests that her reformist reputation was widely accepted, as was the level of influence which she had on her husband. It might also subtly imply that Edward Seymour was rather more reluctant than we might suppose, unlike Anne. He certainly was worried that they were acting too quickly, and he told Van der Delft that he had been pushed further along the reformist path than he had intended at this point in order to oppose other religious sects of anabaptists which had begun to spring up across the country while ambiguity had been allowed to endure. Many still clung to Roman Catholicism despite the previous reforms of Edward Seymour's Protectorate. For example, although the Edwardian Chantries Act in 1547 had essentially obliterated the Catholic notion of the cult of the dead, still men such as Sir John Cotes persisted in leaving in his will money in perpetuity to his local church, St Stephens of Walbrook, for the singing of Placebo and Dirige 'followed by mass for the souls of Sir John, his wives and all Christian souls'. Candles were to be lit at his tomb and the Mass said every year for seven years.[3] As a result it was decreed that candles, oil and some vestments would be permitted whilst people got used to the new religious order. The *Book of Common Prayer* officially came into use in March 1549 and the new form of service was to become compulsory at Pentecost (9 June) but the printing of it had begun long before, perhaps even before the final Lords vote on the matter aiming to ensure that every parish would have a copy. The printing was spearheaded by the king's printer, Grafton, and another, Whitchurch, who together were responsible for printing 'all books concerning divine service or containing any kind of sermons or exhortations that shall be used suffered or authorised in our Church of England and Ireland … being in the English or Latin tongue'.[4] How many were printed remains unclear but we know that they took the form of folio editions whose pages measured approximately 38 by 28 centimetres.[5]

Two of the most staunch opponents of the new measures in regard to religion were Bishops Bonner and Gardiner. Bonner, when his release from the Fleet was agreed upon, ordered that the new book be distributed and used throughout London, but his co-operation did not last long and after he preached about the true Catholic nature of transubstantiation at St Paul's Cross, he was imprisoned at Marshalsea, something for which he laid the blame squarely at Edward Seymour's door. Gardiner, likewise, was sent to the Tower in June; neither man would emerge again whilst Edward VI was king.

Another opponent of course was Anne's great friend Lady Mary. Remarkably the two women seem to have been able to separate religion from their own friendship and it endured. So to, to an extent, did Mary and Edward Seymour's; perhaps she was more willing to compromise with him than she might have liked to for Annes sake. Seymour had allowed Mary to worship as she saw fit up until now, making it clear that he did not wish to know what was taking place behind the doors of her houses, something Mary had accepted as a reasonable compromise until her brother could judge for himself and could rule on such matters independently. Unfortunately for Mary, her cousin, the Emperor Charles, now made an ill-timed attempt to force Seymour to put into writing that Mary could continue to hear Mass without reprisal. Seymour would not agree, telling both that although he would continue to protect her as best he could, he could only do so in 'everything that it is not prejudicial to the king' to whom he bore the greatest loyalty.[6] Edward might have been willing to be patient but others were not. They didn't understand why he was willing to be so lenient and urged firmer measures and Petre and Rich visited Mary to urge her to conform to the new religious doctrine. Instead of doing so, Mary increased the number of times she went to chapel and began to keep Mass with more ceremony. She was adding fuel to a situation which was far more volatile than she realised.

In June a rebellion broke out in what is now known as the 'Western Rebellion'. When a vicar by the name of William Harer tried to introduce the book in the Devonshire church of Sampford Courtenay his parishioners refused to accept it. Soon they had been joined by hundreds of supporters who were not only angry at the religious reforms but also that summer had been ravaged by plague. They were also angry at the increased sheep taxation and the land enclosures taking place. They wanted to halt the Reformation in its tracks and were prepared to commit violence to achieve their aims. Within days justices had been murdered and riots broke out. Down in Cornwall a gentleman named Humphrey Arundell also took up the baton and marched on the road to London, meeting up with the Devonshire men on the way. The long-bearded Sir Peter Carew, who had served as High Sheriff of Devon, was sent by Edward Seymour to deal with the rebellion. He met with the rebels at Crediton, but when a barn was set alight the rebels dispersed and Carew was chastised by Edward Seymour for his mishandling of the situation. Rumours now spread that Carew and his men had deliberately burnt the barn and the common people's anger now turned on local members of the gentry. One story goes that Walter Raleigh, father of the famous explorer, approached Exeter at this time and encountered an old lady saying her rosary. He complained that she was showing disrespect for the new religious laws of the land. When she told those at her parish church it 'caused a great stir in the open church, using very harsh and unseemly speeches concerning religion saying that she was threatened by the gentleman that if she did not leave her beads and give over using holy bread and holy water her house and their houses would be burnt and themselves despoiled of everything'. Whether this was exactly what Walter said or not we shall never know, but the woman was believed and Raleigh was pursued by the rioters and barely escaped with his life.[7] When news of the rapidly deteriorating situation reached Edward Seymour, he dispatched Lord Russel to deal with the situation but this time more gently. He was told to merely 'reside for a time in the west parts of his Majesty's realm as well for the good governance of his highness' counties of Devon, Cornwall, Somerset and Dorset in good order and quiet as also for the better defence of his highness' loving subjects in the same shires incase of any attempt at invasion'.[8] Seymour simply could not afford to pay for Russell to be accompanied by a supporting army, so he hoped that a gentle approach might yet suffice. Russell, meanwhile, was forced to try to recruit what men he could locally, a fairly futile exercise as the men of the West Country did not want to fight against their neighbours, especially in the absence of heavy financial inducement.

Carew, meanwhile, mustered the local justices at Clyst St Mary in an attempt to get the rebels to disperse. He approached a rebel fortified bridge unarmed but he was so hated by now that only the intervention of a local man called Hugh Osbourne prevented a gunner, John Hamon, from killing him there and then.[9] From a safe distance now Carew continued to try to negotiate and sent men to parley but 'the conference here ended … Sir Peter Carew, as soon as he had seen them, asked how they had succeeded; who answered, well enough. And giving no other answer they all rode back to Exeter, deferring the discoursing on the matter until they came thither. Having all supped together the same night; after supper was ended and the servants gone out of the room, Sir Peter demanded of them what they had done, and what agreement they had made with the people at Clyst. They answered that the commons had promised to keep themselves in peaceable order for the future, and attempt nothing further, provided the King and his Council would not alter the religion of the country, but suffer it to remain in the same state as King Henry VIII had left it, until the King himself came to full age. Sir Peter Carew and the rest of the company, not liking this answer, which was very different from what they expected, were for some time in a great dump thereat; but having recovered themselves, Sir Peter Carew, and Sir Courtenay, then sheriff of Devon, openly reproved them in very harsh terms, greatly blaming them for their lukewarmness in so weighty a cause; when they ought rather to have exerted the utmost endeavours towards the quelling of these outrages, than any way seem to have countenanced the rioters in their follies'.[10] When Russell heard Carew's account of these events he ordered him to report back to the Protector, who again told him that they had not been conciliatory enough in their dealing with the rebels.[11] Nevertheless Edward Seymour now knew that firmer action was needed, with the rebels now besieging Exeter. The danger was very real, as Professor Stoyle argues, 'the rebel forces were now strong and had concentrated their forces very quickly, and were preparing to advance upon London likely with the aim of deposing the boy king Edward VI and replacing him with his Catholic half-sister Mary'.[12]

Russell arrived in the area on 2 July but Seymour was still promising them all a pardon if they would disperse, and it seems that this was his own personal policy: He also promised to rethink the Enclosure Act but there was little support either for pardon or policy change amongst the other councillors. Likely this strategy was driven by his need to save money, but his gentle approach did also appear to be working on a small scale.[13] It was not, however, winning him any friends. Paget was becoming increasingly frustrated with him and wrote him a stream of advice. He wrote that peace in England was maintained only by a balance between law and religion, with the Church providing moral guidance and the king's government enforcing law and order. Now the laws had been too relaxed and the Church everyone was familiar with had been outlawed before they understood properly its replacement. He blamed Seymour for this, arguing that he 'had the absolute power of the king but had failed to act as one'.[14] Cranmer was likewise incensed at the actions of the rebels who had marched on Exeter under the banner of the five wounds of Christ, the same banner which had been used during the Pilgrimage of Grace. He furiously replied to their demands that the old religion be restored with the words 'O ignorant men of Devonshire and Cornwall. Standeth it with any reason to turn upside down the good order of the whole world that is everywhere and ever hath been that is to say the commoners to be governed by the nobles and the servants by their masters? Will you now have the subjects to govern their king, the villains to rule the gentleman and the servants their masters? If men would suffer so God will not!'.[15]

Internationally things also began to deteriorate. The French King Henri II was watching the growing unrest both within the council and in the land and took the opportunity to try to destabilise the situation further. When Seymour had instructed Russell that the West Country must also prepare for possible invasion he was not exaggerating the risk. At the beginning of the year Seymour had planned to take further military action against Scotland and France. At the time England seemed strong, but the scandal of Thomas's death in conjunction with religious unrest had seriously weakened her appearance. In addition there was simply no money to pay for military action. Paget, writing from Brussels where he had been sent to negotiate with the Emperor and plan an attack on France, was in despair, stating plainly that England could simply not finance such actions.[16] Paget increasingly felt that his advice was being ignored, which did nothing to improve matters between the two men.

Paget was correct that Seymour's previous military actions had been hugely expensive and his regime was critically short of money, but it must also be remembered that the finances of England had already been in a terrible state when Edward VI acceded to the throne. The last years of Henry VIII's rule had seen him spend huge amounts of money on military ventures himself. By 1545, Henry had been in debt by over 400,000 marks, something ironically that Paget had also warned him about writing in despair that 'I see not how we shall live without some help'.[17] By the end of his reign nearly two million pounds had been spent and in addition the currency was suffering from debasement. In 1544 Henry VIII had begun to order reductions in the gold and silver content of English coinage. For over 400 years English currency had managed to maintain a 92.5 per cent purity; under Henry it dropped from 75 per cent to just 25 per cent.[18] This meant that confidence in the currency was at an all-time low. To combat this, in January Seymour had ordered that new coins – gold sovereigns, half sovereigns, crowns and half crowns – be issued in an attempt to restore currency. These had a higher amount of gold and silver in them but they were also smaller and lighter which made them appear less valuable, even though the coinage was not actually being devalued and its worth improved.

In 1548, Edward had proposed taxes to help pay for the war in Scotland – the so-called Sheep Tax which those in the West were vehemently objecting to. Sheep kept on enclosed land were taxed, as were those on common land and the cloth made from their wool. In March 1549 Edward VI was granted the proceeds of all this tax and it was so unpopular that it is considered probably the shortest lived tax in English fiscal history; it would be repealed in 1550. The income it brought was not enough to make a difference, but it does however show both how important the wool industry was now considered to the nation and its politics and how desperately Edward VI's government needed money. Irrespective of this, Seymour had sent more men to Boulogne against the council's advice, to deal with the French who were beginning to riot themselves.

In England, Lord Russell arrived at the besieged city of Exeter in early July and on 11 July the rioters were ordered to submit to him or lose their lands and their lives would be forfeit. This seemingly harder line, however, was undermined by another declaration on 12 July which stated that if the rebels repented they would be pardoned. The 16th saw the threat of martial law being bandied about, the council's oscillating was doing it no favours, as neither rebel nor nobleman in the West Country seemed certain what was required by the king and his Lord Protector.[19]

Rebellions began to break out in other areas, notably in Oxfordshire where the rebels' attention was on matters of religion. Their grievances theological, Seymour was far less willing to compromise on this matter but still was willing to offer them pardons, twice, before he acknowledged that force would be needed. He wrote on 18 July that he was sending Lord Grey to deal with the rebels in Oxfordshire and that 'a dozen of the ringleaders [should be] delivered unto him whereof at least some shall suffer pains of death as an example to all malefactors'.[20] Lord Grey had been on his way to join Lord Russell but now turned north and King Edward wrote in his journal that Lord Grey ambushed some of the rebels and 'more than half of them ran away and the other that tarried some were slain, some taken and some hanged'.[21] Lord Grey ordered that more executions take place and George Raves, John White and Richard Thompson, a vicar, were to be hung at Banbury, with another eleven men meeting the same fate including the vicar of Chipping Norton who was to be hung from his own steeple.[22] By 9 August the 'Oxfordshire Papists [were] at last reduced to order, many of them having been apprehended and some gibbeted and their heads fastened to the walls'.[23]

Despite this success, yet another rebellion had broken out simultaneously in Norfolk when on 7 July men had torn up the hedges of John Flowerfew on his estate near Norwich; the rioters also began ripping up other enclosures. They were joined a few days later by landowner, Robert Kett, who held a manor at Wymondham and who assumed the leadership of the men in their quarrel with Flowerfew. Kett seems to have agreed that he would tear up his own enclosure hedges and he had soon attracted a large following, which by 9 July numbered several hundred men who camped near Norwich before they moved to higher ground at Mousehold Heath, with its sweeping views down towards the cathedral. The panicked authorities sent urgent messages to the council asking for help as Kett began to organise his men into an army and supply it with food. The council gave firm instruction that they must not be allowed access to the city but after a skirmish the mayor, Thomas Codd, was captured and access gained to the city's supplies. There was a lot of local support for the rebels and soon smaller bands of men were gathering at Downham Market, Ipswich and Bury St Edmunds. Sometime before 17 July Edward Seymour sent the Marquis of Northampton, a poor and inexperienced choice, something Somerset himself was aware of, to deal with the rebels, but he also offered to make serious compromises with them. Again he offered them a pardon and stated that he would consider in Parliament how prices of food and wool as well as the issue of enclosure would be better dealt with. The rebels were not impressed and Kett rejected the offer of pardon that was extended. Northampton was at Norwich by 30 July and he ignored Seymour's orders and he attacked, overwhelming the poorly defended city easily, but that night Kett attacked properly in revenge, Northampton was soundly defeated and Lord Sheffield was killed in the violence. In London, Seymour received a list of the rebel demands, which were wide ranging and somewhat confused. They demanded, amongst other things, that 'no man should henceforth enclose any more land', that rents must be controlled, that 'priests henceforth shall purchase no lands neither free nor bond and the lands that they have in possession may be letten to the temporal men as they were in the first year of the reign of Henry VII'. They asked that marshers be held freely or at low rents, that parishioners should be entitled to choose their own priest or vicar if the current one doesn't please them, that no 'lord, knight or gentleman shall have any spiritual promotion' or that conies must not be kept upon a freehold.[24] Edward Seymour was sympathetic and felt that their grievances were largely 'founded upon great and just causes'.[25] In July he ordered that the commissioners investigating acts of enclosure could actually pull down the enclosures themselves if they wanted, much to Paget's dismay, and he wailed that 'your Grace that you have too much gentleness!'[26] In particular he agreed to replace some of the enclosure commissioners at Thetford and said that he would recall Parliament to address their complaints.[27] Seymour was not oblivious to the need for stronger measures though and he chastised Russell for not taking firmer action against the West Country rebels who were now besieging Exeter. Russell was awaiting reinforcements near to Honiton, but as we have seen Lord Grey had to be diverted. Seymour intended now to send Warwick to his aid but the Norfolk threat put paid to that and on 22 July Russell was informed that he was largely on his own. Instead 1000 men were on their way, but again this order was quickly countermanded as the intended troops were German mercenaries and it was thought that deploying them against Englishmen would make an already tense and serious situation worse.[28] Instead he was informed that Lord Grey would march south once Oxfordshire had been dealt with. Towards the end of July Russell, at the urging of the council, began to move with the forces he had managed to recruit though he 'feared for his own safety [as he could not] depend on the fidelity of those who remained with him'.[29] On 21 July Russell was joined by 150 arquebusiers under the command of a Genoese nobleman called Paolo Spinola and a series of skirmishes broke out which 'thanks largely to Spinola's men and the steadiness of the local billmen led gallantly by the gentleman, Russell got the better of the insurgents who armed with only bows and bills stood little chance against the accuracy and penetration of the professional discipline … Russell's own archers were not very effective'.[30] The rebels were now keen to attack Russell before any reinforcements could arrive and they prepared for battle at Fenny Bridges. Russell still wanted to wait but Carew had his way and they gave battle the next day. Russell's men set about capturing the bridge with a will and the rebels were 'driven back' and 'attacked courageously so that though they withstood him most manfully … much blood was shed on both sides'.[31] They pursued the rebels for three miles before breaking off to await Lord Grey. In a full pitched battle near to Clyst St Mary's the combined might of the two forces met. The royal army 'pitched forward in three parts, each to assail the ramparts defending the entry … with Sir William Francis of Somerset leasing the advance, the barricades were taken and the army entered the village' before retreating in fear of an ambush.[32] They soon regrouped though and the town fell. Lord Grey would later report that he had 'never seen much fight with greater valour and stoutness' but the day belonged to the Royal army and many of the rebels were slaughtered.[33] The royal casualties numbered only about forty killed, with numerous others injured. The highest ranking casualty was Sir William Francis whose body was wrapped to be taken to Exeter for burial. Many men, hearing of the defeat, now began to melt away from the city and Russell 'liberated' the city on 6 August and raised the royal red dragon flag high up on the city walls.[34] Russell wasted no time in dealing with the ringleaders and for over a week remained in the city dealing out summary justice.

The need for Seymour to assert his authority and gain control of the country once again was now becoming urgent. Two days after Exeter was relieved, Henri II declared war on England and Seymour knew that an attack on Boulogne was now imminent.[35] The French had taken control of Ambleteuse and Blackness and were now moving on Boulogne. The council knew that they did not have the ability to respond. As a consequence Seymour was perhaps harsher on Russell than he otherwise would have been and he rebuked him strongly for intending to spare William Paget's brother, Robert, who had been a 'head, Captain of the rebellion' from death.[36] He likewise now saw the necessity of taking harsher measures in Norfolk following Northampton's defeat which had sent shockwaves through London. Seymour assumed command of the army himself on 6 August but then he changed his mind and decided to send Warwick to deal with the rebels. The question as to why Seymour didn't command this force himself is something of a mystery. He was experienced enough to and by associating himself directly with a royal victory he would certainly have improved his position. Some have argued that he did not wish to 'in all conscience confront men with whom he had much sympathy' but this seems very unlikely considering that we now know that he viewed the rebels as 'a plague and fury … the worst of men'.[37] More likely he wanted to distance himself from what was likely to be the large scale slaughter of his own people. Equally, perhaps, following the news of the attack on Boulogne he felt his place was in the Capital, or maybe he simply felt that Warwick was the best man for the job. Dudley amassed his forces and at the beginning of August led 5000 men out of London. He joined up with the Lords Willoughby, Powys and Bray and with his forces now swelled to over 10,000 men he was at Norwich by 23 August. Dudley sent a man out to offer the rebels the king's pardon, to all except Kett. Kett had intended to meet with Warwick but when a young boy made a rude gesture at the royal forces and was shot dead by Warwick's men, order broke down. There was no longer any chance of negotiation and Warwick was in no mood to be patient. He ordered that the city gates be smashed down and his men poured into the streets, forcing the rebels out of the city with brutal efficiency. He had forty-nine rebels hung in the marketplace, after which those who begged pardon were granted it.[38] The rebels retreated and Warwick cut off their supply lines. They attacked the city furiously that night but Warwick held out and the next day the rebels were forced to move away from Mousehold towards Dussindale where a few days later Warwick attacked them, rallying his troops with the words that they 'should now take the rebels not for men but brute beasts imbued with cruelty'.[39] Two thousand rebels were cut down but Warwick was impressed by their valour and offered them a last chance at pardon which many of the remaining men accepted only once Warwick had personally assured them that he was genuine.[40] The next day nine of the rebel leaders were hung, drawn and quartered, their heads cut off and displayed on spikes around the city walls as a warning that this was the fate of all traitors. Three hundred more were executed the next day. The Kett brothers had fled but were soon captured and brought back, to ultimately be taken to London where they were imprisoned in Newgate and paraded through the streets. William was eventually hanged on 7 December from the Abbey tower at Wymondham whilst Robert was hung in chains from the walls of Norwich Castle.

The rebellions had finally been defeated but despite Seymour's intentions it is thought that over 10,000 Englishmen had died in the violence. Where Seymour had personally been during the violence is of interest; both he and Anne had remained in London, where he had directed both the council and the city's preparations for defence. In July he had declared martial law and a watch had been ordered throughout the city in case any forces should advance upon London. A bridge at Staines, over the Thames, was fortified and guarded and scouts were sent to keep watch on the roads. New portcullises were fitted at the city gates and they were armed with guns from the Tower. Six thousand men were assembled to guard the king and Windsor Castle was fortified in case the king needed to retreat there, which he did at the end of July to be on the safe side. Before he did so, on 23 July, Seymour took to the streets to parade alongside the king so that Londoners could see that they were both safe.

Chapter 14

The Tower

England was now at peace but Edward Seymour's position had been much weakened and he had shown himself to be indecisive and flawed. Even worse, he had lost the full support of some of his closest colleagues, including, crucially, the Earl of Warwick. Up until now he and Edward Seymour had been the closest of friends and allies but now Dudley seemed to have grown exasperated by Seymour's refusal to go further in matters of reform and by his constant vacillating. By 15 September Van der Delft was reporting to Charles V that 'matters in this realm [England] are restless for change … the split in the Council is not so well hidden … the ill feeling between the Protector and the Earl of Warwick is well known'.[1] He also wrote that he considered that Paget was to blame for 'all the evil which had befallen the kingdom, since he had been the principal instrument in setting up a Protectorate which would certainly never do good'.[2] Paget replied that Seymour had behaved so poorly because he 'had a bad wife'. This is the first time that any blame is laid at Anne's door and it is clear that this is an attempt by Paget to divert blame from both men; previously even when he was attacking Seymour in numerous letters he never once mentioned Anne.[3]

Anne was by now well established as the first lady of the court, and crucially, on a national scale as a figurehead for religious reform. Aside from welcoming reformists into her household between 1548 and 1551 Anne sponsored eight religious publications, more than any other women in England.[4] Whilst rebellion was raging, John Olde had dedicated his translation of Erasmus' *Paraphrases*, a text which by royal command was to be placed in every parish church after 1547, to 'infuse the Edwardian reformation with even more Erasmusian thought', to 'the most virtuous Lady Anne Duchess of Somerset'.[5] The same year Walter Lynne also dedicated a book to Anne, the first of two he would dedicate to her. Lynne was Cranmer's printer and in 1549 he dedicated his work *A Brief Collection* which included sermons by Martin Luther, to Anne.[6] Lynne called Anne 'the most gracious patroness and supporter both of good learning and also of godly men learned'.[7] He also stated that she was known to make 'chief and daily' study of the Holy Bible.[8] His second book would bear the dedication 'to the right virtuous Lady Anne duchess of Somerset … faithful mother for all good works'.[9] Samuel, Becon and Mildred Cooke would all also dedicate works to Anne. Traditionally it has been asserted that a personal political reality, their practical power, was the basis for such dedications but the fact that every author who dedicated works to Anne was Protestant belies the idea that it was her power and not her faith which was the primary concern for the authors and printers. It is clear that these works were dedicated to Anne because of her religious leaning, proof being that they would continue to be so deep into the reign of Elizabeth I, when she had no power or influence politically.[10] Anne's position as a leading patroness of the reformers made her an easy target for those who now felt that Seymour was going too far, or not far enough. Anne appears to have spent most of the summer at Syon, present and aware of the dangers facing her husband and England. She was also very aware that the relationship between her husband and Warwick was beginning to fragment and we know that she and Jane Dudley must have spent many hours discussing the falling out of their husbands. As we have seen they were close friends, fellow reformists, and their children often shared both tutors such as John Cheke and Roger Ascham and the royal schoolroom.[11] They plotted together how unity might be restored and their closeness is testified to by the fact that the following year they would together manage to bring about the connection of their families through marriage, something which neither of their husbands was, by that stage, disposed to want. The new Imperial ambassador, Jehan Scheyfve, wrote to his master that 'the two mothers between them had made the match'.[12]

At the beginning of autumn we get a glimpse into the marriage of Anne and Edward at this time. By the end of September we know that they were at Odiham in Hampshire where they were 'hunting and sporting' together.[13] The image of the two taking a much needed break from court with their children after the tensions of the summer is a touching one. Anne was not yet done with childbearing and she may well have conceived while she was away from London.

Anne remained behind in Hampshire when Seymour returned to London on 1 October. Putting down the rebellion had drained further Seymour's money and resources and although he now wanted to return to the matter of Scotland, England simply couldn't continue to finance the garrisons there. After eight years the English were 'exhausted and worn to the bones'.[14] Haddington, an English garrison which had been besieged since 1548 in an attempt to 'consume Scottish and French resources', was now under constant assault and disease had broken out.[15] A year ago the commander had written to Seymour describing how the garrison had been stricken with the plague and that 'the state of this town pities me both to see and to write it … many are sick and a great number dead, most of the plague. On my faith there are not here this day of horse, foot and Italians, 1000 able to go to the walls and more like to be sick, than sick to men, who watch the also every fifth night, yet the walls are unmanned'.[16] Since then matters had only deteriorated, with the French stepping up their night raids under French army Marechal Paul de Thermes, and Seymour's stubborn refusal to withdraw had infuriated his council. Now, without the support of Paget and Warwick and with England's forces needed elsewhere, he had no choice but to order a withdrawal. Haddington had been in 1548, 'the fairest town ever fortified in these parts and the "daunter" of Scotland', and Seymour's greatest achievement – a permanent English military presence in Scotland.[17] Now though its men were reduced to eating rats and on 14 September an English relief column of 16,000 men, under the command of the Earl of Rutland, was sent north to relieve the beleaguered town and assist with the withdrawal. Before they left the English razed the fortification and burnt the town leaving behind them, in the words of the indomitable Mary of Guise 'nothing but the plague'.[18] Seymour's plan for Scotland had failed utterly, England was at war with France and the infant Mary, Queen of Scots was well out of his reach. This was one failure too many and now things began to move quickly against Seymour.

Upon his return from Norfolk, Warwick had asked that his son, Ambrose, be granted a post and lands as a reward for his service in Norfolk, where the 19-year-old is recorded as having served alongside his father. Seymour refused, for what reason is unclear, but it did nothing to close the widening gulf between the two men. The man appointed in Ambrose's place, Seymour's secretary Thomas Fisher, wrote and warned Seymour that Warwick posed a serious threat to him and that he should 'be well rewarded' for his actions in Norfolk. Yet once again Seymour took no action.[19] The exact sequence of events in relation to the coup, which now removed Seymour from his post, are hard to piece together, not least because many of those involved were reluctant to commit their view and actions to paper. We do know that Warwick's plot to remove him was well enough established by the beginning of September that Lady Mary was writing about it and she claimed that the plan was to charge him with offences against the Crown. She tells that the plot was spearheaded by Warwick with the support of Arundel, Southampton and St John. Mary believed that her support was going to be solicited and she asked the Emperor, through Van der Delft, how best she should respond. He wisely advised her to say nothing in case the men should use any response she did give as ammunition to attack her religious faith. The idea that Dudley would appoint her Regent for her brother was also rife throughout the rumour mill, but such a plan seems unlikely given Warwick and Mary's differences on matters of religion.

After leaving Anne, Edward Seymour rode to Hampton Court where he was accompanied by Petre, Smith, Paget, St John, Thynne and Cecil. In London, meanwhile, men began to arm and the council met without Seymour. Five days later he issued a proclamation that all loyal men should ride to join Seymour and the king at Hampton Court where they were threatened by 'a most dangerous conspiracy'.[20] Van der Delft wrote an account of these events to his master. He records that 'Last Sunday the Archbishop of Canterbury was summoned by letters from the King, and caused a preacher to proclaim that all those who were loyal to the King should repair to Hampton Court where his person resided, and the same day the same appeal was made in all directions by letters from the Protector. The result was that over 4,000 peasants immediately assembled at court, where the Protector was without any members of the Council except the Archbishop of Canterbury, Controller Paget and Dr Smith, one of the secretaries. On the same day, early, assembled in London the Earls of Warwick and Southampton, the Great Master of the Household, the Earl of Arundel, Mr. Baker, Mr. North, the first secretary Dr Petre, other councillors, the Marquis of Northampton and several more lords, and summoned the Lord Mayor and all the city authorities, all of whom at once came to an agreement, seized the Tower of London, and put a garrison of their men into it. The Protector, immediately informed of this assembly and its doings, produced the King in the presence of the court. The King said he was displeased that an attempt should be made to take his uncle the Protector away from him, and prayed that all would help him in resisting, for he himself was clothed, and ready to arm. The Protector also voiced complaints that his destruction was being plotted on false accusations, and that he should never be found guilty, for it all sprang out of malice and rank treason.[21] Somerset made immediate plans to fortify the building, including the removal of stone paving stones to be hurled from the roof if necessary and raiding the armoury for as much equipment as possible.[22] Men had also answered his summons and were arriving at Hampton Court, most notably Cranmer who brought with him sixty men to help protect the king. Dramatically Seymour also brought Edward VI down to the base court where he delivered a speech Seymour had written which entreated men to remember Richard III usurpation of royal power and that they must oppose Warwick who was conspiring against the king. The speech became a riotous affair after which Edward Seymour declared boldly that 'he would be one of the first to die defending the king' and Edward himself implied that he was 'ready to arm'.[23] Edward VI, through Seymour, also sent Edward Wolf to London to secure the Tower arsenal, a task he failed because St John had already done so. With poor communication and rumours abounding it is hard to judge today just how serious the threat to Edward VI and Seymour was. Certainly Warwick wanted Seymour out, and he was now supported by the majority, but not all the court. Guards had been posted around London to prevent Seymour from entering the city with an armed force. An apparently furious Edward VI wrote to the 'rebel' Lords stating that they were failing in their loyalty to him and they wrote back apologising profusely and assuring him of their loyalty, but in reality the letter changed nothing.[24] It is clear that by now Anne had been summoned by Edward to join him, and that she was now both with him and very concerned. Likely both she and Edward passed a sleepless night and were awake to hear the news that several thousand men had assembled on horseback in the city, close to Ely Place, the residence of the Dudleys and were planning to ride to Hampton Court. Seymour then had the peasants divided into squadrons, and assigned them quarters as if he expected to fight. At about 5pm on Sunday evening Edward sent Anne away to safety and she went out weeping. She was very badly handled in words by the courtiers and peasants, who put all this trouble down to her. Anne was sent to Beddington Park, a house in Surrey which was kept by her brother, Michael Stanhope, and which had belonged to the Carew family since the reign of King Edward III.[25] It had been used by Henry VIII when he was courting Anne Boleyn, and Jane Seymour had stayed there, likely with her sister-in-law in attendance in May 1536. Anne either travelled with or was met there by her sister-in-law, Michael's wife Anne, and the two women must have been relieved to see each other.[26]

Very soon afterwards all the peasants were sent away to their homes and at about 7 o'clock the king and the Protector departed with the guard and other members of the court for Windsor, 'where a great number of peasants are daily assembling'. Sir John Gates was the captain of the king's guard and he was ordered to escort them.[27] Windsor, with its walls several metres thick, was far more defensible than Hampton Court and Seymour's plan seems to have been to hole up there with the king until the rebellious councillors were forced to come to heel.

Unfortunately for Seymour, Edward hated the idea of stealing away like a thief in the night and he protested. Even worse he caught a chill on the night ride and the castle was not prepared or equipped for his arrival. The lack of fires, tapestries and other luxuries that he was used to did not help to improve the young king's mood. He wrote in his journal that that night 'I went to Windsor and there was watch and ward every night'.[28] The following day the council in London, having heard of Seymour's flight with the king, sent supplies 'with a most inestimable care'.[29] Letters flew between London and Windsor with those in London pledging their loyalty to the king, and Seymour trying to judge just how strong the opposition to him was. He now had only Cranmer, Paget and Smith with him; Russell and Herbert supported him theoretically but were not sending any actual assistance. Arrayed against him now were sixteen other councillors. The chief grievance being levelled against Seymour was that he had not listened to his councillors advice. The Lords in London wrote to Windsor on Monday stating that they 'mean nothing else but the surety of his majesties person … [and that] ... if the Duke of Somerset would at any time have heard our advices if he would have heard reason, and acknowledged himself a subject our meaning would have quietly communed with him for redress of all things without any disturbance to the realm'.[30] Seymour, for his part, remained belligerent and had replied that 'It is you that take no other way but violence, our allegiance doth bind us to the extremity of death and put all into God's hands, who giveth victory as it pleaseth him'.[31] Behind the bravado though, Seymour was aware of the reality of his situation, and behind closed doors he gave orders for his goods and valuables, which would be confiscated should he be arrested and charged, to be removed from his great houses at Syon and Sheen. It is a plan which Anne took an active part in, and which she and Seymour must have discussed during those tense days at Hampton Court. Anne took four caskets by boat to Richard Whalley, their chamberlain's house, down in Wimbledon.[32] Key items such as caskets, bedding and coffers were taken down river and hidden effectively in the houses of loyal Seymour servants and supporters.[33] Historian, Margaret Scard notes in particular that 'bedding, carpets, hangings and other items were moved by Somerset's surveyor of works to his own house in Isleworth … the bailiff at Syon even sold as much wood as he could to raise money'.[34] Anne was not content to simply await the outcome of events, she was determined to support her husband and soon after her arrival at Beddington she wrote to Paget asking him to support her husband for she said he well knew that the charges against him were 'untrue and unfriendly… [constructed by] ... some wicked person or persons', and that they were manufactured by those who would see him fall. Her concern for Edward is palpable when she urges Paget to 'comfort my Lord as I trust you do, both with council and otherwise, for I much fear that he is sore grieved at heart'.[35]

Seymour was not without his supporters though, especially amongst the common men of England, and more arrived daily at Windsor. One from Kent brought with him 352 men who stated that he came because 'I was sure that my Lord Protector could be no traitor' and that if he were harmed that 'the king would revenge his uncle's death at his fullest age'.[36] It was not enough though, Russell and Herbert now cast their votes and urged that Seymour 'step aside rather than any blood be shed, which if be once attempted and the case brought to that misery that the hands of the nobility be once polluted each with others blood the quarrel once begun will never end'.[37] The Wars of the Roses which had cost so many lives amongst the nobility were still just within living memory, and neither Russell nor Herbert at least wanted to risk a return to those days of violence. Seymour realised now that he was beaten and that he could not continue as Lord Protector. He offered submission to the king and stated that he was willing to both submit to the will of the council and king and negotiate. He wrote to Warwick, humbly and protesting that he never meant any harm to him.

'My Lord, I cannot persuade myself that there is any ill-conceived in your heart as of yourself against me, for that the same seemeth impossible that where there hath been from your youth to mine so great a friendship and amity between us, as never for my part to no man was greater, now so suddenly should there be hatred; and that without just cause, whatsoever rumours and bruits, or persuasion of others have moved you to conceive; in the sight and judgement of almighty God I protest and affirm this unto you, I never meant worse to you than to myself; wherefore my lord for God's sake, for friendship, for the love that hath ever been betwixt us or that hereafter may be, persuade yourself with truth, and let this time declare to me and the world your just honour and perseverance in our friendship.'[38]

This letter reveals Edward to be both desperate, submissive and also aware of Dudley's character. No letter was more designed to appeal to his sense of honour, as Seymour well knew for all his faults Dudley was a man who was devoted to his family and friends.

Edward VI also wrote to the council and asked them to treat Seymour well, arguing that all men have their faults and making it clear that Seymour was 'our uncle, whom you know we love'.[39] The veiled threat was clear, Edward might be a child but his views still mattered and if they acted harshly against his uncle they would pay for it thereafter. Cranmer, Paget and Smith also acted on his behalf. Hoby travelled to London to take letters of submission from Seymour and he also carried those from the three Lords who had heard that those in London sought Seymour's 'blood and his death', and that instead they wished him, in accordance with the king's wishes, to be treated with 'kindness and humanity, remembering that he hath never been cruel to any of you'.[40] Down in Surrey Anne was being kept well informed by her half-brother as to what was happening and her panic is palpable in the letters she wrote to Paget and others. Her husband was, she knew, innocent and she was puzzled as to what Seymour had 'done to any of these noble men or others that should thus rage and seek the extremity to him'. She, however, was equally sure that her God would protect him as was right and just.[41] Likely she spent a good deal of her time both in writing letters and in prayer when she was not gazing out of the windows for a glimpse of a messenger riding through the park. That she was felt to be in considerable distress is implied by the fact that in early October, Richard Whalley, the Seymour treasurer, was authorised to go to her in order to comfort her.[42] Anne, though, was not content to simply await news and be comforted, she intended to take action and planned a visit to the Dudleys personally to try to speak with the Duke.

The king's messenger, Sir Philip Hoby, was soon heading back to Windsor with the Lord's replies to Seymour's submission; they were cautious. In a curious incident, Hoby turned back halfway through the journey claiming that he had lost the letters for the king. This seems unlikely and is generally regarded as a ruse on the part of the Lords who were waiting to see what Russell and Herbert would do next. They had not been privy to the men's communications with Seymour and therefore were unsure how they might react; this implies that Hoby was in fact on the side of the councillors in London. Sir Philip Hoby had been a reformist supporter of Edward Seymour's but he now seems to have switched allegiance, possibly because he had been looked over for promotion by the Lord Protector, who for his part seems not to have considered Hoby fully as one of 'his' men.

The Lords in London soon received assurance that Russell and Herbert would not militarily support Edward Seymour and Hoby was back at Windsor with very real letters from them on the morning of 10 October. The most important one was addressed to Seymour and read that 'they do not intend, nor will hurt in any case the person of my Lord the Duke, nor none of you all, nor take away any of his lands or goods, whom they do esteem and tender as well as any of you, as they ought, and as one whom they are not ignorant, no more than you, that is the King's uncle. They do intend to preserve his honour as much as any of you would nor meaneth not nor purposeth not, no matter to hurt him but only to give order for the Protectorship which hath not been so well ordered as they think it should have been; and to see that the king is better answered of his things and the realm better governed for the King's Majesty. And for you my Lords and masters of the Council they will have you to keep your rooms and places as you did before and they will counsel with you for the better government of things'.[43] This letter was read aloud by Hoby to the assembled court and the assurance that Seymour would not be harmed was greeted by all with relief. Paget knelt weeping and declared that the councillors were to be praised for their 'generosity and leniency'.[44] All, however, was not what it seemed; other letters addressed to Paget, Cranmer and Smith were much harsher and urged them to keep watch on Seymour and the king stating that if they did not they would 'answer for the contrary at utmost peril'.[45] Hoby set about ensuring that Seymour and his closest associates, such as Anne's half-brother Michael Stanhope, Smith, Thynne and Cecil were placed under armed guard. He was deliberately moved from his previous chamber, which was next to the king's, to another. The next day, 11 October, 500 men arrived from London under Sir Anthony Wingfield, who had served under Seymour but now was sent by the council to escort Edward Seymour to the Tower.[46] Perhaps they hoped that the sympathetic Wingfield would present less of a daunting prospect to both Seymour and the king than Dudley or other of the Lord Councillors.

Anne would no doubt have been relieved to hear that Edward and Henry, their sons who had until now been with the king as his companions, were sent away to safety to rejoin the rest of the Seymour children.[47] News arriving at Beddington would have slowed following Michael Stanhope's confinement alongside his brother-in-law and Anne must have grown increasingly concerned as the days passed, even with Whalley's attempts at reassurance.

Dudley and the Lords arrived at Windsor the next day and begged formally for the king's pardon. King Edward initially was frightened but soon was 'in good health and merry' according to Paget.[48] He welcomed the Lords formally with a 'merry countenance and a good voice'.[49] He asked after their health and then allowed them to kiss his hand for their 'good comfort'.[50] Relieved that the king had accepted their actions, the next day the council issued letters patent which in one swoop removed Edward Seymour from his position as Lord Protector. Seymour's fall from power seemed complete and he was now interviewed by the council as to the motives and intentions behind his recent actions before being escorted back towards London and imprisonment in the Tower. He was guarded by 300 men despite loudly protesting to the crowds that 'he was no traitor but a faithful a servant of the king as any man'.[51] According to the chronicle, he entered the city at St Giles in the Field at his own insistence 'because he would not come by the place he had begun and pulled down divers churches and the cloister in St Pauls to build it'.[52] He was accompanied on his journey by Michael Stanhope, Thynne, Smith and Wolf who would all join him in the Tower, though they were certainly kept apart, and several of his servants were imprisoned including his personal secretary, Fisher. The question of what to do with Edward Seymour was now the matter of the hour; the king for all his cold words in his journal would surely never allow for the execution of his uncle, he had made that very clear. But nor could Edward be allowed to regain any position which would allow him to one day revenge himself upon those who now imprisoned him.

Anne Seymour, meanwhile, was not content to allow her husband to languish forever in the Tower whilst the council debated and at the beginning of December she played her trump card and went to visit Jane Dudley. The two women spoke together and it seems that they plotted together to mend the rift between their husbands. The Imperial ambassador records that Anne was at that time 'always at his [Dudley's] house'.[53] The Spanish Chronicle goes on to give us some details about the sort of meetings which took place between Anne and the Dudleys at this time. The chronicler tells us that 'the Lords Protectors wife was a very prudent woman and saw that she could have to humble herself' and that to this end she threw herself at Dudley's feet and gave an impassioned speech, an almost angry and even threatening speech, although she was on her knees, which was designed carefully to appeal to, and trouble, the character of a man she did after all know very well.

She began: 'My lord I am much surprised that there should have been words which have angered you between my husband and yourself for I always hear him say that the King had no wiser or more prudent councillor in his realm than you, and yet out of mere passion you have had him proclaimed a traitor; an act which neither God nor man can think well. It lies in your hands to make amends and as he has done no treason I pray you consider that he is the king's uncle and although the king is too young to understand, yet he will nevertheless in time come to know the truth if you my lord are the cause of my husband's death'.[54] John Dudley was embarrassed and tried many times to get her to sit on a chair before helping her to do so himself. Anne had more sense than to refute the charges which Dudley explained her husband was guilty of – excessive building for one, and misjudgement in military matters – instead she reminded him that her husband had for a long time been 'a good friend to him'. She also flattered him stating that she knew his current power and position meant that he had the casting vote in the matter. After speaking to John she asked to speak with Jane and the two women retired to Jane's chamber where they 'talked for a long time and Jane was entreated to speak that night to her husband in favour of the Duke' to which she agreed. Anne gave Jane a brooch of diamonds to remind her of this promise. Nothing shows Anne's clear political acumen and intelligence more than this incident. Not only did she know just how to appeal to John Dudley, but she also knew when to stay her hand, when not to protest and that John Dudley would ultimately listen to his wife. If Jane was on the Seymours' side, half the battle for Edward's life was won.

Chapter 15

What to do with Edward Seymour?

What to do with Edward Seymour was a pressing issue but it was also only one of many facing the king's councillors. Edward Seymour's removal had left a power vacuum at the heart of government. John Dudley was intent on ensuring that he was the man in control but he did not intend to declare himself Lord Protector in Seymour's place; rather he sought to fill the council with his allies and supporters. With Seymour safely in the Tower along with most of those who had supported him, five noblemen were now appointed to the king's Privy Council: Dudley, Russell, Wentworth, St John and Northampton. Others included Andrew Dudley, brother to John, Wriothesley, Darcy and Rogers.[1] All of these men were allies of Dudley's and Cranmer also lent his support. It would later be alleged that it was through him that Dudley was able to establish such a powerbase.[2] Security around the king was also to be improved, so that no one could ever again 'abduct' the king away from London without council consent. Edward himself records that 'three of the outer privy chamber gentlemen should always be here, and two lie in the palate and fill the room of one of the four knights; that the esquires should be diligent in their office and five grooms should always be present of which one to watch the bedchamber'.[3]

The issue of religion was another matter which also needed to be settled. Around half of the council were now openly reformist but others such as Arundel and St John still held out hopes for the restoration of the Catholic faith in England. The reformists were by now also very much supported by the maturing king who had concluded that the Pope was 'the true son of the devil, a bad man, an Antichrist and an abominable tyrant'.[4] He expressed these views in an original treatise which he finished writing in August 1549. It was a treaty which he dedicated to his uncle Edward Seymour and in it praises Seymour for his 'great affection towards the divine word and sincere religion'.[5]

With Edward VI's support, by November Dudley openly announced that further acts of religious reformation would be implemented as of Christmastide; these would insist on the use of the new prayer book and implement the destruction of books associated with Catholicism and Latin worship.[6] This caused several Catholics on the council to waiver and in November Arundel offered to join the service of Princess Mary, implying perhaps that he and others would plot to put her on the throne. Mary angrily rejected him, accusing him of being responsible for Seymour's downfall, something which she herself appears to have opposed, perhaps out of loyalty to Anne, perhaps because she had no wish to oppose the legitimate rule of her brother. Most likely it was a mixture of both. Dudley was unsettled by what he saw as a Catholic resurgence and he blocked Arundel's appointment to the council and instead ensured that enough reformists were given positions to give him a majority. These included Thomas Goodrich, the Protestant Bishop of Ely, 'a busy secular spirited man' who opposed 'zealots' on both sides of the religious divide, and the Marquess of Dorset, Henry Grey, another staunch Protestant and longtime ally of Dudley's.[7] At the same time Thomas Wriothesley, Earl of Southampton, another prominent supporter of the old faith fell dangerously ill and Van der Delft wrote that if he should die then 'matters [of religion] might never be righted' because there were no other man with 'sound enough judgement to conduct opposition'.[8] He had helped Dudley bring about Seymour's downfall but now Dudley sought to exclude him from decisions on the basis of his ill health, not entirely unjustly as Wriothesley would die in 1550. Wriothesley was not quite done yet though, and in December he sought to explore whether he could bring down Dudley alongside Seymour. He plotted with Arundel and St John to ensure that Warwick would execute Somerset and then they would arrest Warwick. St John betrayed him however, and Warwick was warned of the plot in advance and accused Wriothesley of seeking his blood.

For now Dudley had subdued his opposition and consolidated his position within the council. On Christmas Day 1549, the reformists were secure enough in their position to issue the order to burn all Catholic books, the Reformation would continue at a pace.

From his prison in the Tower Edward Seymour would have had limited information about these events and been able to do little but sit and wait for Dudley to decide his fate. Dudley softened in part by Anne's relentless petitioning, assurances of friendship, and in part at his wife's urging, now sought to get Seymour out of the Tower alive. To this end Seymour was encouraged to admit his faults and on 23 December he submitted formally to the king and council and asked for mercy. He was accused of and admitted to twenty-nine charges. These included that he had abused his position as Protector, ignored his council's advice and acted without their consent. He was also accused of favouring the rebels during the recent rebellions and of being against the landowners. Further charges concerned the treatment of the king and counsellors and two dealt with his mistakes in war. He was not accused of any offences in matters of religion.[9] None of these amounted to treason although each could have been expanded to include that offence if the council decreed. Two days later, on Christmas Day, Anne was permitted to visit her husband in the Tower; there is some suggestion recorded in the *Chronicle of King Henry VIII* that Anne had been given permission to visit him prior to this and that Warwick had in fact allowed her to visit 'as she pleased'.[10] Her visit on Christmas Day, however, is also verified in other sources and it was noted that Seymour was greatly comforted to see his wife.[11] Now that Warwick had relaxed Seymour's imprisonment enough to allow Anne to visit, the warders of the Tower diligently ensured his comfort, likely at Anne's urging. Their kind treatment of him would later earn them livery and preferment. It was Seymour who would, in 1552, arrange for them to be granted the privilege of wearing the livery of the Yeomen of the Guard, making them the Yeoman Warders 'extraordinary members of the sovereign's bodyguard'.[12] By January, Warwick was 'openly favourable to the Protector' and it was widely reported that Anne was daily at the Dudleys house where she and Jane frequently dined and attended festivities together.[13] Rumours soon abounded in London that Seymour would be released by the New Year. An indication that Anne was not quite as confident as she might have appeared however, can be found in the letters of Richard Scudamore to Sir Philip Hoby in which the former relates that on one day in January Anne was so 'acrased' (distressed) that she remained within her apartment at the Savoy Palace where she had been lodging to be close to her husband and the Dudleys. If the strain was starting to tell on Anne then it is hardly surprising. She was trying to secure her husband's life, as well as that of her half-brother and her own position, and ensure that her children were safe from the machinations in London. It was a tall order.

She was, however, not entirely alone. William Cecil also was lobbying for Seymour's release and the Duchess of Suffolk offered her support.[14] In mid-January it was rumoured that Seymour would be released imminently and a deputation from Parliament questioned him again to be certain that his previous confession had not been given under duress and that he would stand by it. On 14 January he was formally stripped of the title of Lord Protector and 2000 people gathered by the Tower to witness his release. But it did not occur that day; instead a fine was set on his freedom, the exact sum of which is unclear but Seymour wrote to the council and humbly asked for its reduction as it would not be possible for him to pay such an amount.[15] In the end he forfeited around two thousand pounds worth of goods and property as his punishment; it could have been a lot worse.

Edward Seymour was released from the Tower on 6 February 'largely on account of his wife's efforts' according to Van der Delft. He was taken by barge upriver to the house of the Sheriff of York where Dudley was recovering from a 'rheum in the head'.[16] There before the council Seymour doffed his cap and maintained a subservient aspect.[17] How he must act moving forward was explained to him before he could finally take a barge to the Savoy House and be reunited with Anne.[18] The terms of his release included the fact that he had to live at either Syon or Sheen and was not to travel more than four miles from either without the council's express permission. Edward and Anne decided to make their home at Syon and they travelled there directly where they appear to have spent the next few weeks simply relaxing and enjoying each other's company. They no doubt discussed their future as well. To what extent Dudley might one day welcome Edward back at court was a matter of much debate but for now the relief of being together and safe must have been more than enough after the desperate uncertainty of the past few months. Anne's attention, at least, also returned to her children and enquiries were made as to their health and the state of their education. Perhaps during these quiet few weeks Anne also mentioned to her husband an idea which it seems likely she and Jane Dudley had already discussed – that is the possible union of the Seymours and Dudleys though the marriage of their eldest daughter Anne to John Dudley's eldest son, also called John and titled Viscount Lisle.

Anne and Edward's children were growing up and their daughters were by now accomplished young women, the three eldest in particular, Anne was now aged about 14, Margaret about 12 and Jane was a couple of years younger, and through them in 1550 we get a clear picture of their lives and the education which their parents had endowed them with. Few fragments of their lives remain but Jane Seymour, had written to Bucer and Phagius in June 1549, thanking them for sending her and her sisters books and 'commending them on their grace and eloquence to Cicero',[19] implying that they were familiar with the latter. They clearly studied and wrote extensively, and more unusually were known to do so, for when Marguerite of Navarre died in December 1549 they composed 103 (or 104 in a later edition) Latin distichs in her memory. When Nicholas Denisot, their former tutor who had been caught spying for the French and hastily departed, heard this, he sent many letters to the Seymour daughters imploring that they send their verses to him in France where he might have them published.[20] They did so and he published their work under the title *Annae, Margaritae, Janae, sororum virginum heroidum Anglarum, in mortem Dicae Margaritae Valesiae navarrorum Reginae, Hecatodistichon* and it was the first original and formal verse written in Latin by a woman in England.[21] Each sister wrote alternate distichs, all of which were in praise of Marguerite of Navarre, holding her up as a model for all women to emulate her piety and purity. Together Anne, Margaret and Jane 'weave a poem charting Marguerite's progress through life and earth and beyond … she passes from wise virgin with an oil-filled lamp to bride of Christ united with him for all eternity in an apocalyptic vision of the marriage of the lamb'.[22] It is a truly remarkable piece of work, and proved so popular that a second edition was published in 1551 which had a few minor alterations and they were held up both as literary 'sirens' and as model Protestants to be admired and emulated.[23] Anne's pride in her daughter's educational and literary achievement in 1550, which as their mother she was largely responsible for, can easily be imagined. She and Edward had succeeded in raising exemplary Protestant noblewomen. Nevertheless it was for marriage that the eldest daughter, Anne, was destined and throughout the spring of 1550 Anne and Jane Dudley negotiated and cajoled their husbands into supporting the match between her and Viscount Lisle, something which became ever more likely as Seymour's rehabilitation continued. The match was first mentioned seriously as early as March when Van der Delft reported that whilst Warwick maintained that he was ill, in reality he was at Somerset House discussing the marriage.[24] Neither man seems to have initially been keen with Edward Seymour suggesting that Anne might marry Katherine Brandon's son, Henry, instead, the young Duke of Suffolk, but Katherine was against arranged marriages in general especially when the bride and groom were so young and so eventually both men came round.[25] She also claimed that Warwick wanted the match 'for better to show off his friendship, he wanted the duke of Somerset to have her son for his daughter'.[26]

The new Dudley regime was not universally popular, especially amongst the common people and in Braintree, Essex, for example, a rebellion was planned which intended to burn the residence of Richard Rich and kill local representatives of the government. The plan was discovered before any violence took place but it is notable that Seymour remained popular with the 'mob' largely because he supported their position regarding the enclosure acts, and had been unwilling, in their eyes, to proceed against 'ordinary country folk'. However there were no large scale uprisings and John Dudley felt secure enough in his position to lift the bond on Seymour and permit his return to court by the end of March.[27] By April, Edward could be found dining with the very men who had plotted against him and sought his imprisonment. On 8 April he met with the king and by the end of the month he was once again sitting on the Privy Council though he was no longer Lord Protector but rather the Duke of Somerset, and more tellingly the king's uncle. Edward Seymour was also soon regranted many of his houses including Somerset Place and Syon alongside many of his other lands dotted about the Home Counties, ensuring his family's future and position.[28] John Dudley was in control of the government but Edward Seymour had quickly re-established himself with the ambassador, Scheyfve, even arguing that he is preeminent once again at court.[29] In May a visit took place from the French ambassadors to conclude the treaty which would see the return of Boulogne to the French. It must have been galling for Seymour to see Dudley overturn his foreign policies but Dudley's actions made sense. Seymour's instance on maintaining a military presence in England and France had nearly bankrupted the government and Dudley felt that withdrawing from France would give him and England leverage with which to address the question of Scotland. Boulogne was to be returned to France in exchange for a large sum of money – 400,000 ecus. Even more galling for Seymour and Anne was the fact that in April their son, Edward, was sent to France as a hostage for the agreement, though he and the other hostages were returned without incident.[30] Whilst Dudley's actions made sense, they were not widely popular in England. They gained no material advantage in Scotland and Warwick was eventually forced to agree to stop hostilities north of the border. Everything Seymour had sought to achieve, including the marriage of the Scottish Queen Mary to King Edward, lay in ruins. Regardless, Seymour knew he had little choice but to go along with Dudley's policy and to this end he hosted a dinner on the final evening of the French ambassadors visit, which Anne would have arranged and over which she presided. The evening concluded with a bear being hunted through the waters of the Thames and a 'wildfire' display of primitive gunpowder fireworks being shot from boats into the sky.[31] Edward Seymour was also once again in a position to observe and comment upon the latest acts of the Reformation. Warwick was prepared to go far further than Seymour, and was an eyewitness to the growing hostility between the council and Princess Mary, whom he had always taken care to appease, likely, at least in part, on Anne's account. In time he would take a leading role in trying to hash out a religious compromise between the two but initially he was more concerned about testing his own power and establishing where the boundaries of his influence would now lie.

The Seymours recovery was quite remarkable and it was completed by the marriage of Anne Seymour and John Dudley, which took place on 3 June at Sheen Palace.[32] The new Imperial ambassador, Jehan Scheyfve, wrote that the match was both made and brought about by the couple's mothers as it was primarily their wish. There is some evidence that the young John Dudley had in fact spent a good deal of time living in the Seymour household as a child, which as we have seen was usual at the time, and Anne would therefore have known her future husband-to-be quite well.[33] Something everyone involved probably viewed as a great advantage. The king attended the marriage and he wrote in his diary that he, the king 'came to Sheen where a marriage was made between the Lord Lisle and the Lady Anne, daughter of the Duke of Somerset which done and a fair dinner made and dancing finished the king and ladies went into two chambers made of boughs, where first he [the king] saw six gentleman of once side and six of the other run the course of the field twice over'. Anne's brother, Edward, was amongst those who raced. The king continued to recall that 'afterward came three masques of one side and two of another, which ran four courses apiece. Last of all came the Count of Rangone with three Italians who ran with all the gentleman four courses and afterwards fought at a tourney. And so after supper he [the king] returned to Westminster'.[34] At the banquet which followed Scheyfve stated that it was not Anne Seymour or even Jane Dudley who stole the show but Elizabeth Parr, who was gifted a valuable enamelled chain. This, however, appears to be his personal preference as he admired her beauty and he also got many details of the occasion wrong. For example, he claims that the banquet was hosted by Francis de Vandome which was not the case. Regardless, any favour which was shown to Elizabeth can hardly have pleased Anne as her husband, William Parr, had joined Dudley in his plot to overthrow Edward Seymour and had been granted the post of Lord Chamberlain as a reward. Anne's other daughters were in attendance and they, alongside the other ladies, all received presents 'according to their station'.[35] Anne Seymour, now Dudley, was personally given a ring worth forty pounds by her cousin, the king. John Dudley himself was not well enough to attend, either the day's festivities or the marriage the following day of one of his younger sons, Robert, to Amy Robsart, which was also attended by the king and of which William Cecil famously disapproved stating that 'carnal [meaning love] marriages begin in joy and end in weeping'.[36]

Edward and Anne Seymour had always planned impressive marriages for their children. They had long hoped that their daughter, Jane, might prove a match for the king, something which had caused discord when Thomas Seymour had planned for his ward, Lady Jane Grey, to fulfil such a role. Anne and Edward hoped that Lady Jane Grey might marry their eldest son Edward instead. In 1548 they had arranged for their son, Henry, to marry Catherine, the daughter and heiress of the Earl of Oxford. The two were still just children of around 10 and 12, but the match was locked down as tightly as Seymour could make it. If Henry were to die he would be replaced by another of his brothers and in addition to her dowry, Oxford was held by a bond of six thousand pounds to ensure that he did not simply change his mind.[37] Margaret, meanwhile, was to marry the son of the Earl of Derby, Lord Strange.

Chapter 16

Power and Patronage

One matter in which Seymour flexed his political capital was in the matter of a prisoner named John Rybalde, who had been held in the Tower. He was released at Seymour's intercession in June and the same day Seymour supported, if not proposed, the idea that Gardiner, who was currently imprisoned for refusing to accept the acts of religious reformation taking place, be released if he agreed to the new religious order.[1] Gardiner had once been a friend of both Seymour's and Dudley's but now he found himself imprisoned and isolated. He resolutely critiqued Cranmer's approach to religious reform, especially in relation to the doctrine of substantiation, and consistently reaffirmed his belief in it.[2] Despite Seymour's actions, Gardiner remained resolute and when, in 1551, he criticised Cranmer's seminal work *A defence of the True and Catholic doctrine of the Sacrament of the Body and Blood of our Saviour Christ* in his response *An Explication and Assertion of the true Catholic Faith touching the most blessed Sacrament of the Altar, with a Confutation of a Book written against the same*, the council ran out of patience. In his defence, Gardiner not only attacked Cranmer's religious views but also his capabilities, arguing that as he was wrong about the Eucharist, how can he be allied to remain in a position of religious or political power? As a result, Gardiner was deprived of his position as Bishop of Winchester. Edward Seymour had studiously tried to avoid, whilst in power, an actual attack on the Catholic bishops but now he had no choice but to go along with Dudley's more aggressive foreign policy. A policy which is best demonstrated by his burning of a Protestant heretic on 2 May 1550. Although Joan Bocher, also called Joan of Kent, had been arrested and condemned 'to be burned for certain detestable opinions of heresy' under Edward Seymour's tenure as Lord Protector, she had been imprisoned in the Tower and the death sentence was not carried out.[3] Now though, it was determined that the sentence should be implemented and Joan was burnt; at the last Dr Scory tried to convert her but she defiantly told him that he 'lied like a rogue [and that] he should read the scriptures'.[4] The fact that the writ issued for her execution was passed by the council on 27 April when Seymour was known to have been absent is telling and suggests that they would have expected him to oppose it. Dudley and others had long criticised Seymour's more moderate approach. For them he simply had not done enough to advance the Reformation. The fact that the Seymours were still regarded as powerful and authoritative on religious matters can be seen in the fact that theological works were still being dedicated to Anne and Edward, likely in the hope of securing a reward for their efforts, implying that the Seymours were still in a position to offer one. From 1549 to 1551 a man named Walter Lynne dedicated three books to Anne, calling himself her 'daily orator'. He maintained that she was known to be 'the most gracious patroness and supporter both of good learning and also of godly men'. He tells us that she was famous for her 'chief and daily study of the scriptures', and in the final dedication he made he called her 'the most worthy example of all noble women whose Godly study all Christian hearts do rejoice in'.[5] Although these dedications were, of course, designed to flatter it suggests that behind the politics Anne was living a life of religious study and constantly educating herself. Further support for this comes from the fact that upon Martin Bucer's death she bought most of the books in his library. We also know that she continued to employ and speak with men of learning at the heart of the Reformation, and there is no sign that her appetite for either study or religion had been blunted by Seymour's removal from the Protectorate, nor that her reputation was altered in the minds of many of her contemporaries. Other dedications came from a member of her own household, William Samuel, and another from Thomas Becon in his 1550 edition of *The Flower of Godly Prayers*.[6] Mildred Cecil, William's wife, likewise called her a 'very noble and virtuous' lady and a 'good lady and mistress'.[7] A more serious testament to her perceived power comes from Edward Courtenay, who was imprisoned in the Tower on account of the Yorkist blood running through his veins. He hoped that she, as 'the right virtuous lady and gracious princess Anne duchess of Somerset' might plead his case and help to secure his release.[8]

Dudley was threatened by Seymour's position regarding religion, the esteem in which he and his wife were held and his interventions, for example, with regards to Gardiner. He complained to Whalley that the council disliked Seymour's attempts to 'rule and direct the whole Council', given that he had only been released from the Tower due to them.[9] Though they were now related through marriage, Dudley and Seymour clearly still did not trust each other.

It is difficult to tell what extent the rumours that were circulating by August 1550 – that Seymour was planning to overthrow Dudley and resume control of the country – should be believed. Certainly they were relatively widespread and fuelled by the dissent that was spreading throughout the country that summer. Disturbances occurred in Sussex and Kent at Easter, and later throughout the south east forcing Dudley and the council to order that the number of watchmen on duty in London should be increased just in case disturbances should reach the Capital.[10]

It is equally certain that Seymour had by now fully reinserted himself into the business of government. For example, on 25 September 1550 he was at Oatlands Palace where he is named foremost amongst the members of the council who were present and authorised the wages for Robert Barras the captain of the light horsemen who were attendant on the king.[11] Likewise, three days later he also met with an embassy from Scotland, also at Oatlands, who bore letters asking whether now 'the king's highness and council meant that they should enjoy their old loyalties in the manners as they did before the last wars'.[12] Seymour remained with the Lord Treasurer, the Lord Chamberlain, Paget, the Vice Chamberlain, Petre, Cecil and Wootton to debate the response they should make to the treaty.[13] By 6 October, Seymour was still with the council, although they had now moved to Richmond Palace where again he is recorded as taking precedence, and likewise he was present at Westminster on 26 of the month drawing a vivid picture of just how involved with the council and respected he was once again.

Personal tragedy was, however, on the horizon and in mid-October Edward Seymour received news of his mother's death. He had with her 'a bond of blood and natural love towards her confirmed by her most happy fruit of the most virtuous princess the late Queen Jane, grandmother to our sovereign lord the king's majestie'.[14] Anne's reaction to her mother-in-law's death is unrecorded but she can hardly have been pleased when her husband's attempt to grant her a state funeral with full court mourning was rejected. The council told Seymour that in accordance with the new Protestant religion, the black trappings of mourning wear served no purpose and that he must 'set a further example for others' and 'temper his doings … to that duty of love which the child oweth the parent'.[15] Seymour is not recorded as being at the council a few days later, so it is possible that he and Anne travelled back to Wulfhall to mourn and be with their family or that they did so at Syon. If so, he was soon back at Westminster debating the defence of Calais and the dispute which had arisen over boundaries with the French.[16] Margery Seymour, meanwhile, was buried in St Mary's, Great Bedwyn in Wiltshire alongside her husband.

At around this time Edward VI fell ill. The precise nature of his illness is not known but it was serious enough for everyone to be greatly concerned. His 'recovery was despaired of, even the physicians had given up … the news was kept very secret' and special red and white cloth was ordered to decorate his bed and ensure his comfort on 4 November.[17]

Edward VI's ill health seems to have encouraged Seymour to make a move and at this time Scheyfve wrote that 'there are deep causes of discord within the Council. Some take Warwick's side others my Lord Somerset's [who was] doing his utmost to acquire friends and especially to win over the people'.[18] As with many of Scheyfve's observations, they should be treated cautiously, but there is no doubt that tensions on the council were increasing.

The only mention of Anne we have at this time is in a letter which Katherine Willoughby wrote in October to Cecil complaining that Anne had been ungrateful and unhelpful in relation to a suit of her cousin's, again implying that Anne had the power to influence such matters.[19] Perhaps Anne was having trouble assisting those who had watched her husband's downfall passively. Seymour himself possibly was and Nicholas Throckmorton wrote that at this time he felt that Seymour's heart was 'set upon revenge'.[20] However Seymour's good friend, Richard Morison, insisted that Seymour would and did forgive those who had brought him down.[21] Such two widely different views of Seymour's actions and character are difficult to reconcile so perhaps we should see such comments less as illustrative of his character but as an indication of the uncertainty which was pervading the country and court at this time.

By the beginning of 1551 the Reformation was gathering pace and one of its first targets was Anne's friend, Princess Mary. Seymour had promised Mary the freedom to hear Mass, but he was not in power any longer and now King Edward and Dudley were determined that Mary would toe the line. Warrants of arrest for Mary's chaplains were now issued by the council, although she did not issue them, and although she maintained that she was loyal to her brother she would not back down on matters of religion, declaring to the council, in barely respectful terms, that she would continue as she was 'until his Majesty has reached the age to judge for himself … Take this to be my final answer to any letters you might write to me on matters of religion'.[22] Mary, though, had underestimated her brother and Edward was not about to allow his sister to flaunt her opposition to the new laws of the land. Panicked by barely veiled threats from both her brother and the council, Mary stated that she would hear Mass only in private as had previously been agreed. Mary was genuinely frightened and she now wrote to Moronelli, a servant of the now dead Van der Delft, asking that he promise to gain her assistance from the Emperor should she require it. Her hastily scrawled ending, that he was to 'burn this note directly after you have read it', is a clear indication of her genuine fear.[23] This conflict with her brother and council led to the development of two plots to get Mary out of the country, but both ultimately came to nothing. Sadly there is no evidence as to what Anne felt about the treatment of Mary by the council; certainly they were opposed on matters of religion but as we have seen, on a personal level they could overlook that. For her part, Mary remained very much a supporter of Edward Seymour's; she called Dudley 'the most unstable man in England' who was, along with his supporters, guilty of 'envy and ambition' when they attacked Seymour.[24]

Their support of Mary was just one more thing on which Dudley and Seymour differed, although crucially now the growing king seemed to be on Dudley's side. There is some evidence that Seymour was considering making a bid to regain the Protectorate, notably Richard Whalley was arrested and sent to the Fleet prison for trying to gather support for such a bid, but again it is difficult to find evidence to prove that this was at Seymour's instigation.[25] Whalley, it was claimed in an anonymous letter likely written by the Earl of Shrewsbury, had 'practised with me to feel my disposition in friendship towards the duke of Somerset and Dudley'.[26] The scheme had seemed to focus on gathering enough support in Parliament to seriously challenge Dudley in the Commons where he was very unpopular and as a result he, equally seriously, prorogued Parliament for as long as he could. Seymour, it is said, felt that that summer, Parliament would support him as 'the people were oppressed with fresh taxes, the king proper than ever and those in power governed simply after their own caprice without respecting the law and customs of the realm'.[27] Dudley certainly felt the threat and Whalley's arrest was followed by that of another servant in Seymour's household who, it was claimed, had said openly that Seymour was a better master than Dudley. More seriously politically, Sir Ralph Vane was also sent to the Tower, ostensibly in relation to an enclosure dispute with Dudley but in reality because he was known to be Seymour's man. Interestingly Vane's wife, Elizabeth, was a staunch Protestant who would later risk her life and position to support Protestant prisoners and help them flee England under Queen Mary. In 1550 she herself published a small book *12 Certaine Psalms of Godly Mediation* in the manner of Anne and Edward's own daughters. It is interesting to consider the relationship Elizabeth may or may not have had with Anne Seymour. The two women certainly knew each other, as women of the court they would have been in each other's company frequently, but whether or not Anne influenced her or they shared books and ideas is sadly unclear. Elizabeth's later actions are, however, indicative of just how widespread religious dedication was amongst the circle of noble women to which Anne Seymour belonged, and just how far some were prepared to go to further their cause.

When spring finally arrived, after a dull and damp winter, Seymour approached Arundel and the two men began to meet at Syon or at Somerset House to discuss the downfall of Dudley, or at least that is what was later claimed.[28] In addition, Warwick had quarrelled with the Earls of Derby and Shrewsbury, leading him to suspect that they had switched their loyalty to Seymour.[29] The same month the general discontent with Dudley in the country boiled over and the king's diary records that a conspiracy in London was discovered whereby all the people had been encouraged to rise up against Dudley's regime on Mayday. At the same time a riot was being planned to take place in Chelmsford. The Spanish ambassador believed that these two conspiracies were linked and if so a large number of men would have been involved and they could have brought the insurrection literally to the king's door. Moreover, it was also recorded that a man was found to be prowling around Dudley's house with a sword in his hand; the man was considered to be a would-be assassin.[30]

Dudley struck back and at the ceremony of the Order of the Garter he set about trying to diminish Seymour's influence by reducing his claim to kinship with the king. Seymour was uncle to Edward VI, but Dudley now sought to diminish that fact by inserting a note reading 'on his mother's side'.[31] He also increased the king's guard and the number of men he had available to call on should the need arise.

The feud between the two men and their supporters stalled in late summer as a 'hot [or sweating] sickness' was reported in London which quickly swept through the population and swiftly killed nearly a thousand people.[32] The 1551 outbreak would turn out to be the last epidemic of 'the sweat' which was to ravage England and it also gave us our best information regarding the disease's symptoms and cause, courtesy of the work of Dr John Caius, physician to Edward VI and a man whom Seymour would have known, but that would have been little consolation to those who died. Amongst them was Charles Brandon, the 3rd Duke of Suffolk, who died of the disease an hour after his elder brother, Henry, at Buckden Palace, meaning that he has the dubious distinction of having the shortest tenure in the British peerage. His death was a disappointment to the Seymours who had been considering marrying the young Duke to one of their daughters. Perhaps their deaths made Edward Seymour more aware of his own mortality because that summer he made a will.[33]

The court, including Seymour, moved to Hampton Court along with the king in an attempt to escape the disease and he was there in July when he escorted the French ambassador, Marshal Jacques d'Albon, to the king. After which he left to go to Wokingham, and on his way back he was forced to remain at Syon when someone in his household contracted the sickness. Being away from the court was dangerous and Seymour knew it, for it now gave Dudley the chance to chip away at his support and exclude him from council business. It also limited the chances he had for open rebellion. We do not know if Anne was with her husband during this time but it seems likely, and we do know that she was involved in her husband's schemes and plotting at the court. Edward Seymour himself tells us this because a few months later he would instruct Anne and her half-brother, Michael, to 'meddle no more in [conspiratorial] talk with Henry FitzAlan, the Earl of Arundel'.[34]

After a tense few weeks Seymour was summoned back to attend the council on 30 September, but only responded a few days later after a further summons. On 4 October he was one of the councillors who granted Arundel senior's release from the Tower and historian, Margaret Scard, argues that this should be seen as evidence that Warwick was not intending to move against Seymour at this time, Arundel was, after all, known to be one of the Seymour faction.[35] If that was Warwick's intention, he soon changed his mind when on 7 October a man named Thomas Palmer visited Dudley at home and there he revealed to Dudley that there had been a serious plot against him and that the threat remained. He told Dudley that on St Georges day that year, Seymour had gone to 'raise the people' and that 'a device was made to call the Earl of Warwick to a banquet with the Marquis of Northampton and divers others and cut off their heads'. He added that Sir Ralph Vane now had 2000 men ready, and that Arundel had secured the Tower. A man named Miles Partridge was to raise London and capture the Great Seal and that the king's own guard would be slain.[36] Palmer claimed that Seymour and his supporters would then take power. The veracity of these allegations has been debated ever since. Palmer certainly had reason to take revenge on Seymour, who had humiliated him when he had criticised his actions and capture in Scotland. Warwick had also granted him one hundred pounds a year in 1550, making Palmer very much a Warwick man. Most historians today argue that the fact there is no independent evidence for this plot means that it should be taken as the manufactured means by which Warwick sought to remove Seymour once and for all.[37] Indeed, both Palmer and Warwick would later admit that Palmer had made his 'written accusation at Warwick's request'. This, however, might be a little simplistic, as we have seen there was insurrection and we know that Seymour was courting support and making his position clear but there is nothing to prove that he was actually planning a full scale coup. There are, however, a few pieces of evidence that should not be discounted. It is true that Derby and Shrewsbury, allies of Seymour's, had asked to be excused from a St George's Day feast and refused to attend. Did they know that Warwick's assassination was planned?[38] Likewise there had been a disagreement between Seymour and Warwick at this time where 'discord was bruited'; however, if it had been an actual assassination attempt then surely Warwick would have arrested Seymour there and then.[39] It seems likely that Palmer gained knowledge of a few of the facts, such as Seymour's meetings with Arundel and his quarrel with Warwick in April, and embellished them with Warwick's consent and knowledge into outright treason.

Seymour, of course, knew nothing of Palmer's words and entirely in the dark he attended Warwick's ennoblement as Duke of Northumberland, even standing beside him, but the Spanish ambassador was already writing that the plan was now to have Seymour arrested.[40] Seymour's ignorance did not last long. Soon the rumours reached his ears and he did not attend the council on 14th, writing to Cecil that he feared he would 'come by some ill'.[41] Cecil replied that 'if he were not guilty then he might be of good courage; if he were he had nothing to say but to lament him'.[42] It was not a reassuring reply and soon Seymour was fully aware of the gist of the accusations against him, and he sought to defend himself as best he could.

Hearing that Palmer was involved he demanded that he come to see him but Palmer refused.[43]

On 16 October Seymour arrived at the court late and attended Privy Council business, after which the king records that 'after dinner he was apprehended', that is arrested.[44] Following Seymour's arrest, a number of others were arrested in quick succession including Thomas Palmer himself, who was arrested when walking the terrace. Others arrested included Francis Newdigate, Lord Grey, Thomas Arundel and Vane. Interestingly a man called John Seymour and one called David Seymour were also arrested, no doubt kinsmen of Edward. All were in the Tower by nightfall. The Imperial ambassador was present and wrote down what he was told by William Cecil:

> When I arrived, Secretary Cecil acted as spokesman and gave me the following accounts of the occurrence that had moved the Council to send for me. One of the foremost and distinguished of their body, the Duke of Somerset, had laid aside all fear of God, all reverence and duty towards his sovereign and natural Lord and plotted to seize the Tower of London and consequently the royal treasury and military store there kept in order to subdue the town. Moreover he had endeavoured to have several other castles and first, particularly in the north country surprised and occupied by his accomplices and also to rouse the commons and peasantry to revolt this, jeopardising the king's person and his country's welfare without the slightest excuse or reason. Not content with this he had turned his back on all honour and humanity and connived and planned to invite his colleagues of the Council to a banquet to have them struck down and murdered by hired assassins which seems to them a very horrible action and calculated to give a very evil example. The council warned of the danger and had been able [the previous day] to arrest the duke and some of his party without any scandal or disturbance.[45]

The day after her husband's arrest, Anne Seymour was arrested and sent to the Tower, as was Crane, and the following day James Wingfield, Mr Banister, Vaughan and Anne's half-brother, Michael Stanhope, were also apprehended.[46] Edward VI specifically records that Anne was sent to the Tower for 'devising these treasons'; clearly it was felt this time that she had actively participated in her husband's plotting against Dudley and indeed Crane would later testify that she was aware of her husband's schemes and had been working on his behalf along with her half-brother, Michael.[47] Not even her friendship with Jane would save her this time. In contrast though, Seymour's secretary, Thomas Norton, wrote to Calvin that 'some parties are of the opinion that [Anne] was not imprisoned for having committed a crime but to prevent her from committing one'.[48] Warwick clearly did not want to risk her wielding her influence as she had done three years earlier. Norton's letters, written to John Calvin who was anxious for news of the Seymours, also tell us what happened to Anne's children at this time, something which surely was of paramount concern to her. They assure us, and Calvin, that they were safe and well though they had been made wards of court at their parents' arrest.[49] The couple's unmarried daughters, Margaret, Jane, Mary and Catherine, were placed in the care of their aunt, Elizabeth Seymour. Their youngest daughter, Elizabeth, went to stay with another Seymour aunt, Dorothy, and as the king's cousins they were all given one hundred pounds a year to pay for their maintenance and upkeep.[50] Their sons, Edward, Henry and Edward, meanwhile, were placed in the care of the Lord High Treasurer, William Paulet.[51] The Seymour heir, the eldest Edward, was kept a particular watch on, as at 13 he was nearly at the age of majority. The fact that provision was made for Anne and Edward's children so quickly after their imprisonment suggests that their incarceration was intended, right from the start, to be of long duration.[52]

Chapter 17

Edward

Edward Seymour had been in the Tower before but Anne had only visited previously. It is often assumed that as a woman she would have had little to fear but we must remember that no less than two queens whom Anne had known personally had died within the Tower walls, and the memory of Anne Askew must also have been fresh in her mind. Anne Seymour had every reason to be afraid. The king was generous to his aunt and uncle and they were permitted to send for such things as they deemed were necessary. This would have been expected, as luxurious accommodation for high status prisoners was usual; even Anne Boleyn had been allowed to live comfortably in the same rooms she used before her coronation during her confinement in the Tower. Edward Seymour requested 'one gown, one velvet cap, one night cap, two doublets, two pairs of hose, three shirts, two nightshirts, six handkerchiefs, three dozen points, two pairs of shoes, plus table linen and towels'. His list reflects the necessities of life, Anne, meanwhile, included such things as books, silk and thread so she could work at her needlepoint to pass the time. She also requested, amongst other fine clothing, her 'gown of black velvet edged with garnets as well as [numerous] silver dishes and silver spoons'.[1] Anne was also given 20 shillings a week to pay for light and fuel for the fires in her rooms. This was very generous; a pound of tallow wax would have cost around 1.5 pennies at the time and 6.5 pennies if she had wanted wax candles meaning that Anne would have had ample light to sew or read by on the dark winter evenings.[2] At this early stage there is no evidence that she was permitted visitors but Anne was not left entirely to fend for herself, and in more practical terms she was served by two gentlewomen and, at various times, between one and three male servants. Interestingly, the Constable of the Tower at the time, Sir Arthur Darcy, was not given any money to pay for these servants so either he provided them because he felt it to be to his advantage or more likely a private arrangement was made and he was paid by Anne's mother or another relation. Anne was also given an allowance of 11 shillings per day for food, much of which would have been prepared by her own cook. She would have been able to afford to eat roast meats, drink wine, bread and butter and even sweetmeats. An inventory tells us that she took full advantage of this allowance and ate 'mutton, wild game, bread, butter, beer and wine'.[3] The care that she was afforded, however, is unlikely to have, at least initially, compensated for the terrifying situation in which she now found herself. She was not permitted to have contact with her husband and was closely guarded. Edward and David Seymour were not allowed to send any letters so it seems unlikely that Anne was allowed to either.[4] By November, she might also have realised that her husband or even she might face torture when it was authorised by the council if it was felt to be necessary. The torture of women was not permitted but that had not stopped them in the case of Anne Askew and Anne would have remembered very well.

Outside the Tower the council now sought to find more evidence against those incarcerated but it seems that the populace in general were not convinced of Seymour's guilt. Ambassador Scheyfve noted that most felt that Seymour was 'unjustly accused' and resentment against Dudley was growing as a result.[5] They persisted in calling Seymour 'the Good Duke' and as a result Dudley, anxious of reprisals, ordered that more guards be posted and a curfew was enforced. Scheyfve maintained that despite this 'it has proved impossible to persuade the people or impress it upon them, and note a few persons of rank that Somerset really tried to lead such a enterprise [meaning the rebellion] for they believe him to be a good man wrongly accused in this conspiracy and think that the origin of the matter is to be sought in the Duke of Northumberland covetousness and deaf of Somerset'.[6] He also tells us that the cross examination of Somerset's supposed accomplices also took place and that the questioning of his young son, now Earl of Hertford, caused particular consternation.[7] Palmer helpfully, and probably to secure his release, elaborated on the information he had already provided and gave further details of the supposed revolt whereby Somerset would have travelled to the south coast, or even the Isle of Wight, to raise an army against Northumberland and the king.[8] Crane and Arundel were likewise questioned, although they maintained that at most they had intended to imprison Dudley and not execute him. Nevertheless, and whether true or not, the body of evidence against Seymour seems to have been growing. Lady Mary was alarmed and when her opinion was sought she asked Scheyfve how she should respond, and he told her that she should conceal any feeling of liking for the duke or his wife and merely state that she continues to 'pray for the king's welfare'.[9] This implies that she herself was not convinced and had continued affection for the duke and his wife, something which would later be borne out by her actions when queen.

Edward Seymour was interrogated in the Tower, and faced a series of questions largely concerned with his fellow accused and his relationship with them. How Seymour replied is not known but he would certainly have maintained his innocence, though an admission of meeting with Arundel to discuss the possible future arrest of Dudley is recorded.[10] The fact that the king could by now, at age 14, sign and authorise documents and warrants himself played to Dudley's advantage. There was not enough support for his continued actions against Seymour in the council but now he only needed the king to be on board. Only Edward's signature and that of the Lord Chancellor, Rich, who would soon helpfully relinquish the seal, ostensibly on the basis of his ill health but more likely because he opposed the idea of proceeding further against Seymour, was needed. Rich was replaced by the Bishop of Ely, Thomas Goodrich, a 'burly secular spirited man' who was a staunch supporter of Dudley's, although not of dedicated reform as history would later prove.[11] This evidence points to the idea that Northumberland knew that his case was weak and that he needed to move quickly. He was, however, this time determined to proceed against Seymour and to this end the following charges were drawn up: That he had planned to seize the king and assume his right and authority; that he had intended to take the Tower and capture the Great Seal; that he planned to incite the men of London to rebellion; and that he had plotted to arrest Northampton, Pembroke and Dudley himself. As historian Margaret Scard points out though, whilst the charge of intended murder against Dudley was applied to Vane, Arundel, Stanhope and Partridge, it was not applied to Seymour at this time.[12] Dudley, and London, now prepared for Seymour's trial. By 16 November 'good and substantial full juries of knights and esquires of the best sort' had been assembled to review the charges and Seymour's old friend, Paulet, was appointed as High Steward. Twenty-two Lords were sent for to make up Seymour's jury of peers, and despite the lack of solid evidence only the Earl of Shrewsbury, Francis Talbot, refused to attend, stating that he was seriously unwell, although he would live for nearly another decade. Also in attendance were members of the council.

On the night of 30 November Hoby went to the Tower and informed Edward Seymour that his trial would begin the next morning. At the same time he was stripped of his Order of the Garter and in the city a curfew was ordered so that men could not take to the streets. Armed guards were placed at regular points throughout the city and each man was ordered 'to see to his family and keep his house'.[13] With the stripping of the garter, Seymour must have realised that a guilty verdict was certain, all that remained to be decided was his fate.

We do not know how much or how little of these proceedings Anne was aware of, but through her servants, and news from her mother, she cannot have been ignorant. She might even have been officially informed although there are no definitive records of her being so.

The council was so concerned about violence breaking out in the city that Seymour was taken from the Tower at five in the morning, whilst it was still very dark, and torches lit the way as he was hastened into a barge and moved down river at low tide, so as to pass easily under London Bridge, to Westminster.

Edward VI, when he was recording these events, opens his account of 1 December simply with the words 'The Duke of Somerset came to his trial at Westminster Hall'.[14] He goes on to tell us that inside the hall 'the lord treasurer sat as high steward of England under a cloth of estate [then] on a bench between two posts three degrees high all the Lords sat'.[15] There then follows a list of the Lords present and so it was the Dukes of Suffolk and Northumberland, the Marquess of Northampton, the Earls of Derby, Bedford, Huntingdon, Rutland, Bath, Sussex, Worcester and Pembroke and the Viscount of Hereford were present alongside fifteen barons – Bargeiney, Audley, Wharton, Euers, Latimer, Borough, Souch, Stafford, Wentworth, Darcy, Sturton, Windsor, Cromwell, Cobham and Bray.[16] With this set up the council were following the standard procedure as had been instituted by Thomas Cromwell under Henry VIII for the trial of a member of the nobility, to streamline the process which had previously required the defence at least to be heard prior to trial.[17]

The trial began at 8am and there is some discrepancy in the sources regarding exactly what the charges levelled at Seymour actually were, but it seems clear that the charge of his having plotted to kill Northumberland and his allies had been added. Northumberland's Parliament had recently made it treason to plot to attack or otherwise imprison any member of the Privy Council, never mind kill him, so perhaps this late addition was made to throw Seymour off guard. If so it failed. Seymour remained defiant and he made a brilliant and bold defence. He argues, correctly, that the evidence against him was circumstantial at best, that he had never intended to take the Tower, to raise a rebellion or to do anything that might threaten the king's majesty. Likewise, he asserted that the only men he had ever raised were for his own protection as was customary. As before he did concede that he had discussed the best way to influence Northumberland and check his power but he staunchly denied that he had ever intended him any harm. In addition he argued that he had at one time or another had enough men to 'do harm [but] he did not'.[18] The trial lasted for many hours and the debate amongst the assembled peers was fierce; some felt that Northumberland, Northampton and Pembroke should not be permitted to sit on the jury as the charges concerned them and they could not be expected to be impartial. Others argued that whilst Seymour's actions had been 'mean', they were treasonous.[19] The result, however, was inevitable. Whilst they found Seymour not guilty of treason, he was found guilty of 'planning to imprison and kill three councillors'. This was not treason, the jury decreed, but it was a crime and the punishment for it was death.[20] Scheyfve recorded that despite the dispersal orders a crowd had gathered outside Westminster Hall chanting 'God save the Good Duke' to the astonishment of the Lords inside who could hear their shouts. After the verdict of not guilty was returned for treason, he wrote that scenes of jubilation broke out.[21]

Edward Seymour, however, must have known that his fate was sealed the moment he stepped into the Hall, and he greeted the news of his fate stoically. He knelt, begged the Lord's pardon and asked that his wife, children, servants and debts be taken care of. He was then led from the Hall back to the Tower. Usually a condemned man would be moved with an axe carried ahead of him and facing him to signify the death sentence; when this did not appear the crowds believed that their fears had been assuaged and continued their celebrations, believing that he was to be freed. Edward VI heard the commotion and asked what was happening and when he was told, according to the Spanish ambassador he replied that 'he had never believed Somerset could be a traitor'.[22] King Edward's own feelings are hard to ascertain despite his journal as sadly it does not give a glimpse into his mind and soul but rather he simply records events and what he told people. We do know that he did not intervene to save his once beloved uncle, whether this was because he believed him to be guilty or whether he simply did not have the power and influence under the Northumberland regime to do so, is unclear.

When Seymour was rowed back to the Tower the crowds grew increasingly uneasy. Due to the tide he had to finish his journey on foot and as he walked down the streets ever closer to the Tower the people stopped cheering and instead offered quieter 'God save the Duke' and words of encouragement. The strength of London's reaction to the verdict when its true nature became known shocked Northumberland and by the end of December he was 'sorely puzzled at present and does not know how all this will end'.[23] The country was grumbling and everywhere there were rumours circulating that the king himself was ill, and could not live long.

Back in the Tower, Anne cannot have been surprised at the verdict against her husband, and the enforced inaction must have been tortuous for a woman who had taken such decisive action to help save her husband last time. If the rumours of unease and unhappiness at the verdict within the city reached her ears, perhaps they cheered her, but I would suggest that she was far too experienced a political creature by this point to have seriously believed that Northumberland would allow her husband to live if he had any other choice. We also know that she feared for her own life at this time. Christmas was spent by both Edward and Anne separately within the Tower, and whilst the court feasted and danced, for them there was no glimmer of cause for celebration. If the king felt any grief at the impending fate of his uncle he gave no clear indication and recorded in a letter to his friend, Barnaby Fitzpatrick, that Christmas hath been well and merrily passed'. From this we might deduce that he was now fully ensconced in the Northumberland camp and happily watched Dudley's sons 'run and tilt against all challengers' during the festivities.[24] Scheyfve, however, records events slightly differently and that Edward VI was in fact 'grieved and sombre about the imprisonment of his uncle … but he had been so carefully primed with evil accounts of the said Somerset that he shows no feeling for him'.[25] Whatever the truth of the king's feelings it was Northumberland who headed the council and Edward Seymour would have been as aware, as Dudley undoubtedly was, that sooner or later a new year's Parliament would have to be called, and the likelihood was that they would petition to save him, so Northumberland would have to strike before that. This is supported by the fact that the French ambassador records that he had encouraged the king, alongside Northumberland, to convince the reluctant king that

Seymour had to die. For the French ambassador's part, he wanted Seymour out of the way so that negotiations for a marriage between Edward and the French Princess, Elisabeth, would continue. Seymour knew that time was running out.

On 18 January the council determined that Seymour was to die three days later and Goodrich was made Lord Chancellor so that Seymour's death warrant could be properly authorised with the Great Seal. On 21 January, Seymour was informed that his death sentence had been commuted to beheading on Tower Hill rather than hanging, as befitted his rank. With little time to prepare for his death, he wrote inside a small book that he had in his possession. This book is small and covered in red velvet and inside the flyleaf he wrote the poignant following words:

> Fear of the Lord is the beginning of wisdom.
> Put thy trust in the Lord with all thine heart.
> Be not wise in thine own conceit, but fear the Lord
> And flee from evil.
> From the Tower on the day before my death 1551 Edward Seymour.[26]

He also asked for and was granted forty pounds for alms to be distributed on his death. Likely he spent his last night in prayer, and perhaps we can suppose that Anne did too.

Edward VI recorded, with his famous impartiality and sandwiched between his removing to Westminster and the delivering of a token to Lady Elizabeth by Sir William Pickering, that on 22 January 'The Duke of Somerset had his head cut off upon Tower Hill between eight and nine o'clock in the morning'. Whilst he is correct the reality was rather more complicated. Despite an order to remain at home, large crowds had gathered to see 'the Good Duke' meet his end. Given this, he was escorted by a large guard. Did Anne manage to catch a last glimpse of the man who had been her husband, partner and lover for over twenty years? We simply don't know. He was led straight to Tower Hill and to the scaffold where he knelt to commend his soul to God before standing to address the crowd. He was, one of those watching recorded, 'of remarkable alacrity and cheerfulness of mind'.[27] The speech he gave, which exists in several recorded versions all of which vary slightly, shows that Seymour had accepted his fate, though not his guilt. He also mentioned that of which he was most proud: that he had helped to bring England closer to God.

> Masters and good fellows, I am come hither to die, albeit it that I never offended against the king neither by word nor deed, and have always been as faithful and true unto this realm as any man hath been. But as I am condemned by law to die whereunto I am subject, as are we all, and therefore to show obedience I am come hither to suffer death, where unto I willingly offer myself, giving most hearty thanks unto his divine goodness, as if I had received a most ample and great reward… I have to say to you concerning religion; I have always, being in authority, a furtherer of it to the glory of God to the uttermost of my power, whereof I am nothing sorry but rather have cause and do rejoice that I have so done, for the mightiest benefit of God that I ever had, or any man might have in their world beseeching you all to take it so.[28]

His speech was interrupted both by the cheers of the crowd who called out their agreement with him, and by a 'great noise'. Men panicked, and when Sir Athony Browne rode towards them around the scaffold to quiet the crowd, rumour arose that the king had sent his uncle a pardon and panic turned to jubilation with men crying out 'Pardon, pardon is come! God Save the King!' Seymour, however, knew better and raised his hand to quiet the men asking them to calm themselves so that he himself might remain calm. He told them almost gently that 'There is no such thing [as a pardon] good people. It is the ordinance of God thus for me to die, wherewith we must be content and I pray you be quite for I myself and quiet and make you no stirring and I pray you now let us pray together for the king's majesty to whose Grace I have always been [a] faithful, true and most loving subject, desirous always of his most preposterous success in all his affairs and ever glad for the furtherance and helping forward of the commonwealth of the realm'.[29] When they didn't immediately heed him he appealed to them movingly, in a more direct way saying that 'through their tumult, you might trouble me. For albeit if the spirit is willing and ready, the flesh is frail and wavering and through your quietness I shall be more quiet'.[30] This time they listened and silence fell as Seymour knelt and received a scroll containing his confession to God from Dr Cox. He read it then handed the scroll back to Dr Cox before shaking hands with all those on the scaffold and paying and forgiving the executioner as was customary. Seymour then removed his gown and lay down, but the executioner asked him to stand to remove or turn down his collar, presumably because it was covering the back of his neck. He then lay down again, was heard to utter the words 'O' Lord Jesus preserve me' and the axe fell and severed his head in one blow. The crowd wailed and groaned before rushing forward to dip their hands and handkerchiefs in the good duke's blood.[31] Edward Seymour's body was bundled into a cart and drawn back into the Tower to be laid to rest in the Chapel of St Peter ad Vincula without ceremony, ironically alongside that of the brother whom he had himself condemned to the same fate.[32]

Chapter 18

Anne

Edward Seymour was dead, but Anne was not, though inside the Tower she thought that her own execution was imminent. The only action that we know she took for certain in the aftermath of her husband's death is that the next day she asked that John Hooper, her former chaplain, be brought to her so that she might 'settle her conscience'.[1] In this request perhaps we can get a glimpse of the magnitude of her fear and that her primary concern, like her husband's had been, was matters of religion. She was not wrong to fear for her life; writing from the court Scheyfve recorded 'that the Duchess, Somerset's spouse, will soon go the same way as her husband'.[2] This is further supported by the fact that those imprisoned alongside the Seymours began to also go to the block, including Anne's half-brother, Michael Stanhope, who was executed on 26 February 1552, like Seymour, proclaiming his innocence to the last.[3] This was undoubtedly of great grief to Anne who, as we have seen, was often visiting, planning with and in the company of Michael. Sir Thomas Arundel, Sir Miles Partridge and Sir Ralph Vane were all executed alongside him. Stanhope and Sir Thomas Arundel were beheaded, the rest hanged.[4] The Earl of Arundel remained, like Anne, locked up in the Tower, whilst Paget, Crane and Thynne were released but had to pay large fines. The fact that Paget was also expelled from the Order of the Garter as punishment did not endear him to Northumberland. Northumberland, however, seems to have felt that with Edward Seymour's death the threat posed by Anne was past, though he did not release her. Instead she remained in the Tower, to grieve and reflect largely in isolation and cut off from the world. Anne, though, was not entirely forgotten and as time passed the conditions in which she was held improved slightly. In June 1552 we know that she was permitted to receive regular visits from her mother, Lady Page, who as far as we can tell had steadfastly supported her daughter and sent money when she could.

This indicates the closeness between mother and daughter that I mentioned was implied earlier; as others now sought to distance themselves from the disgraced duchess, her mother remained constant.[5] It has later been claimed that Lady Page, in fact, spent so much time with her daughter that she practically moved in and was 'for the most part with the Duchess' from June onwards.[6] With her mother now at least able to visit her regularly, Anne would have been slightly less isolated than previously. No doubt they talked of Anne's children and of events in the outside world. She would surely have been proud to hear of how 'well' her husband had died, the bravery of which had greatly impressed the already pro-Seymour London mob. She would likewise no doubt have been comforted by the fact that for weeks Seymour was being 'deeply mourned' by the city.

Anne would, however, have been furious to learn that Northumberland had created a parliamentary bill whereby all the Seymour land and titles would be forfeit, which as he had not been found guilty of treason should not have been the case. Her sons now had no lands or titles to inherit and when John, Edward's son by Catherine Fillol, was instead granted the lands and property which had belonged to Catherine as part of her dowry, it must have felt like everything she and Edward had strived so hard for had come to nothing. Catherine, however, we must imagine would have smiled at this vagary of fate. John had been imprisoned in the Tower alongside his father and he died in 1552 and was buried at the Savoy hospital but he left instructions that his younger brother, Catherine and Edward's second son, Edward, should inherit everything. His will clearly states that 'I make my brother Sir Edward Seymour … my full executor and I give him all my lands and goods that is bequeathed'.[7] This included, in 1553, the manor and castle of Berry Pomeroy.

Other misfortunes soon befell Anne's other children too, Dudley could do nothing about his son's marriage to Anne Seymour but Henry Seymour's marriage to the daughter of the Earl of Oxford, which the Seymour's had been at such pains to secure, did not take place when the Earl of Oxford petitioned Parliament for the contract to be annulled and the money which had been intended as insurance was not required to be paid.[8] Henry would eventually marry a daughter of the Earl of Northumberland. No further great matches were planned for Anne's children though, they were no longer attractive prospects.

As time passed Anne was allowed further visits. At Easter 1553 Bishop Hooper was allowed to visit Anne again, and she was able to acquire some books. Furthermore she was granted another hundred pounds by the council 'out of the profits arising from the lands of the late Duke of Somerset', to use as she saw fit.[9] She likely also heard from one of her servants, Francis Newdigate, regularly as he sought to salvage what he could of the duke's estates and manage them on her account.[10]

Anne would have heard rumours of the growing unease with Northumberland's regime and of the king's ill health. At some point in early 1553 Edward VI fell ill. Until 1552 he had been healthy but that year he had contracted measles, something which is speculated today may have seriously weakened his immune system. By spring 1553 he was vomiting blood and other matter, and it soon became clear that he was dying. His successor was Anne's friend, and Edward's elder sister, Princess Mary, a staunch Catholic. Under Northumberland and Edward VI the Reformation had taken on a furious pace and Edward was now determined that England should not be left to Mary who would undoubtedly undo all his work to bring the 'true religion' to England. He also knew that his other half-sister, Elizabeth, would never consent to go against their father Henry VIII's Acts of Succession and so he eliminated her as his successor too. Instead he proposed to disinherit both his half-sisters and in his Devise for the Succession, which he signed in May 1553, he left the crown to Lady Jane Grey and her heirs male. Lady Jane was a great-granddaughter of Henry VII through his daughter, Mary Tudor, and was conveniently married to John Dudley's son, Guildford.

Edward VI died on 6 July 1553 and duly Lady Jane Grey was taken to the Tower and declared queen. Again what Anne saw or heard of all the associated events is uncertain but she cannot have been ignorant as to what was happening. She must have prayed for the king's soul, but did she resent him for allowing her husband to die? Or did she remember the young boy who had played alongside her own children and been, according to some, the image of her late sister-in-law? We simply do not know, but her feelings must have been very complicated in regard to the young boy who had promised so much but who had never even taken up the reins of power. Her feelings about Northumberland were likely rather more simple. We know that she never forgave him for her imprisonment or her husband's death. Anne religious faith, however, would have brought an added complication to her feelings around current events. She fervently believed that Mary's Catholicism was false and idolatrous but did her loyalty to Mary override her misgivings about her faith; certainly it did on a personal level but on a political level we simply do not know. I suggest, however, given later events, that Anne would have felt that Mary was her best, and perhaps only chance of regaining her freedom and that regardless of this, as she had such long term affection for Mary she would have supported Mary's accession irrespective of their religious differences. The fact that she later maintained not only her friendship with Mary when she became queen but amiable relations with her Catholic court supports this supposition.

If this was the case then Anne was in agreement with most of the country. Princess Mary had fled to her East Anglian heartlands, to mighty Framlingham Castle, and very soon she had huge numbers of supporters, who, like Anne, may have been in conflict with her on religious grounds but who supported her accession simply because she was Henry's daughter and the people wanted to see a true Tudor on the throne. Northumberland, for his part, took a force to face her but when he saw which way the tide was turning he admitted defeat and gave way. On 19 July Mary Tudor was proclaimed queen to the great rejoicing of the realm and for the first time in history England had a queen regnant. One of Mary's first acts was to release her friends from the Tower and on 11 August Anne Seymour was released and walked free from the Tower after two years of imprisonment, perhaps with one last glance in the direction of her husband's final resting place. Given their religious differences it is clear that this was a personal decision, not a political one, and speaks to the strength of their personal friendship which had endured at this point for over thirty years. No doubt many of their letters and gifts to each other have been lost but those which do survive as we have seen reveal their friendship to have been a deep one of respect, love and laughter. It was a true friendship in every sense of the word and the best evidence we have for this is the speed of Anne Seymour's release, which was not left as an afterthought but rather took place the same day as that of Mary's strongest political supporter, Bishop Stephen Gardiner. Mary went much further than simply granting Anne her freedom, she was restored to her position as Duchess of Somerset and was permitted to stay at and use Syon House, as she had done for a good deal of her married life, in order that she could be close to Mary, the court and live in the manner to which she had previously been accustomed. We do not know exactly where Anne went after her release but we can suppose that she saw her children, thanked the queen and then did in fact go to Syon because in May 1554, Mary asked Anne if she would allow the Imperial ambassador to use it that summer, which implies that until then it had been occupied presumably by Anne herself.[11]

Northumberland went to the block on 22 August, ironically having converted to Catholicism just prior to his death, and Anne surely spared few tears for the man who had plotted and brought about her husband's death. Before his death there is a suggestion that Northumberland admitted that he had fabricated the evidence against Seymour. His execution could not bring Anne's husband back but surely she took some satisfaction both in this admission and his death. Perhaps her feelings were softer toward his widow Jane, who now found herself deprived of her family possessions although Mary permitted her to keep her personal household goods and plate and the use of the confiscated Dudley house in Chelsea.[12] If they did resume something like their former friendship, sadly no evidence of it has survived. Perhaps, though, we should infer that Anne shed more tears for Jane's death in 1555 than she did for Northumberland's.

Her personal connections are difficult to determine during this period but we do get glimpses of them, for example we know that she was friends with William Cecil, who visited her at least twice in 1557/8. Another example of their enduring closeness can be found later in 1570 when she adds a postscript to a letter written by her second husband in which she rather cheekily requests some of his wine, couching her request by referring to herself as his 'loving friend'.[13] We can also perhaps infer that she was unwell in 1555, perhaps temporarily weakened by her time in the Tower, because Archbishop of Canterbury, Reginald Pole, granted her leave to eat meat during Lent.[14]

Anne was certainly not idle during this time, although the specifics of her activities are hard to pin down. We know that she petitioned consistently for the arrears of her jointure and to recover as much of her former wealth and goods as possible. This was a complicated affair given her late husband's attainder and it took many years to be sorted out, but to this issue Anne applied methodical patience and the political acumen that she had under many other monarchs, cajoling and utilising her personal connections.[15] Until, finally, in 1568, she was granted seven hundred pounds annually, in order that the ten thousand pounds she was still owed could be paid to her.[16]

With the Marian regime Anne maintained a good and friendly relationship. This has led some to accuse her of 'selling out' the reformist cause but we must remember that Anne was a survivor and more than that she was a mother, with children whose interests she needed to protect. In addition, her relationship with Mary, as we have repeatedly seen, transcended matters of religion. There is no evidence that Anne ever condoned Mary's

Catholicism but nor did she condemn it; they simply agreed to disagree. Their good relationship is again attested to by the fact that Anne's children were returned to her care and in 1556 Mary granted Anne the means to repair Wulfhall, which was part of her son Edward's inheritance, and which he would inherit the following year when he came of age.[17] Seeking a permanent home of her own, Anne petitioned the queen and in March 1558 she was granted the manor of Hanworth for life. This property was one with royal connections, it had belonged to the Crosby family until Henry VII had acquired it and Henry VIII then inherited it. Henry VIII liked the manor with its local hunting and in 1532 he had granted it to Anne Boleyn for life, and it was extensively modified and dedicated to the couple's tastes. After Anne's death it reverted to the Crown and Henry had given it to wife number six, Katherine Parr, in whose possession it remained until her death before it once again reverted to the Crown meaning that Mary could grant it to Anne for the duration of her life. Anne was certainly already familiar with the manor and she had visited it previously. Situated on the outskirts of London today, in Tudor times it was set in the midst of heathland on which excellent hunting could be found. Queen Mary herself had stayed there, as had Elizabeth, so again such an endowment by the queen is testimony to Mary's regard for Anne.

It is at this point that the man named Francis Newdigate steps to the forefront of Anne's story. Although up until this point he was not of enough consequence to be mentioned, he had in fact been a part of Anne and Edward's household for many years. He had been the duke's steward for many years and had been imprisoned along with the duke and duchess in 1551, before he was released. He then undertook to salvage what he could of the duke's estates and manage them. Perhaps for this loyalty, perhaps for genuine affection, or perhaps simply because she knew her life would be easier with a husband at her side, Anne married Francis in late 1558 or very early 1559. We do not know the exact date, or even where the marriage took place, let alone what Anne's feelings may have been. Everything points to this having been a marriage of convenience but there is also scope for affection to have developed between the couple. Little is known of Francis' early life but we do know that he was born in 1519, which made him 9 years younger than Anne, and was the fifth son of John Newdigate and his wife Anne. At some point in his youth he had become Somerset's steward. In choosing to marry Francis, Anne was following the example of Catherine of Valois and others 'adopting the course which was almost universal in former days with the most illustrious widows, she chose a protector not so much for her person as of her property'.[18] For Francis' part, Anne was by now well past her childbearing years but she could offer him the sort of position and advancement he otherwise could only dream of. It is likely that Anne petitioned for Hanworth Manor on account of her impending marriage, wanting a solid yet different foundation perhaps on which to build her second married life.

1558 for Anne ended on a devastating note. On 17 November her great friend, Queen Mary died, likely of influenza which was tearing through the Capital that summer. Anne must have been devastated on a personal level; in many ways Mary's friendship had been the cornerstone of her life since she was a teenager. The previous year, in 1557, her mother Lady Page had died and been buried on 11 August at Clerkenwell, which must also have been a great loss to Anne and in combination these losses left her more personally isolated than she had ever been before.

The new queen was Mary's Protestant half-sister, Elizabeth, who again Anne knew, though less well than she had Mary. The daughter of Anne Boleyn, Elizabeth was everything Mary was not; she was young, pretty and determined to find a better way in matters of religion for England. Anne soon set about ensuring that she and her husband would prosper under the new Elizabethan regime. In this she was aided by her friendship with Cecil, who was appointed by Elizabeth as her 'eyes'; that is her right-hand man. In 1559 Elizabeth granted Anne and her new husband the use of Chelsea Place in London; the fine, handsome building had been the home of Anne of Cleves until Henry's last surviving wife had died there in 1557. Thanks to some architectural detective work on the part of Dr Johnathon Foyle, it is now thought that panels from Chelsea Place have survived, which bear Anne of Cleves insignia, the emblem of Cleves and a snarling lion's head, and are examples of the type of intricately carved wooden interiors with which Anne Seymour would have been familiar. She may have seen these very panels as, although it is hypothesised that they were removed from Chelsea Place and other locations shortly after Anne of Cleves' death, it could have been several years after meaning that Anne would have potentially lived with them for a while. In 1559, Francis was also appointed, through Anne's influence, to represent the borough of Great Bedwyn, which was a traditional Seymour position close to Wulfhall.[19] Regaining it was an important step for the family and it increased the family's influence. Anne's son was now sitting in the House of Lords, and her husband had a position in the Commons. Her daughter, Jane, was also appointed as one of Elizabeth's maids-in-waiting, and soon became something of a favourite with her mistress.

Anne was not finished with her ambition though, for she now not only sought to advance her husband but also got dangerously involved in the romantic and marital schemes of her children. Her and Edward's eldest surviving son, Edward, now swept her up in potentially the most dangerous situation she had ever faced, for at some point during the latter stages of Queen Mary's reign he had become romantically involved with Lady Katherine Grey. Lady Katherine was born in 1540 and was a great niece of Henry VIII through his sister, Mary. When she was named in the line of succession in Edward VI's will, after her elder sister, Jane, and her heirs male, she became an excellent prospect on the marriage market. Northumberland's plotting had seen her married, in 1552, to Henry Herbert, the son of the 1st Earl of Pembroke, William Herbert, and sent to live with her in-laws at Baynard's Castle. Given their young ages, when Northumberland's coup failed an annulment was secured fairly easily, principally on grounds of non-consummation. At some point Katherine became good friends with Anne Seymour's daughter, Jane Seymour, and through her met Edward Seymour, now 1st Earl of Hertford. The two fell in love and disastrously married in secret, without the queen's consent, in December 1560 at Edward's house in Cannon Row. Jane Seymour was the only witness to the couple's marriage.[20] Initially, it seems that they had intended to seek the permission of Queen Mary, but after her death they proceeded anyway. Katherine was regarded by many as Elizabeth's heir and for her to marry without the queen's permission was tantamount to treason. Following his marriage, Edward Seymour went on tour of the Continent with Cecil's son, Thomas, an excursion on which Anne hoped Thomas would overrule and begin to tame her 'wilful' son.[21] However, he was hastily recalled when Katherine's pregnancy and marriage had been discovered by the queen. Elizabeth was furious and viewed the union of her potential heir with Somerset's son to be a threat to her security and that of England.

It was quickly noted that Anne was against the match, and later writers have implied that she sent Edward abroad because she had uncovered his marriage and hoped he would rethink, but she would deny knowing about it at all, and it seems very unlikely that whatever her ambitions for her son she would have deliberately risked Elizabeth's displeasure in that way. Instead, when the marriage came to light she wrote to Cecil, immediately assuring him that she had known nothing of the matter and that she hoped Edward's actions would 'not diminish the queen's favour'.[22] It evidently did not; Elizabeth never doubted Anne's loyalty and would soon prove it. For now though, Edward and Katherine were sent to the Tower, where Katherine bore her child, a healthy baby boy, something which did not help their cause.

Further tragedy befell Anne in 1561 when her daughter Jane died, traditionally of tuberculosis, aged only 20. As well as being a personal tragedy for Anne, it also meant that the only witness to Edward and Katherine's marriage was now dead. This meant that a year later the marriage was declared to be invalid. Despite this, inside the Tower Edward had bribed someone to allow him to meet with Katherine and soon she was pregnant again, giving birth to a son, Thomas, in 1563. Elizabeth this time was incandescent with rage. Whilst she sent Edward to Hanworth where he was under Anne supervision, Katherine remained in the Tower until plague threatened and then she was sent to her uncle, John Grey in Essex. Her youngest son went with her, but her eldest was placed in Anne's care alongside his father.

It is clear that Anne's star was still in the ascendancy despite her son's actions. Not only was she entrusted by the queen with a potential heir to the throne, Katherine's younger son would also join his brother upon Katherine's death. And Anne was still received 'very honourably' at court.[23] As usual though, Anne was working away behind the scenes to secure Edward's restoration to favour. She wrote to both Robert Dudley, a firm favourite of Elizabeth, and Cecil asking for their help and Dudley, in particular, later wrote to Edward Seymour making it clear to him that he had spoken with the queen but also that 'his mother had done her part'.[24] Katherine Grey's death in 1568 helped to ease the situation a little but Edward Seymour remained under house arrest, although not at Hanworth, where his two sons now lived under Anne's guidance. No doubt she taught them stories of their illustrious heritage as once her first husband had been taught at Wulfhall. Seymour eventually gained some sort of royal favour but threw it away yet again by marrying Frances Howard without permission. He ended up in the Tower (again) for this and for repeatedly trying to have his sons by Katherine Grey declared legitimate. He was released fairly quickly and in 1601 he would marry for a third time and ultimately he managed to survive the reign of Elizabeth I by the skin of his teeth. He died, having gained favour under James I, in 1621.

During this period Francis Newdigate continued to prosper at his wife's encouragement and often thanks to her connections. In 1559 he sat again in Parliament for Chippenham and in 1571 for Middlesex.[25] Anne supported her second husband as loyally as she had done her first and when he felt that he had been insulted by the Earl of Sussex, she was quick to write to Cecil and ask him to make suitable redress.[26] In return he helped to bring about her financial settlement of 1568 and managed her estates, much as he had always done. In 1570, Anne was granted seven more manors and she seems to have continued her religious interests for in 1570 her servant, Edward Crane, dedicated another book to her. 1575 saw Elizabeth grant her Somerset House, Seymour's huge building project, which perhaps felt to Anne like coming home. She had certainly come full circle and was now, as we have seen, happily in a position to grant favours. For example, in 1576 she wished for Cecil to advance a Mr Druse, something which it appears he did.[27] Another clear sign of her position in high royal favour was the fact that Elizabeth stayed with her at Hanworth when she was on progress in 1577. On Thursday, September 12 during her visit, the queen dined with Anne and her Page of the Robes, Charles Smyth, who had worked with Anne to ensure that all was ready for the queen's visit. It is also likely that it was on this visit with Anne that Elizabeth sat for a now lost portrait by artist Cornelius Ketel. A 1604 biography of him records that 'in 1578 Ketel portrayed the Queen of England from life, Her majesty sat at the request of the Earl of Hertford at the house of Hanworth where she stayed/dined with the Duchess of Somerset mother of the same Earl'.[28] Assuming Ketel did indeed paint Elizabeth during this visit, it would be in keeping with Seymour's patronage of Protestant artists as he was one of numerous exiled artists who came to the Elizabethan court in the 1570s.

A year later Anne and the queen exchanged New Year gifts and Anne appears to have been often at court and she again dined with the queen at Hanworth in 1580, on 25 August.[29] In between royal visits and court duties a lot of Anne's life during this period would have been taken up with visiting her family, and raising her grandsons. Her son, Edward, had been restored as Earl of Hertford in 1559 and whilst his sons remained illegitimate, Anne was almost certainly behind her grandson's acquisition of the title Viscount Beauchamp, one of his father's lesser titles, and her efforts would ultimately ensure that despite his illegitimacy he was his father's heir. Into this we can perhaps read both a fondness for her grandson and Anne's desire to see the Seymour position fully restored. Her eldest daughter, Anne, was by now a mother of seven children but suffering from ill health, the nature of which was said to be psychological, so perhaps she visited her, or perhaps the children were some of those mentioned as staying often at Hanworth.[30] She also maintained a close relationship with her brother Michael's children and in 1581 petitioned Cecil successfully, to ask that her nephew, Edward Stanhope, be granted the position of Master of Requests.[31] All was not perfect though and there is evidence that Anne, during this period, quarrelled with her daughter, Mary, who until now had been a frequent visitor to Hanworth. This quarrel was serious enough for Mary to ask Cecil to intervene on her behalf, as Anne had forbidden her to speak with her after hearing some unfortunate rumours, the nature of which remains unclear.[32] This is an indication of the control and influence which Anne wielded over her family. There is also ample evidence that they remained close, and of genuine affection between them. In 1582 we get a glimpse of her two grandsons reading Latin letters to her, and the translation into English they had made, Anne was clearly a hands-on grandmother. The same year her son, Edward, was concerned to receive a report from her servant that she had a bad cough; like all anxious children Anne's kept a close eye on her health as she aged.[33] We do not know when Anne's daughter, Katherine, died but it must have been at sometime during this period as she was dead by 1585.

Anne had clawed back the Seymour inheritance and position and we get a glimpse of the properties she and Francis had come to possess in 1580 when her second husband drew up his will, likely because his health was already failing. In his will, Francis left everything to his wife, to whom he acknowledged he owed everything. This included the Canon Row house, the Bull Inn at Isleworth, Littleton Manor in Middlesex, Little Ashtead and Great Ashtead in Surrey.[34] Anne's second husband died in January 1582 and she passed the manor of Ashtead to her son Henry, to then go to his younger brother, Thomas, should Henry have no heirs. In the absence of her husband, Anne assigned the management of this issue to Cecil, now Lord Burghley, and Ephraim Pagitt, who was a clergyman and writer.

If her 1582 cough had temporarily ailed her, Anne was back in good health by 1585 when she was back at court and exchanging gifts with the queen. She had also mended her quarrel with her daughter Mary and Mary reported to her brother, Hertford, that they had been at court together and that Anne was very well indeed.[35] Anne also ensured that she maintained her status as a religious patron and in 1586 the young Ephraim Pagitt dedicated his work *The Book of Ruth* to Anne and thanked her for her support and 'for the comfort' that she and two others had provided.[36] It was to be her last act of religious patronage.

By now Anne was in her mid-seventies and she felt death drawing near. It appears that she was now suffering from what she termed a long-term illness which 'God hath blessed' her with and two doctors, Thomas Penny and Thomas Muffit, attended her. On 1 July 1586, Anne made her will, which was drawn up by William Clarke, her preacher, and she appointed Edward, Earl of Hertford to be her executor, despite the queen asking her to use her son Henry, instead. She made numerous bequests as befitted the matriarch of a large and powerful dynasty. She left bequests for her son, Hertford, his wife Frances Howard, her son Henry, her daughters Mary and Elizabeth and her grandson and his wife. Her daughter, Anne, was not left anything probably due to her mental illness which would have likely rendered her unable to inherit. She also mentioned her wider friends and family, leaving goods and money to her godchildren, Richard and Anne Knightley, her nephews John and Michael, the sons of her late brother, although she did not mention the eldest nephew, Edward, perhaps feeling she had assisted him enough in helping him achieve the position of Master of Requests. There were also bequests for her nieces, servants and friends as well as poor university students in London and prisoners.[37] The goods she had to leave included a rope of a thousand pearls and a fair great diamond. The text of the will below is testament to just how wealthy Anne was upon her death, and just how far she had risen.

In the name of God. Amen. The xiiij day of Julie, in the yeare of our Lord God 1586. I, Anne, by the goodness of God, Duchess of Somerset, considering the many yeres wherwith God hath blessed me, and the sicknes wherwith I am visited, doe in perfect mynde and remembrance make this my last will and testament in manner and forme following. First, I thank God in Christ Jesus that he hath long agoe called me to the knowledge and love of the Gospell, and ever since kept me therein to an assured hope of life everlasting, thorough faith in the righteousnes of Jesus Christ alone. In which faith I recomend my bodie to the dust whence it was taken, and my soule into the most mercifull handes of him that redemed it, to be kept of him till it shalbe reunited to the bodie in that glorious daye of the resurrection of all flesh. Secondly, I geve thanks to God allso for the temporall blessings of my landes, goodes, and chatells, which I dispose to my childeren, servaunts, the poore, and others, as followeth.

First, I geve to my sonne the Earle of Hertford, and his heyres for ever, all my mansion howse situate in Chanon rowe, within Westminster, in the Countie of Middlesex, with the howsholde and furniture therof. Item, I geve him a glasse of cristall dressed with gould, a basen and ewer all gilt plaine, a payr of gilt pottes, a payer of flagons newe bought, iij gilt trenchers, a spone of gould not foulded, iiij other spones gilt antique fashion. Item, I geve him ij of the fayrest gilt bowles with covers, a salt of cristall, and my beast cheane of greate pearle with long beades of goulde betwene, a fayer juel of diamondes, and a greate pearle worth by estimation about xxx l.

Item, I geve to his wife my daughter of Hertford a fayer tablet to weare with antique work of one syde and a row of diamondes on the other syde. Item, I geve her a clock of gould work worth about xxx l.

Item, I geve to my sonne the Lord Henry Seymour xiij hundred powndes of lawfull English monie, over and above the vij hundred I have allreadie geven him towards the payment of his debts. Item, I geve him a fayer jewel of an egret with divers stones. Item, I geve him ij bowles of silver and gilt, with ewers, and a basen and ewer of sylver.

Item, I geve to my daughter the Ladie Marie Rogers all my lease and tearme of yeres in the manner and ferme of Ashford, in the countie of Middlesex, which I have fernied of [blank]. Item, I geve her a harkenet of pearle, in number about c.c.c. two ropes of perle, in number about ij thousand, a lace with small pearle, a jewel of jacinth rownd with small pearle, a cople of bowles with covers, a spice box of sylver with the furniture of it, a ladle sylver and gilt, and my saddel embroydered with black velvet.

Item, I geve to my daughter the Ladie Elizabeth Knightley a greate cheane of pearle with true-loves, a jewel of a balist, ij great standing cuppes sylver and gilte, a jugge of stone fayer dressed with sylver and gilt, and a skellet of sylver.

Item, I geve to my sonne Beuchamp [a grandson] ij hundred powndes of lawfull English monie and a cheane of pearle and gould with friers' knottes, the gould by estimation worth about Lxxx l.

Item, I geve to my Sonne Thomas Seymour [another grandson] a hundred powndes of lawful English monie, and a cheane worth about Lxl.

Item, I geve to my sonne Beuchampes wife a booke of gould kept in a grene purse, and a payer of bracelets without stones.

Item, I geve to my daughter Maries husband a clieane of gould black.

Item, I geve to my daughter Elizabethes husband one of my ringes that hath the best diamonds.

Item, I geve to my goddaughter Anne Knightley five hundred powndes of lawful English monie and a rope of small pearle, in number about a thousand.

Item, I geve to my Lord Treasurer a jugge of cristall with a cover dressed with sylver and gilt, and a ring with an emerald.

Item, I geve to my nephew John Stanhope the fortie powndes he oweth me.

Item, I geve to my nephew Michael Stanhope a piller of gould with viii diamondes.

Item, all the reast of my plate not geven before I geve to my fower childeren, equally to be devided betwene them. Item, I geve a cofer of sheetes and pillowberes and a case standard with fine white naperie to my two daughters, equally to be devided. Item, I geve to the same my ij daughters my apparell, equally allso to be devided.

Item, I geve to my servant Win. Dickinson tenne powndes of lawfull English money, to be paide him for an annuitie or pension by myne executor during his life. Item, I geve to Richard Saunders, my servant, five powndes of lyke lawfull English monie, to be paide him by myne executor for a yearly pension during his life. Item, I geve to Richard Lanckeshire, John Trodde, and mother Gardener, to every one of them a yerely pension of 40s. to be payde them by myne executor during there lives. Item, I geve to all the rest of my gentilmen, yeomen, and gromes, and others in ordinarie, a yeres wages.

Item, I geve to Margaret Ashhurst all my wearing linnen, which is in her keeping, and a new black satten gowne. Item, I geve to Anne Jones 40s. Item, I geve to Mrs. Ansley a gowne of wrought velvet furred thorough with cunnie. Item, I geve to Jane Seymour 100l of lawfull English mony.

Item, I geve to godly and poor students in the ij Universites xxl, xl to the one and xl to the other.

Item, I geve to the poor prisoners in London xx markes, willing that these ij legacies be distributed by ij godly preachers.

The rest of all my landes, tenements, rentes, plate, Jewells, with other goodes, leases, chattles, horses, mares, geldinges, oxen, shepe, and all other stock and store, together with all mony, debts, now or hereafter dew, by bonde, covenant, or otherwise, my debts and legacies being payd, I geve to my sonne the Earle of Hertford, whom I make and appoint my sole executor, to see my debts payd and my legacies faithfully performed, and my funeralls discharged according to this my last will and testament. In witness whereof, to this my last will and testament, I have subscribed my name with myne own hande, and putte my seale this daye and yere abovesayd.

Signed, Anne Somerset.

Postscriptum. Memorandum, that there is no materiall enterlyning, but the gown geven to Mrs. Ashhurst, these wordes, 'lawfull English monie', and abowt the recitall of the goodes, tenements, leases, &c. Witnesses. Tho. Penney. Tho. Muffet. W. Clarke.

Endorsed. This was acknowledged and avowed by her Grace the Duchess of Somerset to be her last will and testament, we witnesses whose names are underwritten.

Tho. Penney. Tho. Muffet. W. Charke.[38]

Her full estate was assessed at an enormous nine thousand eight hundred and twenty nine pounds nineteen shillings and eight pence.

Anne Seymour died peacefully at Easter on 16 April 1587 at Hanworth with most of her family at her side. Anne was laid to rest in the chapel of St Nicholas in Westminster Abbey, at Elizabeth's wish, another sign of the royal favour which Anne enjoyed to the last. A magnificent memorial was erected to her memory on which she is declared to be 'a princess of noble lineage', paying tribute to her distant descend from King Edward III. Her memorial itself is colourful and stunning, projecting the exact image she had sought to maintain her entire life, that of a powerful and wealthy political manoeuvre and mother of a great dynasty. Almost certainly Anne commissioned and designed her own tomb and in the inscription she references her first husband, though not her second, and mentioned both her son Hertford and her grandson Beauchamp, making it clear that she had achieved her aim of continuing and restoring the Seymour dynasty. The full inscription reads:

> Heare lieth entombed the noble duchesse of Somerset, Anne, deere spouse unto the renowned prince Edward Duke of Somerset, Earle of Hertford, Viscount Beauchampe and Baron Seymour, Compaignon [Companion] of the most famous knightly Order of the Garter: uncle to King Edward the Sixt, Gouvernor of His Roial Person and most worthie Protector of all his realmes, dominions, and subiectes: Leiutenant Generall of all his armies: threasoror and Erle

> Marschall of England, Gouvernor and capitayne of the Isles of Guernsey and Jersey: under whose prosperous conduct, glorious victory hath ben so often and so fortunatly obteyned over the Scottes, vanquished at Edinburgh, Leth [Leith], and Musselborough Field.
>
> A princesse discended of noble lignage, beinge daughter of the worthie knight Sr Edward Stanhope, by Elizabeth his wyfe that was daughter of Sr Foulke Bourghchier Lord Fitzwarin, from whome our moderne earles of Bathe ar spronge, sonne was he unto Willm. Lord Fitzwarin, that was brother to Henry, Earle of Essex and Ihon [John] Lord Berners: whome Willm. their sire sometyme Earle of Ev in Normandy, begat Anne the sole heire of Thomas of Woodstock, Duke of Gloucester, yonger sonne to the mighty Prince, Kinge Edward the Third, and of his wyfe Aleanore, coheire unto the tenth Humphrey De Bohun that was Erle of Hereford, Essex and Northampton, High Constable of England.
>
> Many children bare this lady unto her Lord, of either sort: to witte Edward, Erle of Hertford, Henry, and a younger Edward: Anne, Countesse of Warwike, Margaret, Jane, Mary, Katherine, and Elizabeth. And with firme faith in Christ in most mylde maner renred she this life at XC yeres of age on Easter day, the sixtenth of Aprill Anno.M.CCCCC.LXXXVII.
>
> The Erle of Hertford, Edward her eldest sonne, in this dolefull dutie carefull and diligent, doth consecrate this monument to his deere parent: not for her honor wherewith lyvinge she did abounde and nowe departed flourisheth: but for the dutifull love he beareth her, and for his laste testification therof.[39]

Anne shares St Nicholas' chapel with her daughter, Jane, who had died in 1560, something which again perhaps she chose herself. A strong and remarkable woman, Anne had survived all of Henry VIII's wives, four Tudor monarchs and the execution of her husband, an almost impossible feat. Anne was the ultimate Tudor survivor.

Almost as soon as she was laid to rest, Anne Seymour began to suffer the fate of many powerful women, and writers and historians alike began to slander her. Quickly she became characterised as that of 'malevolent mischief maker who ruled her husband and successfully sought the death of her brother-in-law and brought down her own husband'.[40] She has been described by later historians as a harridan and the worst of all wicked women. I hope I have shown that Anne was none of those things, though neither was she a saint. Proud, ambitious and sometimes sharp, she was a real woman, flesh and blood who strove to further her faith and advance herself and her family, and in doing so made mistakes. Fiercely loyal to her friends and family and devoted to her husband and the Crown, Anne was a shrewd political manoeuvrer in her own right and a major force in religion and politics. It is time that she is recognised as such, and as the woman she really was.

Epilogue

It would not have pleased Anne or Edward to know that Catherine Fillol gets the last laugh in dynastic terms, even though she has all but been erased from history. After two hundred years, the line of Anne Stanhope's children failed and today it is the descendants of Catherine's children by Edward who hold the Dukedom of Hertford. I hope that would have pleased her.

Endnotes

Introduction

1. BL Stowe MS 1066. The date of 1551 is not incorrect, Somerset was using the old Julian calendar. The book would also be used by Somerset's daughter-in-law, Katherine Grey, when she was in the Tower between 1561 and 1563.
2. Foxe, *Acts and Monuments*, vol. VI, pp.293–5. See also: *Annales*, p.1026; *Diary of Henry Machyn*, p.14.
3. Wriothesley, Charles, *A Chronicle of England During the Reigns of the Tudors from AD 1485 to 1559*. Camden Society, p.65–66.
4. Ibid.
5. Ibid., p.14. See also: CSP Spain X, p.453.
6. Acts of the Privy Council (APC) IV, pp.465–6. See also: Robinson, *Original Letters*, vol. II, p.579.

Chapter 1. Three Families

The Seymours

1. St Maur, H., *Annals of the Seymours*. London, 1902, p.2.
2. Ibid., p.3.
3. Loades, D., *The Tudor Court*. London, 1985, p.65.
4. St Maur, p.3.
5. Ibid., p.4.
6. Lewis, Christopher, 'The Norman Settlement of Herefordshire under William I' in Brown, Reginald Allen (ed.), *Anglo-Norman Studies VII:*

Proceedings of the Battle Conference 1984, vol. VII. The Boydell Press, 1985, p.208.

7. Sanders, I. J., *English Baronies: A Study of Their Origin and Descent 1086–1327*. OUP: Oxford, 1960, p.27.
8. St Maur, p.5.
9. Pipe Roll 21 Henry II.
10. Cott MS 106 August 11.
11. St Maur, p.8. Her feast day falls on 20 July.
12. TVAS Archaeological report 'Church Row Farm, Frome Road, Rode, Somerset: An Archaeological Evaluation', July 2008. www.tvas.co.uk.
13. St Maur, p.8.
14. Calendar of the Close Rolls 1259–1261, pp.277 and 330.
15. St Maur, p.8.
16. MSS Dugdale.
17. Loades, p.25.
18. Jean le Bel, Nigel, E. (trans.), *The True Chronicles of Jean le Bel*. Woodbridge: Boydell Press, 2011, p.173.
19. MSS Dugdale.
20. Page, William (ed.), 'Houses of Augustinian Canons: The Priory of Stavordale' in *A History of the County of Somerset*, vol. 2. London, 1911, pp.139–141.
21. Baronage in the College of Arms, no.20, Vincent.
22. Giles 1889 1:10, pp.34–5.
23. Morgan and Wakeman, 1867, pp.10–11.
24. CChR 3:99. no.6 and no. 7; PRO Chancery Scutage Role 29 Henry III C 72/7 m.1.
25. CChR 3:105.
26. Dugdale, 1817–30, vol. 5, p.269, no.2.
27. CCR 1337–39, p.117.
28. Vincent MS Camden, quoted in St Maur, p.366.
29. St Maur, p.14.
30. Bruce, C., *The Wardens Of Savernake Forest*. London: Routledge and Kegan Paul, 1949, pp.310–2.
31. Loades, p.29.
32. St Maur, p.15.
33. Calendar of the Close Rolls 1483–1494, p.452.
34. Collins Peerage I, p.149.

35. Loades, p.35.
36. L&P I, ii, no.2575.
37. Norton, E., *Jane Seymour: Henry VIII's True Love*. Chalford: Amberley Publishing, 2009, p.11.
38. NMM Warship Histories: Rodger Safeguard of the Seas, pp. 476 and 483.
39. Spont, A. *Letters and Papers relating to the war with France 1512–13*, 1897, pp.27–33.
40. St Maur, p.18.
41. Loades, p.39.
42. McElroy, A., *Educating the Tudors*. Pen & Sword, 2023, p.2.
43. Ibid.

The Filliols

1. Scard, p.19.
2. Bryson, S., *Sexual Intercourse in Tudor Times*, 2015. www.tudorsociety.com.
3. Gristwood, S., *Blood Sisters: The Women Behind the Wars of the Roses*. New York: Basic Books, 2013, p.48.
4. Locke, Audrey, *The Seymour Family History and Romance*. London: Constable and Company Ltd, 1911, pp.5–6, 31–4, 74–5, 365.
5. The National Archives Website, Discovery: Mi D 4817; Nottingham University Library, Department of Manuscripts and Special Collections; GB 159 Mi – The Family and Estate Papers of the Willoughby Family, Lords Middleton, of Wollaton, Nottinghamshire, Middleton, Warwickshire and Birdsall, Yorkshire c.1150–c.1986; Mi D 4817 – Marriage settlement of Edward Willoughby and Anne, daughter of William Fyloll. http://discovery.nationalarchives.gov.uk/details/rd/18e47833-2dca-4ea5-aebb-a2e2f4976371.
6. Kentish, B. L., *Kelvedon and its Antiquities*. Phillimore and Co. Ltd: London and Chichester, 1974, p.20.
7. Ibid.
8. www.opcdorset.org.
9. Anne would later marry Edward Willoughby. The National Archives Website, Discovery: Mi D 4817; Nottingham University Library, Department of Manuscripts and Special Collections; GB 159 Mi – The Family and Estate Papers of the Willoughby Family, Lords Middleton,

of Wollaton, Nottinghamshire, Middleton, Warwickshire and Birdsall, Yorkshire, c.1150–c.1986; Mi D 4817 – Marriage settlement of Edward Willoughby and Anne, daughter of William Fyloll. http://discovery.nationalarchives.gov.uk/details/rd/18e47833-2dca-4ea5-aebb-a2e2f4976371.

10. Orme, N., *The Medieval Church: Your Guide to Religion and Worship in the Middle Ages*. www.historyextra.com.

The Stanhopes

1. Warnicke, Retha M., 'Anne Seymour [nee Stanhope], Duchess of Somerset (*c*.1510–1587), noblewoman and literary patron' in *Oxford Dictionary of National Biography*, 2004.
2. Licence of York, dated August 19, 1459.
3. Henry VII Inquisition 1493 refers to Edward Stanhope as both his cousin and heir apparent.
4. Noble, T. (ed.), *The History Gazetteer and Directory of the County of Derby*, Part II. Derby: Henry Mozley and Son, 1829, pp.163–4.
5. Ibid.
6. Pollard, A. F., 'Stanhope, Michael' in Lee, S. (ed.), *Dictionary of National Biography*, vol. 54. London: Smith, Elder and Co., 1898, p.21.
7. Bryson, S., *Childbirth in Medieval and Tudor Times*, 2015. www.tudorsociety.com.
8. Gunn, S. J., 'Brandon, Sir Thomas' in *Oxford Dictionary of National Biography*, online edition. OUP, 2004.
9. Norton, E., *The Hidden Lives of Tudor Women: A Social History*. New York: Pegasus Books, 2017, p.54.
10. Margaret Roper (trans.), *A devoute treatise upon the Pater Noster*, preface by Richard Hyde. London: Thomas Berthelet, 1531, pp.1–6.

Chapter 2. Edward and Catherine

1. L&P vol. 1, no. 3357.
2. CSP Venice vol. 2, no. 505.
3. CSP Venice vol. 2, no. 510.
4. Baumgartner, F. J., *Louis XII*. St Martin's Press: New York, 1996, p.143.

5. Ibid. and L&P vol. 1, no. 3357.
6. Masek, R., *Women of England: From Anglo-Saxon Times to the Present*. Archon Books: Hamden, 1979, p.141.
7. Norton, E., *Jane Seymour: Henry VIII's True Love*. Kindle edition, pp.184 and 493.
8. Foster, J., *Alumni Oxonienses 1500–1714*, vol. 4. Parker and Co., London and Oxford, 1892, p.1335.
9. Crumb, L., *Cromwell and the English Universities*, p.1.
10. Ibid., p.9.
11. L&P vol. 2, no. 3473; quoted in Loades, D., *The Seymours*, p.99.
12. Scard, M., p.19.
13. L&P Henry VIII Foreign and Domestic vol. 3, no. 1201.
14. Martin Luther's Declaration: www.luther.de.
15. L&P Henry VIII Foreign and Domestic vol. 3, no. 1201.
16. Ibid., no. 1297. See also BL MS 15387 f.88.
17. Ibid., nos. 1208 and 1210.
18. Ibid., no. 3288.
19. Gunn, S. J. 'The Duke of Suffolk's March on Paris in 1523' in *The English Historical Review,* 101, no. 400 (1986), pp.596–634. http://www.jstor.org/stable/571478.
20. Ibid. See also L&P Henry VIII Foreign and Domestic vol. 3, no. 3516.
21. *Oxford Dictionary of National Biography*, vol. 49, p.861.
22. Fox, J., *The Infamous Lady Rochford*, pp.28–9.
23. Ibid.
24. Loades, D., p.100.
25. They increased from 17/18 men per county to 30/40 men. See: Loades, D., *Politics and the Nation 1540–1660: Obedience, Resistance and Public Order*. London: Fontana Library, 1974, p.122.
26. Elton, G. R., *England Under the Tudors*. London: Putnam and Co. Ltd., 1959, p.418.
27. L&P Henry VIII Foreign and Domestic vol. 4, no. 1512.
28. Murphy, B., *Bastard Prince Henry VIII's Lost Son*, p.29.
29. Lloyd, Simon, 'William Longespee II: The Making of an English Crusading Hero (Part I)' in *Nottingham Medieval Studies*, 1991, 35: 41–69, p.42.
30. BL MS Egerton 2642 f.7.
31. Ibid.
32. CPR 1396–1399, p.334. Quoted in Amin, N., *The Beauforts*, p.38.

33. Ives, E., *Anne Boleyn*, p.265.
34. CSP Henry VIII vol. 4, p.135.
35. Loades, D., p.100.

Chapter 3. Catherine

1. Inquisition post mortem c.142/46/25 19 Henry VIII PRO.
2. Ibid.
3. www.folger.edu. Interview given June 22, 2021, A closer look at pregnancy, midwifery, and breastfeeding in the Tudor Period.
4. Weir, A., *The Six Wives of Henry VIII*; Denny, J., *Jane Seymour*.
5. Power, Eileen E., *Medieval English Nunneries 1275–1535*. Cambridge University Press, 1922, p.4.
6. Ibid., p.40.
7. Ibid., p.30. See also: *The Testamenta Vetusta* 1, p.74.
8. Valor Ecclesiastica i. 280.
9. Ibid.
10. Cal. Fine. R 1272–1307, no. 207.
11. Power, p.317.
12. Exeter Register Stapeldon, pp.317–8.
13. Power, p.138.
14. Ibid.
15. VCH Oxon. II, p.104.
16. VCH Yorkshire III, p.172.
17. Power, p.394.
18. Ibid., p.403.
19. Tes Ebor, p.262.
20. Liveing op-ed., pp.245–6.
21. Manus to Wolsey, 22 July 1528, no. 6516.
22. Scard, p.25.

Chapter 4. Anne

1. Tytler 1839, pp.51–2.
2. James, S. E., *Kateryn Parr: The Making of a Queen*. Aldershot: Ashgate Publishing, 1999, p.13.

3. Starkey, D., *The Six Wives of Henry VIII*, 2003, p.459.
4. Ives, E., *The Life and Death of Anne Boleyn: The Most Happy*. London: Wiley Blackwell, 2005.
5. Ibid.
6. Chapuys.
7. Hall, p.798.
8. Cranmer Letters p.245. See also Hall, E., p.804.
9. Ives, p.183.
10. L&P vol. 6, no. 63.
11. LP Foreign and Domestic Henry VIII vol. 19, part 1, 1544, p.620.
12. Frederick Madden (ed.), *Privy Purse expenses of the Princess Mary, Daughter of King Henry the Eight Afterwards Queen Mary*. London: William Pickering, 1831. As examples, pages 33, 46, 49, 57, 58, 97, 113, 143, 149, 184.
13. Ives, pp.260–1.
14. CSP 1558–9, no.1303, p.532.
15. Ives, p.279.
16. Ibid., p.284.
17. Ibid.
18. For example in a letter from John Husee to Lord Lisle, dated 13 January. LP Henry VIII January 1535, 11–20, no. 45.
19. Bush, M., 'The Lisle-Seymour Land disputes: A Study in Power and Influence in the 1530s' in *The Historical Journal*, vol. 9, 1966, pp.255–74.
20. Holinshed, 1557.
21. Heyman, P., Simons, L. and Cochez, C., 'Were the English Sweating Sickness and the Picardy Sweat caused by Hantavirus?' in *Viruses*, January 2014, pp.151–171. www.ncbi.nlm.nih.gov.

Chapter 5. Edward and Anne

1. L&P Henry VIII vol. 8, January–July 1535, March 1535, 1-10, p.361.
2. Fraser, A., *The Six Wives of Henry VIII*. London: Weidenfeld and Nicolson, 2009, p.235.
3. L&P vol. 9, no. 620.
4. Martinsen, *Queen Catherine Parr*, p.125.

5. Norton, E., *Jane Seymour*, p.41.
6. Ibid.
7. L&P vol. 10, no. 601.
8. Ives, E., *Anne Boleyn*, p.127.
9. Ibid.
10. L&P vol. 10, no. 915.
11. L&P vol. 10, no. 1047.
12. L&P vol. 10, no. 1058.
13. Norton, p.130.
14. APC June, Grants 1536, Pat.p.3.m.9.
15. St Maur, p.377.
16. Byrne, M. St. C., *The Lisle Letters*, vol. 4, p.139.
17. L&P vol 12, part 2, no. 973.
18. Quoted in MacKay, L., *Inside the Tudor Court: Henry VIII and His Six Wives Through the Eyes of Ambassador Chapuys*. Amberley Publishing, 2015, p.258.
19. Ibid.
20. L&P vol 10, no. 1369.
21. Haigh, C., p.144.

Chapter 6. Dynasty

1. L&P vol. 12; vol. 1, no. 483.
2. Madden, F., *Privy Purse Expense of Princess Mary*, pp.16–19.
3. Scard, p.43.
4. L&P vol. 11, no. 717.
5. Ibid., no. 780.
6. Serjeantson, R. M. and Adkins, W. R. D. (eds.), 'Houses of Cistercian Nuns: The Priory of Catesby', in *A History of the County of Northampton: Volume 2*. London, 1906. *British History Online* https://www.british-history.ac.uk/vch/northants/vol2/pp121-125.
7. L&P vol. 11, no. 5.
8. Lisle Letters vol. 4, p.144.
9. L&P vol. 12, part 2, no. 802.
10. *Wriothesley's Chronicle*, vol. 1, p.65.
11. Jackson, p.176.

12. L&P vol. 12, part 2, no. 939.
13. BM MS 6 133 f.87.
14. L&P vol. 2, part 2, no. 911.
15. Ibid.
16. Weir, A., *Why did Jane Seymour Die in childbed*? 2018. www.tudortimes.co.uk.
17. Ibid.
18. Merriman, R., *Life and Letters of Thomas Cromwell*, vol. 2, p.98.
19. Grants November 1547, no. 44.
20. L&P vol. 12, part 2, no. 1157.
21. L&P vol. 13, part 2, no. 1280, f.55.
22. Madden, p.46.
23. L&P vol. 12, part 1, no. 24.
24. L&P vol 13, part 2, no. 1280, f. 17.
25. L&P November 1538, no. 884.
26. *Lisle Letters*, pp.282 and 285.
27. Ibid.
28. Ibid., p.508.
29. Seymour, W., *Ordeal by Ambition*, p.125.
30. L&P vol. 14, part 1, 1539, no. 947.
31. Jackson, p.174.
32. L&P vol. 13, part 2, no. 1280, f. 17.
33. Ibid., no. 1018.
34. Jackson, p.7.
35. Scard, p.59.
36. Loades, p.114 quoting L&P vol. 14, part 2, no. 572.
37. L&P vol. 15, no. 21.
38. L&P vol. 12, part 2, no. 911.
39. King, J. N., Patterson, H. M. (ed)., 'Patronage and Piety: The Influence of Catherine Parr' in *Silent but for the word: Tudor Women as Patrons, translators and writers of religious works*. Kent: KUP, 1985, p.53.
40. Hosington, Brenda M., 'England's First Female-Authored Encomium: The Seymour Sisters' "Hecatodistichon" (1550) to Marguerite de Navarre. Text, Translation, Notes, and Commentary' in *Studies in Philology* 93, no. 2 (1996), pp.117–63.
41. King, p.53.
42. Becon, Thomas, Syre, J. (ed.), *The Early Works of Thomas Becon*, Cambridge: CUP, 1843, p.396.

Chapter 7. Anne

1. Warnicke, R., *Inventing the Wicked Women of Tudor England.* Quidditas, p.21. See also Soberton (2018, pp.39–40) where Soberton asserts that 'Anne Seymour joined Katherine Howard's household as an experienced lady-in-waiting but she did not establish a close relationship with her'.
2. PRO SP 1 167 and 163. Transcribed by Jennifer Rowley-Williams.
3. Scard, p.69.
4. L&P vol. 17, November 1542, no. 1067.
5. Ibid.
6. Ibid., nos. 1067, 1094 and 1215.
7. Parr, p.71.
8. Ibid.
9. L&P vol. 17, no 1212.
10. Weir, *Six Wives*, p.494.
11. Wilson, D., *The Queen and the Heretic.* Lion Books: London, 2018, p.131.
12. L&P vol.18, part 1, no. 418
13. Ibid., no. 873.
14. Porter, L., p.143.
15. James, *Kateryn Parr*, p.129.
16. Weir, pp.151–61.
17. PRO WARD 9/149 f. 136.
18. King, p.57.
19. Blatcher, M. (ed.), Report on the Manuscripts of the Most Honourable Marquess of Bath Preserved at Longleat Volume 4; Seymour Papers 1532–1686. London: Her Majesty's Stationery Office, p.99.
20. Foxe, J., *The Acts and Monuments of John Foxe: A New and complete edition.* Stehen, Reed, Cattkey: London, pp.553–4.
21. Franklin-Harkrider, *Women, Reform and Community*, p.49.
22. L&P, vol. 19, part 2, no. 688.
23. Mueller, *Katherine Parr the Complete works and Correspondence*, p.79.
24. L&P vol. 19, part 2, no. 688.
25. Scard, p.85.
26. Ibid., p.11.
27. Mueller, p.112.

28. Hall, pp.865–6.
29. L&P vol. 21, part 2, no. 360.
30. CSP Spain vol. 8, no. 130.

Chapter 8. The Queen's Lady

1. White, M., *Women Reformers of Early Modern Europe*. Fortress Press, 2022.
2. Foxe's *Book of Martyrs* is the earliest source for this quote and contains a woodcut showing Tindel's death.
3. Wilson, D., *The Queen and Heretic*. Lion Books: London, 2018, pp.134.
4. Matzat, p.126.
5. Beilin, 1996, pp.127 and 187.
6. Scard, p.106; L&P Henry VIII vol. 21, part 1 July 1–5, no. 1181.
7. Quoted in Soberton, 2018, p.44.
8. Matzat, p.124.
9. James, *Kateryn Parr*. Digital Location 4386.
10. Watt, D., *Oxford National Biography*. Oxford: OUP, 2004.
11. James, BL 4415.
12. Ibid., p.236.
13. Ibid.
14. Ibid.
15. Ibid., p.258.
16. L&P Henry VIII, vol. 21, part 2, no. 1546.
17. Ibid., nos. 21, 31, 128.
18. CSP Spain vol. VIII, no. 325.
19. Ibid., vol. VI, pp.533–4.
20. Ibid.
21. L&P vol. 21, part 2, no. 493.
22. Scard, p.110.
23. Ibid., p.11.
24. Pollard, *England Under Protector Somerset*, p.17.
25. Ibid., p.18.
26. L&P vol. 21, part 2, no. 662.
27. APC Dasent J.R., 46 Volumes 1890–1964, vol. 2, p.10.
28. L&P vol. 21, part 2, no. 752.
29. Weir, p.496.
30. L&P vol. 21, part 2, no. 760.

Chapter 9. Fight the Good Fight

1. NRO FM c.21–7 July 1549.
2. L&P vol. 21, part 2, no. 760.
3. CSP Spain vol. IX, p.100 and APC II 1549, pp. 3–6.
4. Nichols, J. G., 'The Second Patent appointing Edward Duke of Somerset Protector' in *Archaeologia*, 1844, vol. 30.
5. CSP Spain IX, p.19.
6. CSP Foreign Edward VI 1547–1553, no. 6.
7. Ibid., no. 8.
8. Nichols, J. G (ed.), *A Biographical Memoir of Edward VI.* London: Nichols and sons, 1857 p.ccxcv.
9. Scard, p.145.
10. Haynes, S., *Collections of State Papers Relating to the Affairs of the Reign of King Henry VIII, King Edward VI, Queen Mary and Queen Elizabeth, From the Year 1542–1570, Left by William Cecil Lord Burghley at Hatfield House*. London, 1740, p.96.
11. Tallis, N., *Young Elizabeth*, 2024, p.124.
12. Scard, p.159.
13. Foxe vol. 6, p.36.
14. CSP Spain vol. IX, p.50.
15. Haynes, p.102.
16. CSP Spain vol. IX, p.340.
17. Mueller, *Katherine Parr*, p.135.
18. Tallis, p.126.
19. James, p.269.
20. Mueller, p.133.
21. Ibid., p.146.
22. Ibid.
23. Warnicke, p.92.
24. Madden, p.200.
25. Mueller, p.130–131. Independent author and scholar, Sylvia Barbara Soberton, asserts that Katherine 'blamed Anne, whom she believed influenced her husband'. Soberton, 2018, p.51.
26. Ibid., p.141.
27. Warnicke, p.92.
28. NA SP10/1 f.41.
29. Mueller, p.140–41.

30. Quoted in Scard, p.195.
31. Warnicke, p.90.

Chapter 10. Anne

1. CSP Edward VI vol. 2, pp. 96–7.
2. Scard, p.177.
3. Ibid., p.182.
4. CSP Edward VI, no. 29.
5. Battlefields Trust Report UK FOC, no. 280.
6. Scard, p.178.
7. Bain, J., CSP Scotland 1547–1563, vol. 1. Edinburgh and NRS Arrans Household Book E 31/9 ff.57-9, 1898.
8. Philips, G., *The Anglo-Scottish Wars 1513–1550*. Boydell Press, 1999, pp.191–92.
9. Philips, G., *The Anglo-Scottish Wars: Battle of Pinkie Cleugh*. Boydell Press, 1999. www.history.net.
10. Philips, G., *The Anglo-Scottish Wars 1513–1550*. Boydell Press, 1999, p.196.
11. William Patten, 'The expedition into Scotland 1548' in *Fragments of Scottish History*, Layell, J.G (ed.), 1798.
12. The Scottish Chronicles record the lists of the dead, for example in the Chronicle of Lindsay of Pitscottie, *History of Scotland*, 1728, p.195. See also: Paul J.B., *Accounts of the Treasurer of Scotland*, vol. 9. Edinburgh, 1911, p.140.
13. CSP Spain 1547–1549, vol. 9, pp.150–153 contains an account of the battle.
14. BL MS 22047.
15. CSP Scotland vol. 1, Edinburgh, 1898, p.102, no. 207.
16. Patten entry dated 18 September 1547.
17. CPR II pp.27–29.
18. Mueller, J. A. (ed.), *The Letters of Stephen Gardiner*. Cambridge, CUP, 1933, p.xxiv.
19. Heylyn, Peter, *Ecclesia Restaurata: The History of the Reformation of the Church of England*, vol. 1. Cambridge: CUP, 1849.
20. Sander, N., *The Rise and Growth of the Anglican Schism*. London: Bruns and Oates, 1877.
21. Hayward, J., Barrett and Beer (eds.), *The Life and Raigne of King Edward the Sixth*. Kent State University Press, 1993.

22. James, D., *Art and Humanities*, p.6. Soberton (2018, p.56) argues that Anne now 'believed that she was the most important woman in the kingdom' which naturally led to tensions.
23. Tallis, p.136.
24. Ibid., p.124.
25. Haynes, *State Papers*, p.99.
26. Ibid.
27. CSP 1542–1570, p.99.
28. Norton quotes Tallis, p.134.
29. Tallis, p.134.
30. CSP 1542–1570, p.99.
31. LP Henry VIII vol. 18, part 1, no. 66.
32. St Clare, *Lisle Letters*, vol. 3, p.378.
33. Russell, G., *Young Damned and Fair: The Life of Catherine Howard, Fifth Wife of Henry VIII*, p.238.
34. CSP Spain vol. IX. 23 February 1548.
35. Haynes, p.96.
36. Tallis, p.142.
37. Warnicke, p.26.
38. Ibid.
39. CSP Domestic 1547–1580, no. 14.
40. CSP 10/3 f. 15: 20 January 1548.
41. Mueller, pp.168 and 170.
42. Ibid., p.173.
43. MacLean, *The Life of Sir Thomas Seymour*, p.67.
44. Matzat, p.142.
45. Warnicke, p.22.
46. Ibid., p.98.

Chapter 11. Edward

1. Scard, p.234.
2. Mueller, J., *Stephen Gardiner and the Tudor Reaction*. London, 1926, pp.173–180.
3. Scard, p.220.
4. Bush, M. L., *The Government of Protector Somerset*. Montreal: McGill Queen's University Press, 1975, p.104.

5. Seeger Hampson, M. R., *Thomas Becon and the English Reformation: The Sick Man's Salve and the Protestantism of English Popular Piety*. Dissertations, Thesis and Masters Projects, William and Mary Paper 1539625996, 1995.
6. Ibid. p.18.
7. Willes, M., *The Making of the English Gardener*, 2011.
8. Robinson, *Original Letters* vol. 1, p.69.
9. Scard, p.221.
10. Songes, pp.102–103, 143, 145.
11. Letter from Jane Seymour to Bucer and Phagius, 12 June 1549, Syon. Original Letters Parker Society 53, 1846, no. 2.
12. Letter to Anne Seymour, 15 July 1549, Geneva. Original Letters Parker Society 53, 1846 no. 703.
13. Ibid.
14. Robinson, pp.702–3.
15. Ibid., p.702.
16. Westfall, S., p.278.
17. Stowe, J., *Anne's London*, 1631, p.595.
18. Sir Thomas Smith's defence of his conduct and character. Address to the Duchess of Somerset, p.126.
19. Bindoff, S., *The House of Commons 1509–1558*, vol. 1. Boydell and Brewer London, 1982, p.464.
20. Scard, p.242.
21. Summerson, J., *Architecture in Britain 1530–1830*. Fourth Edition, 1963, pp.347–349.
22. Somerset House and King's College in *Old and New London* vol. 2, 1878, pp. 89–95.
23. Needham, R. and Webster, A., *Somerset House Past and Present*, 1905, p.47.
24. Ibid.
25. Jackson, Canon J. E., 'The Seymours of Wolf Hall' in *Wiltshire Archaeological Magazine*, vol. 15.
26. Needham and Webster, pp.46–51.
27. Ibid., p.50.
28. Literary Remains of Edward VI, vol. 1, cxi.
29. Bowden, C. M. K., *Cecil Mildred, Lady Burghley*. OUP Dictionary of National Biography, 2008.
30. Alford, S., *Burghley William Cecil and the Court of Elizabeth I*. New Haven: Yale University Press, 2008, p.36.

31. Croft, P., 'Mildred, Lady Burghley: The Matriarch', in Alford (ed.), *Kingship and Politics in the Reign of* Edward VI. Cambridge, 2002, p.284.
32. Loades, *Dudley John*. Oxford Dictionary of National Biography. Jane Dudley was believed to be 'infected' by reform at the same time as Anne Seymour (see Soberton, 2018, p.43 and p.104).
33. Barrett, L., *Northumberland: The political career of John Dudley Earl of Warwick and Duke of Northumberland*. Kent: Kent University Press, 1973, p.68.
34. Alford, p.36.
35. Strype, J., *The Life of the Learned Sir John Cheke*, 1821, p.46.

Chapter 12. Edward Versus Thomas

1. Haynes State Papers, p.102.
2. Ibid., p.73.
3. Ibid.
4. Ibid., p.72.
5. Tallis, p.150.
6. Haynes State Papers, p.70.
7. Ibid., p.80.
8. HMC Salisbury, p.55.
9. Haynes State Papers, p.80.
10. Ibid., p.69.
11. Alford, S., *Kingship and Politics in the Reign of Edward VI*. Cambridge, 2002, p.92.
12. MacLean, p.60.
13. Primary sources are cited at www.jamesgray2.me.
14. Will of Richard Page PROB 11.34.
15. www.clivefarahar.com/book/5319/hertford-edward-seymour-earl-of-1500-1552.
16. Tallis, p.152.
17. Norton, E., *The Temptation of Elizabeth Tudor*, pp.226–9.
18. PRO State Papers FO.44.
19. APC vol. 2, p.238.
20. CSP Edward VI 1457–1553, no. 111.
21. Beer, B. L., 'A critique of the Protectorate: An unpublished letter of Sir William Paget to the Duke of Somerset' in *Huntington Library Quarterly,* vol. 34 no. 3, 1971, pp.277–283.

22. CSP Edward VI 10/6/12 quoted in Scard, p.266.
23. CSP Spain vol. IX p.332.
24. Ibid.
25. Haynes State Papers, p.74.
26. Ibid., p.90.
27. SPO MSS Edward VI vol. VI, no. 2–4.
28. Scard, p.267.
29. Haynes State Papers, pp.106–107.
30. Scard, p.273.
31. APC vol. 2, p.246.
32. Ibid., p.247.
33. Ibid. Pages 247–256 list the text of the document in full.
34. Ibid., p.247.
35. Ibid., p.257.
36. Ibid., p.259.
37. Ibid., p.260.
38. Ibid.
39. Ibid.
40. Ibid.
41. Ibid.
42. Ibid., p.261.
43. Ibid., pg.262.
44. Porter, L., *Katherine Parr.*
45. Warnicke, p.92.
46. Ibid., p.93.
47. Hugh Latimer, *Secret Sermons*, p.143.
48. Foxe, p.283.
49. Warnicke, p.93.
50. Meuller, p.187.
51. Ibid., p.185.

Chapter 13. I Predict a Riot

1. STC 3287, 3815-6, 4080, 4435, 5195, 6082, 11383-4, 11802, etc.
2. CSP vol. 9, 10 September 1539.
3. PRO PROB. 11/31 FO. 232. See also: Scard, p.281 for further discussion.

4. Blayney, P. M. W., *The Printing and the Printers Book of Common Prayer 1549–1561*. Kindle Edition.
5. Ibid., Location 842.
6. CSP Spain vol. IX, pp.375–382.
7. Hooker, pp.8–9.
8. Pocock, N., *Troubles Connected with the Prayer Book of 1549*. Camden Society, 1884, p.8.
9. Hooker, p.44.
10. Ibid., p.45–46.
11. Rowse, A. L., *Tudor Cornwall*. Macmillan, 1969, p.268.
12. Stoyle, M. A., *A Murderous Midsummer: The Western Rebellion of 1549*. Yale: YUP. 2022.
13. Pocock, p.24.
14. Scard, p.302.
15. Cox vol. 2, pp.164–187.
16. For an example see: NRO FM c. 21 12 March etc.
17. Richardson, E. C., 'Some financial expedients of Henry VIII' in *The Economic History Review*, no. 1, vol. 7, 1954, pp.33–48.
18. Deng, S., 'The Great Debasement and its aftermath' in *Coinage and State Formation in Early Modern English Literature*. Palgrave MacMillan: New York, 2011, p.1.
19. Tudor Royal Proclamations, no. 339–341.
20. Pocock, p.29.
21. Literary Remains, p.228.
22. SP Domestic Edward VI, vol. VIII, p.32.
23. The Western Rebellion, p.393.
24. www.thehistoryofengland.co.uk. Robert Kett's Petition translation.
25. Shagan, *Protector Somerset and the 1549 Rebellions*, p.59.
26. PRO SP 10/8/4.
27. Scard, p.308.
28. Pocock, p.23.
29. Hooker, pp.87–88.
30. Rowse, p.132.
31. Hooker, pp.89–90.
32. Rowse, p.277.
33. Skidmore, C., *Edward VI*, p.124.
34. Hooker, p.98.
35. Scard, p.312.

36. Youngs, J., *The South Western Rebellions of 1549*, p.17.
37. Strype, *Ecclesiastical Memorials*, vol. II, p.425.
38. Skidmore, p.127.
39. Ibid., p.128.
40. Ibid.

Chapter 14. The Tower

1. CSP Spain vol. IX, p.429.
2. Ibid.
3. Warnicke, p.91.
4. Ibid., p.81.
5. Frere, W. H., *Visitation article and injunctions of the period of the Reformation 1536–1558*. Longman, Green and Co. 1910, pp.177–8. See also: Erasmus, D., *Paraphrases on Romans and Galatian*, vol. 42 of the Collected Works of Erasmus. University of Toronto, 1984, p.30.
6. Walter, L., *A Briefe Collection of all such texts of the scripture … Whereunto are added two sermons by Martin Luther*. London, S. Mierdman for Walter Lynne dwelling on Somers haye by Billings Gate, 1549, p.2.
7. Ibid., p.2
8. Ibid.
9. Nicholas Lesse (trans.), *A Work of the Predestination of Saints written by the famous Doctor St. Augustine*. London: Aldersgate Street the widow of John Hertford for Walter Lynne, p.2.
10. PPP, p.111
11. Hannay, M., *Philips Phoenyx: Mary Sidney Countess of Pembroke*. Oxford: OUP, 1990, p.4.
12. CSP Spain vol. X, p.98.
13. Malkiewicz, A. J., An eye witness accounts of the coup d'etat of 1549 in the *English Historical Review*, vol. 70, no. 277, October 1955, pp.600–609.
14. Scard, p.317.
15. Merriman, M., *The Rough Wooings*. Tuckwell, 2000, pp.313–314.
16. CSP Scotland vol. 1, Edinburgh, 1898, pp.165–166.
17. COSP Scotland, p.288. no. 1111.
18. Urwin, 2006, p.80.
19. BL MS 48126 F. 7–8.

20. Scard, p.325
21. Skidmore, p.137.
22. Russell, G., *The Palace*, 2023, p.115.
23. CSP Spain vol. IX, p.457.
24. APC vol. II, p.332.
25. Prosser, G. F., *Select Illustrations Of the County of Surrey*. 1828.
26. Raleigh, W., *The Works of Sir Walter Raleigh*, p.175.
27. Russell, p.115.
28. Skidmore, p.141.
29. Ibid.
30. CSP Domestic 1547–1549, p.457.
31. Ibid.
32. Pocock, p.121.
33. CSP Domestic 1547–1549, pp.458–460.
34. Scard, p.332.
35. Letters of Sir William Paget, p.33.
36. PRO SP 10/10/18 f.48 and 48v.
37. PRO SP 10/9 f.30r-30v.
38. Bodleian Rawlinson MS D 1087 f. 17c-18r. Quotes in John Stowe's *Annals of England*, 1615, p.598.
39. BL Harley MS 353 f. 76-77.
40. Scard, p.334.
41. NRO MS f M c.21–28 October 1549.
42. Warnicke, p.96.
43. BL Harleian MS 353 f. 77.
44. BL Add MS 48126 f. 13-13v.
45. Skidmore, p.146.
46. Wingfield, M. E., *Muniments of the Anglo-Saxon family of Wingfield*. Mitchell and Hughes, 1904, pp.29-30.
47. Scard, p.337.
48. Skidmore, p.147.
49. Ibid.
50. BL MS Cotton Caligula B VIII f. 410.
51. *Greyfriars Chronicle*, p.64.
52. Ibid.
53. CSP Spain vol. IX, 19 December 1549.
54. Ibid. For a full discussion of these events, see Soberton, 2018, pp.105–109.

Chapter 15. What to do with Edward Seymour?

1. Scard, pp.343–344.
2. Skidmore, p.149.
3. *King Edward's Chronicle*, p.26.
4. Skidmore, p.149.
5. Ibid.
6. Tudor Royal Proclamations I, 1549, no. 353.
7. Chisholm. H. (ed.), *Encyclopaedia Cambridge*. CUP, 1911, p.238.
8. CSP Spain vol. IX p.468.
9. Stowe's *Annals*, pp.1015–1018.
10. Hume, M.A., *A Chronicle of King Henry VIII*, pp.190–192.
11. Letters of Philip Scudamore to Sir Philip Hoby, vol. 39. Camden Fourth Series, p.104.
12. www.hrp.org.uk. Yeoman Warders.
13. CSP Spain vol. X, 18 January 1549.
14. PRO SP 10.10.2.
15. Skidmore, p.157.
16. Scudamore Papers, p.91.
17. CSP Spain vol. X, pp.13 and 28.
18. Scudamore Papers, vol. 39, Camden Fourth Series, p.118.
19. Original Letters relative to the English reformation, vol. 1:2, letter no. 2.
20. APC vol. III, pp.10–11.
21. Hosington, B., *Anne, Margaret and Jane Seymour*, p.ix.
22. Ibid., p.x
23. Ibid., p.xi.
24. CSP Spain, 8 March 1550.
25. Knighton, 1992, p.163.
26. Warnicke, p.98.
27. *Literary Remains*, vol. 2, p.255.
28. CPR Edward Vi vol. 3, pp.339 and 430–432.
29. CSP Spain vol. x p.109.
30. Ibid.
31. Literary Remains, vol. 2, p.273.
32. Haydes, E. G., *Islands of the Vale*. Smithe, Edler and Co: London, 1908, pp.136–7.

33. Loades, 1996, p.224.
34. Jordan, W. K. (ed.), *The Chronicle and Political Papers of Edward VI*, pp.32–33.
35. CSP Spain vol. X, 17 June 1550.
36. Literary Remains, vol. 2, pp.273–275.
37. CPR Spain vol. 1, pp.376–380.

Chapter 16. Power and Patronage

1. APC vol. III, p.43.
2. Allen, A. W., *The Eucharistic Debate in Tudor England: Thomas Cranmer, Stephen Gardiner and the English Reformation*, p.7. The book offers an in-depth analysis of the issues between and positions of the two men.
3. Becke, Edmon, *A brefe confutacion of this most detestable, and anabaptistical opinion, that Christ dyd not take hys flesh of the blessed Vyrgyn Mary, nor any corporal substaunce of her body: for the maintenaunce whereof Jhone Bucher, otherwise called Jhone of Kent was burned in Smythfyelde, the .ii. day of May.* 1550. (Available to read on Google Books.)
4. Ibid.
5. Warnicke, p.100.
6. Ibid. p.99.
7. Ibid.
8. Ibid.
9. APC vol. III, pp.54–5.
10. Stowe's *Annals*, p.1021.
11. APC vol. III, p.130.
12. Ibid., p.132.
13. Ibid.
14. Ibid., p.142.
15. Ibid.
16. Ibid., p.147.
17. Skidmore p.177.
18. CSP Spain vol. X, p.186.
19. Skidmore, p.178.
20. CSP Foreign no. 489.

21. Skidmore, p.179.
22. SCP Spain vol. X, pp.205–209 and 410–411.
23. Ibid., p.219.
24. Warnicke, p.93.
25. APC vol. III, pp.215 and 248.
26. Skidmore, p.190.
27. Jordan, *Edward VI: The Threshold of Power*, p.76.
28. APC vol. III, pp.244–246.
29. CSP Spain vol. X, pp.161–167.
30. Bridden, S., *London and The Reformation*, 1989, p.508.
31. CSP Spain vol. X p.291.
32. Scard, p.372
33. HMC Bathe vol. 4, p.114.
34. Skidmore, p.214.
35. Scard, p.171.
36. *Edward VI Chronicle*, pp.87–88.
37. Jordan, p.73.
38. Haigh, *Reformation and Resistance,* pp.141–142.
39. *Edward VI Chronicle*, p.60.
40. CSP Spain vol. X, p.381. See also: Loades, 1996, p.180–181.
41. *Literary Remains*, vol. 2, p.353.
42. Ibid., p.354.
43. Literary Remains, vol. 2, p.354.
44. Ibid.
45. Ibid., 18 October 1551.
46. Ibid., pp.354–355.
47. Warnicke, p.98.
48. Robinson, p.342.
49. Ibid., pp.339–342.
50. Ibid., p.354.
51. Ibid. p.341.
52. Warnicke, p.100.

Chapter 17. Edward

1. Nichols, Anne, Duchess of Somerset 373–374 in Henry Ellis (ed.), *Original Letters, Illustrative of England.* London: Harding, Triphook and Leonard, 1836.

2. www.medieval.ucdavis.edu. Help in determining these figures was provided by Tudor historian and author, Amy McElroy.
3. Warnicke, p.100, note no. 107.
4. Literary Remains, vol. 2, p.358.
5. CSP Spain vol. X, pp.386–393.
6. Ibid.
7. Ibid.
8. Literary Remains, vol. 2, p.356.
9. CSP Spain vol. X, 10 October 1551.
10. Scard, p.383.
11. Chisholm, p.328.
12. Scard, p.384.
13. Skidmore, p.215.
14. *Literary Remains*, vol. 2, p.370.
15. Ibid., p.371.
16. Ibid.
17. Ibid.
18. Ibid., p.373.
19. Skidmore, p.217.
20. CSP Spain vol. X, p.407.
21. Ibid.
22. Skidmore, p.217.
23. CSP Spain vol. X, pp.407–409.
24. Feuillerat, *Revels*, p.47.
25. CSP Spain vol. X, pp.436–443.
26. BL Stowe MS 1066.
27. Skidmore, p.221.
28. BL Cotton Charter IV 17.
29. Ibid.
30. Ibid.
31. CSP Spain vol. X. pp.452–453.
32. Ibid.

Chapter 18. Anne

1. APC vol. 3, pp.465–466.
2. CSP Spain vol. X, p.453.

3. Pollard, 1898, p.22.
4. Loades, 1996, p.190.
5. APC vol. 4, p.90.
6. Nichols, J. G., 'Anne Duchess of Somerset' in *Gentleman's Magazine*, April 1845, pp.373–374.
7. PROB 1/29 No. 3137788.
8. APC vol. 4, pp.656–666.
9. Strype, vol. 2, pp.254–255.
10. Warnicke, p.24.
11. APC vol. 5, no. 29. Anne Seymour had regained custody of her children in 1553 (Soberton, 2018, p.132).
12. Wilson, 1981. p.67.
13. Warnicke, p.102.
14. NA Longleat Manuscripts SE/VOL IV/32, 7 March 1555.
15. Warnicke, p.100.
16. Ibid.
17. CSP Domestic 1566–1579, p.448.
18. Nichols, p.374.
19. Blatcher, *Newdigate, Francis*, p.126.
20. De Lisle, L., *The Sister Who Would be Queen*. London: Harper Press 2017.
21. CSP Domestic 1547–1580, p.174.
22. Ibid., p.184.
23. Ibid., p.236.
24. Ibid.
25. Blatcher, pp.125–126.
26. Ibid., p.127.
27. Nichols, p.380.
28. Karel Van Mander, Miedema, Hessel (ed.), *Lives of the Illustrious Netherlandish and German Painters*. Doornspijk, 1994, p.358.
29. www.folgerpedia.folger.edu. 1577.
30. Warnicke, p.102.
31. Nichols, p.380.
32. Warnicke, p.103.
33. Ibid.
34. Nichols, pp.374–375.
35. Warnicke, p.103.

36. Lavater, Ludwig, *The Book of Ruth Expounded in Twenty Eight Sermons Published in Latin and Translated by Ephraim Pagitt.* London, Robert Palgrave, 1586.
37. Nichols, p.375.
38. Transcribed from Burghley Papers MS Lands 50. Art. 90.
39. Transcribed from Anne Seymour's tomb in Westminster Abbey. See also: www.westminster-abbey.org. For a full account of Anne's funeral and burial, see Soberton, 2018, pp.256–258.
40. James, 2019, p.2.

Select Bibliography

Primary Sources

BL Add. MS 48126 f.13-13v.
BL Cotton MS 106.
BL Cotton Caligula B VIII F. 410.
BL MS Egerton 2642 F. 7.
BL Harley MS 353 F. 76-77.
BL Stowe MS 1066.
College of Arms No 20. Vincent.
MSS Dugdale.
NRO FM c.21-27 July 1549.
NRO MS F.M 21-28 October 1549.
Pipe Roll 21 (Henry II).
PRO PROB 11//31 FO. 232.
PRO Chancery Scutage Roll 29 Henry III C7 2/7 m.1.
PRO State Papers F. 44.
PRO SP 1 163 and 167.
PRO WARD 9/149 f. 136.
SPO MSS Edward VI Vol. VI No. 2-4.

Printed Primary Sources

Acts and Monuments of John Foxe, Rev. J. Pratt (ed.) in 8 vols. London, *c.*1877.

Acts of the Privy Council of England (APC), J. R. Dasent (ed.) in 46 vols. London,
1890–1964.

'A Journal of Matters of State' in *Religion, Politics and Society in Sixteenth-Century England*, I. W. Archer (ed.). Cambridge, 2003.

'An epistle or exhortation to unity and peace' in *The Complaynt of Scotland*, J. A. H. Murray (ed.). London, 1872.

Calendar of Close Rolls, Henry VII in 2 vols. London, 1955–63.

Calendar of Letters, Despatches and State Papers, Spanish, G. A. Bergenroth *et al.* (eds.) in 13 vols. London, 1862–1954.

Calendar of the Patent Rolls, Henry VII in 2 vols. London, 1914–16.

Calendar of Patent Rolls for the reign of Edward VI in 6 vols. London, 1924–29.

Calendar of State Papers: Domestic Series, of the reign of Edward VI, 1547–1553, C. S. Knighton (ed.). London, 1992.

Calendar of State Papers, Foreign series, of the reign of Edward VI, 1547–1553, W. B. Turnbull (ed.). London, 1861.

Calendar of the State Papers relating to Scotland and Mary Queen of Scots, J. Bain *et al.* (eds.) in 13 vols. Edinburgh, 1898–1969.

Calendar of State Papers, Venetian, R. Brown *et al.* (eds.) in 38 vols. London, 1864–1947.

Chronicle of the Grey Friars of London, J. G. Nichols (ed.). London, 1852.

Chronicle of Henry VIII of England, M. A. S. Hume (ed.). London, 1889.

Collection of State Papers relating to affairs in the reigns of King Henry VIII, King Edward VI, Queen Mary and Queen Elizabeth, 1542–1570, of William Cecil at Hatfield House, S. Haynes (ed.). London, 1740.

The Early Works of Thomas Becon, J. Ayre (ed.). Cambridge, 1843.

Foxe, J., *Narratives of the Days of the Reformation*, J. G. Nichols (ed.). London, 1859.

Grafton, R., *Grafton's Chronicle*. London, 1809.

Hall, E., *Chronicle: Containing the History of England*. London, 1809.

Hayward, J., *The Life and Raigne of King Edward the Sixth*. Ohio, USA, 1993.

Historical Manuscripts Commission, Calendar of the Manuscripts of the Marquis of Bath at Longleat House in 5 vols. London, 1904–80.

Historical Manuscripts Commission, *Report on the Records of the City of Exeter*. London, 1916.

Holinshed, R., *Chronicles of England, Scotland and Ireland* in 6 vols. London: J. Johnson, 1807.

Jean le Bel, Nigel, E. (trans.), *The True Chronicles of Jean le Bel*. Woodbridge: Boydell Press, 2011.

Journals of the House of Lords, 1509–1577. London, 1771.
Letters and Papers, Foreign and Domestic of the Reign of Henry VIII, J. S. Brewer *et al.* (eds.) in 21 vols. 1965.
Letters of John Calvin, J. Bonnett (ed.) in 2 vols. Edinburgh, 1855–57.
'Letters of William, Lord Paget of Beaudesert' in *Camden Miscellany*, vol. XIII, 4th series, B. L. Beer (ed.). London, 1974.
'The Letters of Richard Scudamore to Sir Philip Hoby, September 1549–March 1555' in *Camden Miscellany*, vol. XXX, S. Brigden (ed.). London, 1990.
The Lisle Letters: An Abridgement, Muriel St. Clare Byrne (ed.). London, 1983.
Literary Remains of King Edward VI, J. G. Nichols (ed.) in 2 vols. London, 1857.
Machyn, H., *The Diary of Henry Machyn, Citizen and Merchant-Taylor of London*, J. G. Nichols (ed.). London, 1848.
Madden, F. *Privy Purse Expenses of the Princess Mary*. London, 1831.
Margaret Roper (trans.), *A devoute treatise upon the Pater Noster*, preface by R. Hyde. London: Thomas Berthelet 1531.
Original Letters Illustrative of English History, H. Ellis (ed.), 1st series, 3 vols. London, 1824.
Original Letters Relating to the English Reformation, Rev. H. Robinson (ed.) in 2 vols, Cambridge, 1846–47.
Patten, W. 'The expedition into Scotland of the most worthily fortunate prince Edward Duke of Somerset' in *An English Garner* in 8 vols. London, 1877–96.
Ponet, J., *A Short Treatise of Politike Power*. Amsterdam, 1972, facsimile of 1556 edition.
Sermons of Hugh Latimer, G. E. Corrie (ed.). Cambridge, 1844.
State Papers: King Henry the Eighth, A. Strahan *et al.* (eds.) in 11 vols. London, 1830–52.
Statutes of the Realm, in 10 vols. London, 1810–28.
'The Travels and Life of Sir Thomas Hoby' in *Camden Miscellany*, vol. X, E. Powell (ed.). London, 1902.
Troubles connected with the Prayer Book of 1549, N. Pocock (ed.). London, 1884.
Tudor Royal Proclamations, P. L. Hughes and J. F. Larkin (eds.) in 3 vols. New York, 1964.
Wriothesley, C., *A Chronicle of England During the Reigns of the Tudors from A.D. 1485–1559*. A Camden Society Publication.

Secondary Sources

Beer, B. L., *Rebellion and Riot: Popular Disorder in England During the Reign of Edward VI.* Kent, Ohio, 1982.

Beer, B. L., 'The Commoyson in Norfolk, 1549' in *The Journal of Medieval and Renaissance Studies*, 6 (1), 1976, pp.73–99.

Beer, B. L., 'A Critique of the Protectorate: An Unpublished Letter of Sir William Paget to the Duke of Somerset' in *Huntingdon Library Quarterly*, 34 (3) 1971, pp.277–283.

Bindoff, S. T., *The House of Commons 1509–1558* in 3 vols. London, 1982.

Bruce, C., *The Wardens of Savernake Forest.* Routledge and Paul, 1949, pp.310–312.

Burnet, G. A., *History of the Reformation of the Church of England* in 2 vols. London, 1681, 1683.

Bush, M. L., *The Government Policy of Protector Somerset.* London, 1975.

Bush, M. L., 'Protector Somerset and Requests' in *The Historical Journal*, 17 (3) 1974, pp.451–464.

Bush, M. L., 'The Lisle-Seymour Land Disputes: A Study of Power and Influence in the 1530s' in *The Historical Journal*, 9 (3), 1966, pp.255–724.

Demen, P., 'The Seymour Sisters Elegizing Female Attachment' in *The Sixteenth Century Journal*, 30 (2), 1999, pp.343–65.

Dent, E., *Annals of Winchcombe and Sudeley.* London, 1877.

Dictionary of National Biography in 22 vols. London, 1998.

Foster, J., *Alumni Oxonienses: the Members of the University of Oxford, 1500–1714* in 4 vols. Oxford, 1892.

Gasquet, F. A. and Bishop, E., *Edward VI and the Book of Common Prayer.* London, 1890.

Gristwood, S., *Blood Sisters: The Women Behind the Wars of the Roses.* New York, 2013.

Haigh, C., *English Reformations: Religion, Politics and Society Under the Tudors*. Oxford, 1995.

Ives, E.W., 'Henry VIII's Will: The Protectorate Provisions of 1546–7' in *The Historical Journal*, 37 (4), 1994, pp.901–914.

Ives, E., *The Life and Death of Anne Boleyn: The Most Happy*. London: Wiley Blackwell, 2005.

Jackson, J. E. 'Wulfhall and the Seymours' in *Wiltshire Archaeological and Natural History Magazine*, 15, 1875, pp.140–207.

James, S. E. 'A Tudor Divorce. The Marital History of William Parr, Marquess of Northampton' in *Transactions of the Cumberland and Westmorland Antiquarian and Archaeological Society*, 90, 1990 pp.199–204.

James, S. E., *Kateryn Parr: The Making of a Queen*. Aldershot: Ashgate Publishing, 1999.

Jordan, W. K., *Edward VI: The Threshold of Power*. London, 1970.

Jordan, W. K., *Edward VI: The Young King*. London, 1968.

King, J. N., 'Protector Somerset, Patron of the English Renaissance' in *The Papers of the Bibliographical Society of America*, 70, 1976, pp.307–31.

Lewis, C., Brown, R.A. (ed.), 'The Norman settlement of Herefordshire under William I' in *Anglo-Norman Studies VII: Proceedings of the Battle Conference 1984,* vol. VII. Boydell Press, 1985.

Loades, D., *The Tudor Court*. Headstart History Publishing: London, 1992.

Loades, D., *The Seymours of Wolf Hall: A Tudor Family Story*. Amberley Publishing: Gloucestershire, 2015.

Locke, A., *The Seymour Family: History and Romance*. London. 1911.

Maclean, J., *The Life of Sir Thomas Seymour*. London, 1869.

Machyn, H., *A London Provisioners Chronicle 1550–1563*. 1564. www.quod.lib.umich.edu.

Matzat, D., *Katherine Parr: Opportunist, Queen, Reformer: A Theological Perspective*. Amberley Publishing, 2020.

McElroy, A., *Educating the Tudors*. Pen and Sword, 2023.

Mueller, J., *Katherine Parr: Complete Works and Correspondence*. Chicago, University of Chicago Press, 2014.

Miller, H., 'Henry VIII's Unwritten Will: Grants of Lands and Honours in 1547' in *Wealth and Power in Tudor England*, E.W. Ives (ed.). London, 1978.

Muller, J. A., *The Letters of Stephen Gardiner*. Cambridge, 1933.

Muller, J. A., *Stephen Gardiner and the Tudor Reaction*. London, 1926.

Murphy, B., *Bastard Prince: Henry VIII's Lost Son*. London, 2001.

Needham, R. and Webster, A., *Somerset House Past and Present*. London, 1905.

Nichols, J. G., 'Anne, Duchess of Somerset' in *The Gentleman's Magazine*, 2nd series, 23, (1845), pp.371–81.

Nichols, J. G., 'The Second Patent appointing Edward, Duke of Somerset, Lord Protector' in *Archaelogia*, 30, 1844.

Norton, E., *Jane Seymour: Henry VIII's True Love*. Chalford: Amberley Publishing, 2009.

Norton E., *The Temptation of Elizabeth Tudor*. Kindle edition, 2015.

Norton, E., *The Hidden Lives of Tudor Women: A Social History*. New York: Pegasus Books, 2017.

Page, W (ed.), 'Houses of the Augustine Canons: The Priory of Stavordale' in *A History of Somerset*, vol. II. London, 1911.

Pollard, A. F., *England under Protector Somerset*. London: Paul, Trench, Truber & Co., 1900.

Power, E., *Medieval English Nunneries 1275–1535*. London, 1922.

Russell, G., *The Palace: From the Tudors to the Windsors: 500 years of Royal History at Hampton Court*. London: William Collins, 2023.

Sanders, I. J., *English Baronies: A Study in Their Origins and Descent 1086–1327*. OUP: Oxford, 1960.

Scard, M., *Tudor King in All But Name: The Life of Edward Seymour*. The History Press, 2020.

Skidmore, C., *Edward VI: the Lost King of England*. Weidenfeld and Nicolson, 2007.

Soberton, S. B., *The Forgotten Tudor Women: Anne Seymour, Jane Dudley and Elisabeth Parr*. Independently published and accessed on Kindle, 2018.

Spont, A., *Letters and Papers relating to the war with France 1512–13*, 1897.

Strype, J. (ed.), *Ecclesiastical Memorials*. Oxford: Clarendon Press, 1822.

Tallis, N., *Young Elizabeth: Princess. Prisoner. Queen*. London: O'Mara, 2024.

Thames Valley Archaeological Report 'Church Row Farm, Frome Road, Rode, Somerset: An Archaeological Evaluation', July 2008. www.tvas.co.uk.

Wall, Sarah E., 'Editing Anne Askew's examination: John Bale, John Foxe and Early Modern Textual Practices' in *John Foxe and His World*, J. N. King and Christopher Highley (eds.). 2002.

Warnicke, R. M., 'Anne Seymour [nee Stanhope] duchess of Somerset c.1510–1587, noblewoman and literary patron' in *The Oxford Dictionary of National Biography*, 2004.

Warnicke, R. M., *Inventing the Wicked Women of Tudor England, Queenship and Power Series*. Palgrave MacMillan, 2012.

Weir, A., *The Six Wives of Henry VIII*. London: Vintage, 2011.

Index